GW00888842

ADVENTURES WITH THE CONNAUGHT RANGERS, 1809–1814

NAPOLEONIC LIBRARY

William Grattan

ADVENTURES WITH THE CONNAUGHT RANGERS, 1809–1814

Edited by Charles Oman

Greenhill Books, London
Presidio Press, California

Greenhill
Books

This edition of *Adventures with the Connaught Rangers, 1809–1814*
first published 1989 by Greenhill Books, Lionel Leventhal Limited,
Park House, 1 Russell Gardens, London NW11 9NN
and
Presidio Press,
31 Pamaron Way, Novato, Ca. 94947, U.S.A.

This edition © Lionel Leventhal Limited, 1989

All rights reserved. No part of this publication may
be reproduced, stored in a retrieval system or
transmitted in any form by any means electrical,
mechanical or otherwise without first seeking the
written permission of the copyright owner
and of the publisher.

British Library Cataloguing in Publication Data available
Grattan, William
Adventures with the Connaught Rangers, 1809–1814
(Napoleonic Library 12)
1. Napoleonic wars. Peninsular campaign.
Army operations by Great Britain, Army – Biographies
I. Title   II. Oman, Sir Charles, 1860–1946   III. Series
940.2'7'0924

ISBN 1-85367-032-4

Publishing History
Adventures with the Connaught Rangers 1809–1814
was first published in 1902 and is reproduced now
exactly as the original edition, complete and unabridged.

Greenhill Books
welcome readers' suggestions for books that might be
added to this Series. Please write to us if there are
titles which you would like to recommend.

Printed by Antony Rowe Limited,
Chippenham, Wiltshire

PREFACE

WHILE engaged during the last ten years in the task of mastering the original authorities of the history of the Napoleonic wars, I have had to peruse many scores of diaries, autobiographies, and reminiscences of the British military and naval officers who were engaged in the great struggle. They vary, of course, in interest and importance, in literary value, and in the power of vivid presentation of events. But they have this in common, that they are almost all very difficult to procure. Very few of them have been reprinted ; indeed, I believe that the books of Lord Dundonald, Sir John Kincaid, Gleig, John Shipp, and Colonel Mercer are wellnigh the only ones which have passed through a second edition. Yet there are many others which contain matter of the highest interest, not only for the historical student but for every intelligent reader. From these I have made a selection of ten or a dozen which seem to me well worth republishing.

Among these is the present volume—the reminiscences of a subaltern of the Connaught Rangers, the old 88th. William Grattan was one of the well-known Dublin family of that name—a first-cousin of Thomas Colley Grattan the novelist, and a distant kinsman of Henry Grattan the statesman ; he joined the regiment as ensign on July 6,

1809. He went out to the 1st Battalion, and reached it on the Caya late in 1809; he served with it till the spring of 1813, when he went home on leave, having obtained his lieutenancy on April 12, 1812. Thus he was for more than four years continuously with the colours, and saw Busaco, Fuentes d'Oñoro, El Bodon, the storms of Ciudad Rodrigo and Badajoz, Salamanca, and the disastrous retreat from Burgos. He was only off duty for a few weeks in 1812, in consequence of a wound received at Badajoz. In the ranks of the 3rd Division—the "Fighting Division" as he is proud to call it—he saw a greater portion of the war than most of his contemporaries, though he missed Vittoria and the invasion of France which followed.

Grattan as an author had two great merits. He had a very considerable talent for describing battles—indeed some of his chapters would not have disgraced the pen of William Napier. Of the many memoirs which I have read, I think that his is on the whole the most graphic and picturesque in giving the details of actual conflict. His accounts of Fuentes D'Oñoro, Salamanca, and above all of the storm and sack of Ciudad Rodrigo and Badajoz, are admirable. The reader will find in them precisely the touches that make the picture live. His second virtue is a lively sense of humour. The Connaught Rangers were the most Irish of all Irish regiments, and the "boys that took the world *aisy*," as Grattan calls them, were as strange a set to manage as ever tried an officer's temper. "I cannot bring myself to think them, as many did, a parcel of devils," writes Grattan; "neither will I by any manner of means try to pass them off for so many saints" (pp. 128-129); but whether good or bad, they were always amusing. For the exploits of Ody Brophy and Dan Carsons, of Darby Rooney and Barney Mackguekin, I must refer the reader to the book itself. Their doings, as recorded by the much-tried commander of their company, explain clearly enough Sir Thomas Picton's addiction to drum-head court-martials, and Lord Wellington's occasional bursts of plain and drastic language.[1] But no one with any sense of the ludicrous can profess any very lasting feeling of indignation against these merry if unscrupulous rascals.

It is clearly from the domestic annals of the 88th that Charles Lever drew the greater part of the good stories which made the fortune of *Charles O'Malley*. The reader will find many of the characters of that excellent romance appearing as actual historical personages in Grattan, notably the eccentric surgeon Maurice Quill, whose fame was so great throughout the British army that the novelist did not even take the trouble to change his name. His colleague Dr. O'Reily was almost as great an original. Many of the humours of Mickey Free seem to be drawn directly from the doings of Grattan's servant Dan Carsons. Comparing the "real thing" with the work of fiction, one is driven to conclude that much of what was regarded as rollicking invention on Lever's part, was only a photographic reproduction of anecdotes that he had heard from old soldiers of the Connaught Rangers.

Military diaries are often disappointing from one of two causes. Either the author slips into second-hand and second-rate narratives of parts of the campaign which he did not himself witness—things which he had better have left to the professed historian—or he fails to give us those small traits of the daily life of the regiment which are needed to make us realise the actualities of war. Grattan sometimes

[1] See, for example, his remarks on the 88th to Sir James M'Grigor, on page 259 of the latter's autobiography.

b

falls into the first-named fault, but never into the latter. He seems to have had an instinctive knowledge of what future generations would want to know concerning the old Peninsular army—its trials in the matter of pay, food, and clothing, its shifts and devices, its views of life and death. If any one wishes to know why Sir Thomas Picton was unpopular, or what the private and the subaltern thought about Lord Wellington, they will find what they seek in these pages. Nowhere else have I seen the psychology of the stormers of Ciudad Rodrigo and Badajoz dealt with in such a convincing fashion; let the reader note in particular pages 144-5 and 193-4.

I have to confess that in various parts of this reprint I have used the Editor's license to delete a certain amount of the author's original manuscript. Grattan had two besetting sins considered as a literary man. The first was one to which I have already made allusion. Not unfrequently he quitted his autobiographical narrative, and inserted long paragraphs concerning parts of the war of which he had no personal knowledge, e.g. about the movements of Hill's corps in Estremadura, or of the Spaniards in remote corners of the Peninsula. These, as is natural, are often full of inaccuracies: sometimes (and this is a worse fault) they turn out to be taken almost *verbatim* from formal histories, such as those of Colonel Jones and Lord Londonderry. In one place I found thirty lines which were practically identical with a passage in Napier. In all cases these relate to parts of the war which did not come under Grattan's own eyes: I have therefore ventured to omit them.

Grattan's other weakness was a tendency to fly off at a tangent in the middle of a piece of interesting narrative, in order to controvert the statements of writers with whom he

disagreed. He had one special foe—Robinson, the biographer
of Sir Thomas Picton, on whom he wasted many an objurgatory paragraph. These small controversial points, on
which he turns aside, break the thread of his discourse in the
most hopeless fashion, and are now of little interest. I have
often, though not always, thought it well to leave out such
divagations. At the end of the work, in a similar fashion,
a long criticism on a certain speech of the Duke of Wellington in the House of Lords has been omitted. It deals with
the story of the long-delayed issue of the war-medal for the
Peninsula. The whole point of Grattan's remarks (caustic
but well justified in most respects) was removed when the
medal was at last actually distributed, a few months after he
had made his complaint.

The present volume stops short at the end of the Peninsular war. Grattan's pen travelled farther. Encouraged by
the success of his first book, he issued two supplementary
volumes : these are of very inferior interest, being mainly
concerned with the doings of the 88th in their early campaigns, before the author had joined them. There is much
about Buenos Ayres, the Low Countries, and Talavera. The
rest is composed of amusing but very rambling reminiscences
of garrison life in Canada in 1814, and in France in 1815-
1816, and of character sketches of some of Grattan's contemporaries, such as the unfortunate Simon Fairfield, concerning whom the reader will find certain information on pages
130-1 and 324 of this reprint. The whole of these two
volumes consists of mere *disjecta membra*, much inferior in
interest to the first two which the author had produced.

Grattan's military service, which had begun in 1808,
ended in 1817, in consequence of the enormous reductions
in the effective of the army which were carried out after the

evacuation of France began. His name last appears among combatant officers in the army list for March 1817, the month in which the 88th was reduced from two battalions to one, and many of its officers placed upon half pay. But he lived for thirty years longer, frequently descending into print in the *United Service Journal*, to controvert those who seemed to him to undervalue the services of the 88th or the old 3rd Division. In 1836 we find him residing at New Abbey, Kilcullen, and issuing a *Vindication of the Connaught Rangers*, which seemed so convincing to the officers of his old regiment, that they presented him with a present of plate to the value of 200 guineas "as a mark of their personal esteem and regard, and also in token of their warm admiration of his triumphant vindication of his gallant regiment from the attacks of the biographer [Robinson] of the late Sir Thomas Picton." In 1847 he published the two volumes from which the present reprint is taken. In the following year he received his long-deserved Peninsular Medal. His last appearance in print was the publication of the two supplementary volumes of *Anecdotes and Reminiscences*, mentioned above, in the spring of 1853.

C. OMAN.

Oxford, *November* 1902.

THE OFFICERS OF THE 88TH
1809–14

GRATTAN's Memoirs cannot be fully understood without a list of the comrades whom he is perpetually mentioning in the narrative. I therefore append the names of the officers of the 88th from the Army List of 1809-10. I have added to each of those who were killed or wounded during the war a note specifying the casualty. No less than 49 of the 103 names bear this addition!

Colonel

William Carr Beresford, Major-General, wounded at Salamanca, 22.7.12.

Lieutenant-Colonels

Alexander Wallace.   John Taylor.

Majors

Richard Vandeleur, died at Campo   John Silver, killed at Busaco,
   Mayor, 5.11.09.   27.9.10.
Daniel Colquhun.   R. Barclay M'Pherson.

Captains

Robert B. M'Gregor.   Joseph Thomson, killed at Badajoz,
Campbell Callendar.   6.4.12.
John Dunne   Richard R. Browne, wounded at
William C. Seton.   Busaco, died at Pinhel, 1810

Barnaby Murphy, wounded at Badajoz, killed at Salamanca, 22.7.12.

Charles John Peshall, wounded at Badajoz, 6.4.12.

James P. Oates, wounded at Badajoz, 6.4.12.

William Adair M'Dougall.

William Hogan, killed at Salamanca, 22.7.12.

Charles Tryon.

John Groffer.

Christopher Irwine, killed at Fuentes d'Oñoro, 5.5.11.

Peter Lindsay, killed at Badajoz, 6.4.12.

H. G. Buller.

Walter W. Adair, wounded at Salamanca, 22.7.12.

Robert N. Nickle, wounded at Toulouse, 10.5.14.

Henry M'Dermott, wounded at Vittoria, 21.6.13; killed at Orthez, 27.2.14.

George Henry Dansey, wounded at Busaco, 27.9.10.

J. Macdonald.

Robert Christie.

Lieutenants

Duncan Robertson, Adj.

George Bury.

John Bower Lewis.

Richard Bunworth.

William Flack, wounded at Ciudad Rodrigo, 19.1.12.

William Mackie.

James Flood, wounded at Vittoria, 21.6.13.

Richard Fitzpatrick, wounded at Vittoria 21.6.13; wounded at Orthez, 27.2.14.

Nathan Gregg.

Henry Johnson, killed at Busaco, 27.9.10.

John Smith, died at Salamanca, 1812.

Thomas North, killed at Badajoz, 6.4.12.

John D. Hopwood.

Alexander Graham.

John Armstrong, wounded at Rodrigo, 19.1.12; wounded at Badajoz, 6.4.12.

John Stewart, wounded at Fuentes, wounded at Badajoz.

Timothy Richard James.

William Nickle, wounded at Salamanca, 22.7.12.

Isaac Walker.

John Davern, wounded at Badajoz; wounded at Orthez, 27.2.14.

David Weir.

Ralph Mansfield, killed at Badajoz, 6.4.12.

Pat. Heron Cockburn.

Leigh Heppenstal, killed at Foz d'Aronce, 15.3.11.

Edward Cotton, killed at Badajoz, 6.4.12.

Frederick Meade, wounded at Salamanca, 22.7.12.

Hercules Ellis.

Samuel M'Alpine, wounded at Fuentes, 5.5.11; killed at Badajoz, 6.4.12.

George Johnson, wounded at Rodrigo, 19.1.12.

William Hodder.

William Whitelaw, wounded at Busaco, 27.9.10; killed at Badajoz, 6.4.12

Robert Hackett, wounded at Fuentes, 5.5.11 ; died on return voyage.
George F. Faris.
Bartholomew Mahon.

Peter Pegus.
Thomas J. Lloyd.
Jason Hassard.
Geoffrey K. Power.

Ensigns

Christian Hilliard.
John Graham.
Maurice O'Connor.
Thomas Leonard, killed at Busaco, 27.9.10.
William Rutherford.
Simon Fairfield.
Parr Kingsmill, wounded at Salamanca, 22.7.12.
William Kingsmill, wounded at Rodrigo, 19.1.12.
Maurice Mahon.

William Devereux Jackson.
Joseph Owgan, wounded at Fuentes, 5.5.11.
John Fairfield.
William Grattan, wounded at Badajoz, 6.4.12 ; wounded at Salamanca, 22.7.12.
John Christian.
John M'Gregor, died on landing at Portsmouth, invalided 1812.
George Hill.

The following additional officers joined the regiment, either as ensigns or by exchange as lieutenants and captains from other corps, between 1810 and 1814.

T. Moriarty, killed at Orthez, 27.2.14.
John D'Arcy.
L. Beresford, killed at Ciudad Rodrigo, 19.1.12.
Walter C. Poole, wounded at Orthez, 27.2.14.
T. Rutledge, died at Lisan, 12.9.13.
Richard Holland, wounded at Orthez, 27.2.14.
James Mitchell, wounded at Orthez, 27.2.14.
Charles G. Stewart, wounded at Orthez, 27.2.14.

D. M'Intosh, wounded at Orthez, 27.2.14.
—— Gardiner.
Thomas Taylor.
Charles Crawford Peshall.
Samuel Fisher.
Oliver Mills.
Barnard Reynolds, killed at Orthez, 27.2.14.
John Atkin.
Albert W. Sanders, killed at Vittoria, 21.6.13.
James M'Clintock.
George Bunbury.
William Smith.
James Wright.

CONTENTS

CHAPTER I

The Author leaves the depot at Chelmsford, and proceeds to join his regiment in Portugal—The *Samaritan*—Arrival at Lisbon—Measures adopted by General Junot—A night's rest—Portuguese barbers—Priest Fernando and Major Murphy—March to Aldea Gallega—First sight of the Connaught Rangers .

CHAPTER II

Headquarters of the 88th Regiment—Its losses from sickness—Unhealthy state of the country—The British army leaves the Alemtejo—General Picton takes the command of the 3rd Division—Remarks on the general's conduct—His apology to Colonel Wallace—The Connaught boy and the goat

CHAPTER III

Masséna's invasion of Portugal—Fall of Ciudad Rodrigo and Almeida—Craufurd's fight on the Coa—Anecdote of Colonel Charles Napier—The British retire to the position of Busaco

CHAPTER IV

Battle of Busaco—Daring advance of the French—The achievements of the 88th—Adventure of Captain Seton—Alcobaça—Remarks on the battle .

CHAPTER V

Occupation of the Lines of Torres Vedras—An army in motley—An Irish interpreter—Death of the Marquis de la Romana—Retreat of Masséna's army from Portugal—Indulgence of Lord Wellington—The amenities of a subaltern's existence .

CONTENTS

CONTENTS

CONTENTS

CHAPTER XXIV

CHAPTER XXV

CHAPTER XXVI

CHAPTER XXVII

LIST OF ILLUSTRATIONS

xxi

MAP OF SPAIN AND PORTUGAL.

xxii

ADVENTURES

WITH THE

CONNAUGHT RANGERS

1809–1814

CHAPTER I

The Author leaves the depot at Chelmsford, and proceeds to join his regiment in Portugal—The *Samaritan*—Arrival at Lisbon—Measures
adopted by General Junot—A night's rest—Portuguese barbers—
Priest Fernando and Major Murphy—March to Aldea Gallega—
First sight of the Connaught Rangers.

On the 10th day of October 1809 I left the depot at
Chelmsford, and proceeded to Portsmouth for the purpose
of joining the first battalion of my regiment (the 88th) in
Portugal.

The newspapers announced that a fleet of transport
vessels would sail in a few days from Portsmouth for Lisbon,
and although I belonged to the second battalion, at that
period stationed at Gibraltar, I waived all ceremony, and
without asking or obtaining leave from the general in command at Chelmsford (General Colburn), I took the first
coach for London, where I arrived that evening, and the
next day reached Portsmouth.

I waited upon Colonel Barlow, who commanded at Hilsea,

B

and from him received an order to be admitted on board
a transport ship named the *Samaritan*. No questions were
asked as to my qualification for this request, as it was much
easier in those days to get out to Portugal than return from
it. I then requested of the Colonel that he would give me
an order for "embarkation money," which I told him I
understood was allowed to officers on going to Portugal.
He laughed at the demand, and treated me with so little
courtesy that I was glad to be rid of him.

I have said the name of the ship in which I was to
make my first voyage was the *Samaritan*. So it was. But
it most certainly could not be fairly called the *Good
Samaritan*, for a more crazy old demirep of a ship never
floated on the water. She was one of those vessels sent out,
with many others at this period, to be ready to convey our
army to England in the event of any disaster occurring to
it. On board of her were ten or a dozen officers, who, like
myself, had seen little of the world. We had no soldiers on
board, and an inadequate ship's crew; but those deficiencies
were amply made up for by the abundance of rats which
infested the vessel, and which not only devoured a great
portion of our small supply of provisions, but nearly ourselves into the bargain. One officer, ill from sea-sickness,
was well-nigh losing half of his nose, and another had the
best part of his great toe eaten away. Providence, however,
at length decreed that we should soon be rid of these tor-
ments, and on the 29th day of October the Rock of Lisbon
presented itself to our view.

It is difficult to convey to the eye, much less to the
imagination of those who have not seen it, a more imposing
or beautiful sight than Lisbon presents when seen from the
deck of a vessel entering the Tagus; its northern bank,

upon which the city stands, sweeping with a gentle curve along the extent of the city, shows to great advantage the vast pile of buildings, including palaces, convents, and private dwellings, standing like a huge amphitheatre before the view of the spectator; the splendid gardens and orange groves, the former abounding with every species of botanical plant, while the latter, furnishing the eye with a moving mass of gold, presents a *coup d'œil* which may be felt or conceived, but which cannot be described.

Our vessel had scarcely reached the river when a pilot boat came alongside of us, and for the first time I had an opportunity of looking at the natives of Portugal. I confess I was inexpressibly disgusted; the squalid appearance of those half-amphibious animals, their complexion, their famished looks, and their voracious entreaties for salt pork, gave me but a so-so opinion of the patriots I had heard of and read of with so much delight and enthusiasm. Their bare throats, not even with muscle to recommend them, their dark eyes portraying more of the assassin than the patriot, and their teeth, white no doubt in comparison with their dark hides, was sufficient to stamp them in my eyes as the most ill-looking set of cut-throats I had ever beheld. Their costume, too, is anything but striking, except strikingly ugly. Short *demi* petticoat trousers of white linen, a red sash, and their arms and legs naked, give them the appearance of a race of bad bred North American Indians.

On landing at Lisbon, your foot once upon *terra firma*—

> The cloud-cap'd towers,
> The gorgeous palaces—

and the fine gardens all vanish, not into *thin* air, but into the most infernal pestiferous atmosphere that ever unfortunate traveller was compelled to inhale. Here is a hideous change from what the first view led you to expect. It is, indeed, "love at first sight."

You are scarcely established in the first street, when you behold a group of wretches occupied in picking vermin from each other; while, sitting beside them, cross-legged, holding a distaff and spindle in her left hand, and fanning her *fogareiro* with her right, is a woman who sells chestnuts to any one whose stomach is strong enough to commence the process of mastication in so filthy a neighbourhood.

The appearance of everything in Lisbon is so novel to an Englishman, that he is at a loss what most to fix his attention upon. But the number of beggars and the packs of half-famished dogs which infest the streets are in themselves sufficient to afford food for the mind, if not for either the beggars or the dogs. The latter crowd the streets after nightfall and voraciously devour the filth which is indiscriminately thrown from the different windows, and it is a dangerous service to encounter a pack of those famished creatures.

> In every country there are customs known,
> Which they preserve exclusively their own;
> The Portuguese, by some odd whim infected,
> Have Cloacina's temple quite rejected.

The French general, Junot, whatever his other faults might be, did a good thing in ridding Lisbon of this nuisance. On the fourth day after his arrival he ordered all dogs found in the streets after nightfall to be shot; and the proprietor of every door before which was found any dirt, after a certain hour in the morning, he caused to pay a fine according to the quantity found in front of his premises. But Junot had been too long driven from Lisbon to have his orders respected at the period I write of, and we

were in consequence subjected to the annoyance of being
poisoned by the accumulated filth, or to the danger of being
devoured by the herds of dogs who seemed to consider these
windfalls as their particular perquisite.

The beggars, offensive as they were, were less so than the
dogs, because in Portugal, as in most countries professing the
Roman Catholic religion, the giving of alms is considered an
imperative duty; and according to their means, all persons
supply the wants of the poor. From the gates of the
convents, and from the kitchens of the higher classes, food
is daily distributed to a vast number of mendicants, and
those persons actually conceive they have a right to such
donations; long habit has in fact sanctioned this right, and
secure of the means to support their existence, they flock
daily to their respective stations, awaiting the summons
which calls them to the portal to receive the pittance intended for them. Thus it is that strangers suffer less
inconvenience from this description of persons than they
otherwise would, for the laziness of these wretches is so
great, that although they will not hesitate to beg alms from
a passing stranger, they will barely move from their re-
cumbent posture to receive it, much less offer thanks for it.

Satisfied with my first evening's excursion, I returned to
the hotel where we had bespoken our dinner and beds. The
former was excellent; good fish, for which Lisbon is proverbial, *ragoûts*, and game, all well served up, gave us a *goût*
for our wine. We discussed the merits of divers bottles,
and it was late ere we retired to our chamber,—I was going
to say place of rest—but never was word more misplaced,
had I made use of it. Since the hour of my recollection, up
to the moment that I write these lines, I never passed such
a night. From the time I lay down, in hopes of rest, until

the dawning of morning, I never, for five minutes at a time, closed my eyes. Bugs and fleas attacked me with a relentless fury, and when I arose in the fair daylight, to consult my looking-glass, I had scarcely a feature recognisable. I was not, however, singular, for all my companions had shared the same fate. But it was absolutely necessary, before we attempted to perambulate the streets, that something should be done to render our appearance less horrible. We accordingly summoned the landlord with the view of ascertaining the name of some medical person who could administer to our wants; but he laughed at the idea of calling in surgical aid for so trifling a matter, which he said, and I believe him, was an everyday occurrence at his hotel. He recommended to us a man, as he was pleased to say, " well skilled in such cases," and one who had made a comfortable competency by his close residence to the hotel we occupied. The person who could have doubted the latter part of our host's harangue must have indeed been casuistical, because the number of patients which, to our own ears, not our sight, for sight we had none, fell to him in one night, was a sufficient guarantee that his yearly practice must be something out of the common.

The person thus described, and almost as soon introduced, was no other than the far-famed Jozé Almeida Alcantaro de Castreballos, half-brother to the celebrated Louiranna well known in Lisbon. A man, who as he himself jocosely said, had taken many a British officer by the nose. He was, in fact, neither more nor less than a common barber, who gained a livelihood by shaving, bleeding, and physicking his customers.

The Portuguese barbers are like those of other countries, great retailers of scandal, and amply stocked with a fund of

amusing conversation. They know everything, or seem to
know everything, which, to nine-tenths of those they meet,
is the same thing! This fellow told us all the news of the
day, and added to it a thousand inventions, which his own
fertile imagination supplied. He described the retreat of
Wellington from Talavera as one caused by the want of the
Portuguese army to co-operate with him : and if his account
was to be given credit to, the whole world put together did
not contain such an army as that of Portugal. He said that
General Peacock, who commanded in Lisbon, invented stories
every day, and that no intelligence from the army ought to
be considered sterling, except what emanated from his (the
barber's) shop. But then, said he, shrugging up his shoulders,
and in broken English. " It is not one very uncommon ting,
to see one Peacock spreading a tail!" He laughed at his
pun, and so did we; but I have since heard that the merit
of it did not belong to him.

" But, gentlemen," resumed the barber, " I come here as a
professional man, not as a wit, though for that matter I am
as much one as the other—but to the point, gentlemen! you
seem to have suffered, and I am the man, able, ready, and
willing to serve you. Look here," said he, holding up a
white jar, having a superscription on the outside to the
following effect : " *bixas boas* " (good leeches): " I am none of
your quacks, that come *unprepared!* I do not want to write
a prescription that will cost my customers a mint of money!
Well did I know what you stood in need of when you sent
for your humble servant. Within the last ten days, that is
to say, since the arrival of the fleet of transports from
Portsmouth, I have given employment to one thousand
leeches in this very house. This hotel has made my fortune,
and now, with the blessing of God and the Virgin Mary, I'll

add to the number, already made use of, one hundred more, on the faces of those to whom I have the honour of addressing myself."

There was so much truth and sound sense in what the barber said, that we all submitted to the operation of leeching, which was of material service to us. Old Wright of the 28th, already, from a wound, blind of one eye, now began to peep a little with the other, and it was amusing enough to those who could see it, to witness the coquetting between him and the barber. Indeed it would be difficult to say which of them was most pleased—he who received his sight, or he who was the means of restoring it. Quantities of cloths, steeped in warm water, were applied to our faces, and the crimson hue with which every basin was tinctured showed but too plainly that the "*bixas boas*" of the barber Jozé, were of the right sort. We kept our rooms the entire day, ate a moderate and light dinner, and at an early hour retired to our chambers, not without some misgivings of another night-attack. But the barber assured us there was no danger; and whether it was that the vermin, which nearly devoured us on the preceding night, had gorged themselves, or that the applications which Jozé Almeida had administered to our wounded faces was of that nature to give them a nausea towards us, I know not, but, be this as it may, we enjoyed, unmolested, a comfortable night's repose, and in the morning our features had resumed their original shape and appearance.

We were seated at breakfast when the barber again made his appearance. He congratulated us upon our recovery, received his fee, which was extremely moderate, and took his leave. I have not since seen him, or is it likely I ever shall. In 1809 he was approximating to his sixtieth year; now thirty-seven years added to sixty would make him rather an elderly person. However, should he be still alive, and able to fulfil the functions of his calling as well as he did when I met with him, I recommend him to all those who may visit Lisbon and require his aid ; on the other hand, should he be no longer in the land of the living, I have paid his memory a just tribute—but not more than he deserved.

At twelve o'clock I took a calash and reported myself to Major Murphy of the 88th, who commanded at Belem. By him I was received with great kindness, and asked to dine with him at six o'clock. I returned to our hotel, where I found my companions awaiting my arrival. Although not perfectly restored to their good looks, they agreed to accompany me in a stroll through the town, which was a different quarter from that we had before explored. It was more obscure, and overstocked with beggars of every grade.

At six o'clock I arrived at Major Murphy's quarters at Belem, where were several officers of the depôt. Just as we were about to enter the dining-room a note was handed to Murphy from the celebrated priest Fernando : he was an intimate friend of Murphy, and called the 88th his own regiment, because when that corps landed in Lisbon it was quartered in the convent of which Fernando was the head. Nothing could exceed his kindness and hospitality, and, being the principal of the Inquisition, he was a man of great authority. His note was in these words :—

"Priest Fernando will cum dis day in boat to dine with Mr. Major Murphy."

He was as good as his word, for the note had been scarcely read aloud by Murphy when Fernando made his appearance. He was a remarkably handsome man, about forty years of age ; full of gaiety and spirits, a great talker, a prodigious feeder, and a tremendous drinker. So soon as I was introduced to him he took out a book from his pocket which he opened and handed to me, requesting that I would write down my name in it. This book contained the name of every officer in the first battalion, and according as any died, or were either killed or wounded in action, it was regularly noted after his name. His conduct was of the most disinterested kind, and one of his first questions invariably was —" Did we want money ? " It was late before we broke up, and next day an order was issued, directing us to be in readiness to march to join the army on the day but one following.

It did not require many hours' preparation to complete our arrangements, as there were several experienced officers to accompany the detachment, and they not only brought their own animals and provisions, but aided us by their advice in the purchase of ours. At the appointed hour all was in readiness, and the detachment, consisting of fifteen officers and two hundred and twenty men, composed of different regiments, marched from Belem, and embarked on the quay in boats which were prepared to carry us to Aldea Gallega. A short sail soon brought us across the Tagus, and towards evening we disembarked and took up our quarters at Aldea for the night. Our route, which was made by easy marches, was uninterrupted by any circumstance worthy of notice. We passed through the different towns of the Alemtejo, in each of which we were hospitably received by the inhabitants; not so on our arrival at Badajoz, the headquarters of Lord Wellington. Nothing could exceed the dogged rudeness of the Spaniards ; and it was with difficulty we could obtain anything even for money. Civility was not to be purchased on any terms, and one of the

detachment was killed in a fracas with some drunken mule-
teers. Next morning we left this inhospitable town, and
each party took their respective routes, with the view of
rejoining their regiments. Mine, the 88th, was stationed
at Monforte, distant one march from Badajoz, and here, for
the first time, I saw the " Connaught Rangers."

CHAPTER II

Headquarters of the 88th Regiment—Its losses from sickness—Unhealthy state of the country—The British army leaves the Alemtejo—General Picton takes the command of the 3rd Division—Remarks on the general's conduct—His apology to Colonel Wallace—The Connaught Boy and the goat.

THE 88th at this period, although one of the strongest and most effective regiments in the army, did not count more than five hundred bayonets. The fatigues of the late campaign, and the unhealthiness and debility of many of the soldiers in consequence, caused a material diminution in our ranks; added to this, the country in the neighbourhood of the Guadiana was swampy and damp, and what between ague, dysentery, and fever, the hospitals were in a few weeks overstocked. Not less than ten thousand were on the sick list, or about one-third of the entire force, as borne on the muster-rolls; and there was a great paucity of medical officers; many of those had been left at Talavera with the wounded, that were of necessity obliged to be abandoned, and others, either catching the contagion that raged throughout the country, or infected by their close attendance in the hospitals, were lost to us. The consequence was that the men and officers died daily by tens and fifteens, and this mortality was not confined to the old soldiers alone, for the young militia men, who now joined the army from England,

12

suffered equally with those who were half starved on the
retreat from Talavera, and during the occupation of the
bridge of Arzobispo. For several days the rations of those
soldiers consisted of half a pound of wheat, *in the grain*, a
few ounces of flour twice in the week, and a quarter of a
pound of goat's flesh; and regiments which a few weeks
before were capable of exertions that were never equalled
during the remainder of the Peninsular contest, were now
unable to go through an ordinary march.

It was not to be wondered at that men who had so
suffered should be now attacked with disease when all
excitement was over, and a reaction of the system was the
natural consequence; but the young men who joined from
England at this period could not be so classed, and as it was
manifest that the air of the country was unwholesome, Lord
Wellington decided upon marching his army to the north-
eastern frontier; yet before quitting the Alemtejo it was
necessary that the safety of Seville should be guaranteed by
a sufficient Spanish force.

Early in December the army left the Alemtejo, and by
the first week in January the 3rd Division was distributed
in the different villages in the neighbourhood of Trancoso.
The villages of Alverca and Frayadas, distant about two
miles from each other, were allotted for the 88th Regiment.
Midway between the two was a plain of considerable extent,
and upon this plain the regiment exercised every day for
several hours.

At the end of six weeks Colonel Wallace had his battalion
in the most perfect state of discipline that it is possible to
conceive; the men left in hospital were speedily joining the
ranks, and the stragglers which were from necessity left
behind in the north of Portugal were now coming in fast to

their different regiments. It may be remembered that the troops commanded by Lord Beresford in the spring of 1809 suffered great fatigues in their advance through the province of Tras os Montes ; the 88th Regiment formed a portion of this force.

The best-regulated army during a campaign, even if carried on under the most favourable circumstances, always becomes more or less relaxed in its discipline ; and when it is considered that the wreck of the 88th Regiment, after its capture at Buenos Ayres, was made up by drafts from the second battalion, that a few short months only were allowed it to recruit and reorganise before it was again employed in Portugal, it may be matter of regret, but certainly not of surprise, that it did not form an exception to the general rule.[1] Many stragglers were left behind. Some preferred remaining with the Portuguese, and never joined the army again. Nevertheless, many of the good soldiers who had been worn down by fatigue and were obliged to make a short stay, soon rallied, followed the track of their different regiments, and joined them by sixes and sevens. Others of a different stamp preferred remaining where they were, and continued under the hospitable roofs that had given them shelter, and made themselves useful to the inhabitants by assisting them to till their fields and gardens. Others, fatigued with the sameness of the scene, went through the country under pretence of seeking their different regiments, and in many instances committed acts that were disgraceful ; and, strange to say, not the slightest effort was made to look after those stragglers and collect them.

[1] The Wellington despatches for the summer of 1809 contain two angry notes to Donkin, the brigadier commanding the 87th and 88th, concerning the vast number of men absent from the ranks.

Lieut. Gen. Sir T. Picton, G.C.B.

London Edward Arnold, 1902

Several of these men were shot by the peasants, while others were made prisoners and were marched by the militia of the country to the nearest British depôt. There they were either flogged, hanged, or shot, according to the nature of their different offences. Others were sent under escorts to whatever corps they belonged. All this relaxation of discipline commenced, as we have shown, in the early part of 1809, while the regiments of which those marauders formed a portion, between that period and the end of the year, had marched over hundreds of miles, fought a battle in the heart of Spain, occupied a line of posts on the Guadiana, and finally, after the lapse of ten months, took up new ground on the north-eastern frontier of Portugal.

It was at this time, and when the 3rd Division were stationed as has been described, that General Picton joined the army. It would be impossible to deny that a very strong dislike towards the General was prevalent. His conduct at the island of Trinidad,[1] while Governor of that colony, and the torture inflicted, by his order, on Louise Calderon, a torture which, by the way, had been given up in our army as being worse than flogging, had impressed all ranks with an unfavourable opinion of the man. Besides this, the strong appeal made by Mr. Garrow, the Attorney-General, to the jury by whom he was tried and found guilty, was known to all, and a very general, and I do believe a very unjust clamour was raised against him. From what I have just written it will be seen in what sort of

---

[1] Sir Thomas Picton, while Governor of Trinidad, then recently conquered from Spain, had allowed torture to be used to extort confession from a woman accused of theft. This was, he supposed, legal because the island was still under Spanish law, which permitted the practice. His action led to the case of *Rex* v. *Picton*, and brought immense odium upon his head. The torture was "picketing."

estimation General Picton was held, and as we of his division had never seen him, his first appearance before his troops was looked for with no little anxiety.

Our wishes were soon gratified, for, in a few days after his arrival at Trancoso, a division order was issued stating that on a certain day, which was named, the division should be under arms and ready to receive the General.

Punctual to the appointed time, General Picton reached the ground, accompanied by his staff; every eye was turned towards him, and, as first impressions are generally very strong and very lasting, his demeanour and appearance were closely observed. He looked to be a man between fifty and sixty, and I never saw a more perfect specimen of a splendid-looking soldier. In vain did those who had set him down in their own minds as a cruel tyrant, seek to find out such a delineation in his countenance. No such marks were distinguishable; on the contrary, there was a manly open frankness in his appearance that gave a flat contradiction to the slander, and in truth Picton was *not* a tyrant, nor did he ever act as such during the many years that he commanded the 3rd Division.

But if his countenance did not depict him as cruel, there was a caustic severity about it, and a certain curl of the lip that marked him as one who rather despised than courted applause. "The stern countenance, robust frame, caustic speech, and austere demeanour," told in legible characters that he was one not likely to say a thing and not do as he said. In a word, his appearance denoted him as a man of strong mind and strong frame.

The division went through several evolutions, and performed them in a very superior manner indeed; the line marching and the echelon movements, for which the 88th,

under Wallace, was so celebrated, seemed to surprise the
General; he however said little. Once he turned to Wallace
and said, in rather a disagreeable tone, " Very well, sir." The
parade was about to be dismissed, and the General about to
return to his quarters, when two marauders of the 88th were
brought up in charge of a detachment of Portuguese militia.
They had stolen a goat on their march up to join their
regiment. The complaint was at once made to Picton, who
ordered the men to be tried by a drum-head court-martial
on the spot. This was accordingly done; the men were
found guilty, and flogged on the moment in presence of
the General.

This act was considered by all as not good taste in
General Picton on his first appearance amongst his troops;
the offence committed by the soldiers could have been as
well punished in front of their own regiment as in the
presence of the entire division; and, besides this, there was
no necessity for the General's remaining to witness the
punishment. This act on his part caused those who had
formed a favourable opinion from his appearance to waver,
and the word " tyrant " was more than muttered by many of
the division.

So soon as the two soldiers were removed after having
received the number of lashes it was thought necessary to
inflict, the General addressed the brigade in language not
of that bearing which an officer of his rank should use, for
turning to the 88th he said, " You are not known in the
army by the name of ' Connaught Rangers,' but by the
name of Connaught *footpads*!" He also made some remarks on their country and their religion.

Language like this was enough to exasperate the lowest
soldier, equally with the Colonel, who had done so much for

the regiment during his command ; and Colonel Wallace, directly the parade was over, waited on General Mackinnon, who commanded the brigade, and requested that he would go to General Picton, and intimate to him that he conceived the abusive language which he had made use of towards the 88th was not just to the corps, or to himself as commanding officer of it.

Mackinnon was a strict disciplinarian, but a man of an extremely mild temper, and he felt greatly annoyed at what had taken place. He readily complied with Colonel Wallace's request, and received for answer from Picton, that he would remove those impressions when he again had an opportunity of assembling the division.

A long period elapsed before the division was again brought together, and when it was Picton neglected, or perhaps forgot, to fulfil the promise he had made. Immediately after the parade Wallace reminded General Mackinnon of what had before passed on the subject, and Mackinnon, for the second time, waited on Picton. The latter requested that Wallace should call upon him, which was immediately complied with, and then took place a memorable interview.

When Wallace reached Picton's quarters he found the General alone ; a long conversation took place, which Colonel Wallace never repeated to me, nor was it necessary that he should, because my rank did not entitle me to such disclosure, but I have reason to think that it was very animated, and what I am now about to write I have from under Colonel (now General) Wallace's own hand. It is as follows:—

"After a conversation which it is here unnecessary to recapitulate, General Picton paused for a little and said, 'Well, will you dine with me on —— ?' I replied, 'Most certainly, General, I shall be happy to do so.' When I

went to dinner on the day appointed, I found almost all the
superior officers of Picton's division, and the troops quartered
in the vicinity of Pinhel, assembled. General Picton then
addressed himself to Colonel Mackinnon, commanding the
brigade, and said, 'I understand that Colonel Wallace has
taken offence at some observations made by me relative to
the corps he commands, when addressing the division. I
am happy to find that I have been misinformed as to their
conduct for some time past; and I feel it but justice to him
and them, to say that I am satisfied every attention has been
paid to the conduct and appearance of the corps. I certainly
did hear, on my way up to the army, of irregularities that
had been committed, but I am happy to say that I have
had every occasion to be satisfied with the general conduct
of the corps since my joining the divis.on.' I made no
reply, but bowed to the General. Dinner was announced,
and General Picton came up to me and asked me to sit
beside him at dinner. There ought always to be a deference
given to a general of division by an officer inferior in rank,
and under these circumstances I considered General Picton's
conduct to have been arranged in a very gentlemanlike and
handsome manner. From that period General Picton and
myself were always on the best terms, and though from
prejudice he often signified that he suspected the *Connaught
Boys* were as ready for mischief as any of their neighbours,
he always spoke of them to me as good soldiers while I was
with his division."

Thus ended the matter, and I never knew or heard that
Picton ever again made use of a harsh expression towards the
regiment; indeed his biographer says that he often gave
them "unqualified praise." Perhaps he did, but for nearly
four years that Picton commanded the 3rd Division, not

one officer of the 88th was ever promoted through his recommendation, though it is well known in the army that many deserved it.

Shortly after this period a laughable circumstance took place between Picton and a soldier of the 88th, which put the General in great good-humour, and he often repeated the story as a good joke. He was riding out one day, accompanied by his aide-de-camp, near the river Coa, when he saw, on the opposite bank of the river, a man of the Connaught Rangers with a huge goat on his back.

We had received but scanty rations for some days previously, and such a windfall as the old goat was not to be neglected. I am not prepared to state whether it was the cries of the animal, or the stench of his hide—for the wind was from that point—attracted Picton to the spot; howbeit, there he was.

It would be difficult to say, with truth, whether the General was most angry or hungry, but he seemed, in either case, resolved not only to capture the goat, but also the "boy." That he would have done the one or the other, perhaps both, there can be little doubt, had it not been that a stream, whose banks had been the theatre of other scenes of contest, separated the parties. This stream was the Coa, and although its different fordable points were well known to Picton, his *vis-a-vis* neighbour was by no means ignorant of some of the passes ; and as the General had not time to consult his chart, and find out the nearest "ford," nor inclination to plunge into the river, he made a furious, but quite an ineffectual, attack of words against the "Connaught boy."

"Pray, sir," said, or rather roared Picton, addressing the soldier, "what have you got there ?"

Sol. "A thieving puckawn, sir."

Pic. "A *what ?*"

Sol. "A goat, sir. In Ireland we call a buck-goat a puckawn. I found the poor baste sthraying, and he looks as if he was as hungry as myself."

Pic. "What are you going to do with him, sir ?"

Sol. "*Do* with him, is it ? To bring him with me, to be sure ! Do you think I'd lave him here to starve ?"

Pic. "Ah! you villain, you are at your old tricks, are you ? I know you, though you don't think it ! "

Sol. "And I know you, sir, and the ' boys of Connaught ' know you too, and I'd be sorry to do anything that would be displaising to your honour; and, sure, iv you'd only let me, I'd send your sarvent a leg iv him to dhress for your dinner, for by my sowl your honour looks could and angry—hungry I mane."

He then held up the old goat by the beard, and shook it at Captain Tyler, the General's aide-de-camp, and taking it for granted that he had made a peace-offering to the General, or, probably, not caring one straw whether he had or not, went away with his burden, and was soon lost sight of amongst a grove of chestnut-trees.

"Well," said Picton, turning to Tyler, who was nearly convulsed with laughter, "that fellow has some merit. What tact and what humour ! He would make a good out-post soldier, for he knows, not only how to forage, but to take up a position that is unassailable."

"Why yes, sir," said Tyler, "when he held up the goat's head, he seemed to *beard* us to our faces ; and his promise of sending you a leg was a capital ruse ! "

"It was, faith," replied Picton, "and if the fellow is found out, he will, I suppose, endeavour to make *me* the ' scape-goat ' ! "

The General used often to tell this story as one of the best things of the sort he had ever met with.

It is a remarkable circumstance that a few days before the battle of Waterloo, Picton met Wallace in London, when he spoke highly of the regiment, and said if it returned from America in time to join the army under the Duke of Wellington (being then on their passage home), and if he joined the army, the 88th would be one of the first regiments he would ask for his division.

CHAPTER III

Masséna's invasion of Portugal—Fall of Ciudad Rodrigo and Almeida—
Craufurd's fight on the Coa—Anecdote of Colonel Charles Napier
—The British retire to the position of Busaco.

In the month of January, 1810, Lord Wellington established
his headquarters at Viseu, in Upper Beira, and the different
brigades of cavalry and infantry were quartered in the
neighbouring villages. General Hill was left with five
thousand British, and about as many Portuguese, at
Abrantes; and with his army posted as has been described,
the British General awaited the development of Masséna's
plan of invasion. The amount of the French force at this
period in the Peninsula counted over three hundred and
sixty thousand troops of all arms; but the army commanded
by Masséna, and called "the army of Portugal," did not
amount to ninety thousand. The amount of the British and
Portuguese forces has been already stated to be about fifty-
five thousand men; and it will be recollected that of the
Portuguese army scarcely one man in one hundred had ever
discharged a musket against an enemy. As to the British,
when Lord Wellington moved his army from the Guadiana
its numbers counted about thirty thousand, but those under
arms scarcely reckoned twenty thousand; the remainder
were in hospital, and many of those in the ranks were but

23

ill able to carry their knapsacks and firelocks, having not yet recovered from the effects of past illness.

The French preparations were so formidable, our own force so small, that in the British ranks it was generally believed that the entire army would retreat on Lisbon when the French advanced, and embark there. The same was asserted in England ; the Portuguese dreaded it ; the French army universally believed it, and the British ministers seem to have entertained the same opinion ; for at this time an officer of engineers arrived at Lisbon, whose instructions, received personally from Lord Liverpool, though unknown to Lord Wellington, commenced thus : " *As it is probable that the army will embark in September.*"

Fortunately for us, the French lingered long ere they began their invasion. It was not till June 1810 that Ney began the siege of Ciudad Rodrigo, while Masséna still remained at Madrid. The garrison of the fortress amounted to about six thousand men, and was commanded by the Spanish general, Herrasti, an old and gallant man who had served his country with honour for more than half a century. The town was amply supplied with artillery, provisions, and stores of all kinds ; and the vigorous resistance which was expected was made by Herrasti and his brave garrison.

General Robert Craufurd, with his superb division, occupied the line of the Coa, while General Cole, with the 4th Division, and Picton with the 3rd, were posted at Guarda and Pinhel ; and these troops were directed to be in readiness to render any support that could with safety be given to the Spanish governor. That assistance could never be given, and Ciudad Rodrigo fell, after sustaining a siege of upwards of a month. Its gallant defence reflected great credit on both the governor and garrison, and the delay it caused the French army was of the greatest importance to Lord Wellington's plan of resistance, because the heavy rains which were almost sure to fall in the autumn would greatly aid in the defence of the country.

After his capture of Rodrigo, Masséna lost no time in laying siege to Almeida, and it was hoped that this town, which was, though by no means a model of perfection, a more regularly constructed fortress than Ciudad Rodrigo, would hold out for at least as long. But here we were to be bitterly disappointed. On August 26, 1810, the bombardment began: in a short time a great portion of the town was in flames, and it was found impossible in the confusion that prevailed to put a stop to the calamity. But this mattered little; no great damage had been done to the walls, and the guns of the garrison replied with vigour. But at midnight a terrible explosion was heard, the castle was rent into a thousand pieces, and the entire town disappeared, as if swallowed by an earthquake. This tremendous crash was heard for a distance of many leagues. The main magazine had been blown up by a French shell, and the Governor, Colonel Cox, was obliged to surrender next day.

While these events were taking place, a variety of movements between our advance and that of the enemy occurred. Upon one occasion a portion of the 14th Dragoons came in contact with a body of the enemy's infantry, and their commanding officer, Colonel Talbot, fell in the midst of a square against which he made a gallant, but fruitless charge. But this was of little import in comparison with what took place with the Light Division, under Craufurd, on the banks of the Coa. His force consisted of four thousand infantry, a thousand cavalry, and a brigade of guns.

The force opposed to him was about six times his own

number, but yet he, with a hardihood bordering on rashness, held his post, and fought a very dangerous battle—contrary to orders, I believe—and lost upwards of three hundred men, with nearly thirty officers, and had it not been for the superior description of the troops he commanded, the division would have been destroyed to a man. The French, it is true lost three times the number Craufurd did ; but what of that ? Masséna could have better spared one thousand men than Wellington one hundred !

It has been said that Craufurd fully expected Picton would have joined him with the 3rd Division, stationed at Pinhel. The division of Picton were within hearing of the fire, but not a man was ordered to move to the support of Craufurd. The wounded men and officers of the Light Division came into Pinhel in the best manner they could, some on foot, others on cars, and the 3rd Division were much excited at not being allowed to join their old companions.

Colonel Wallace held the 88th in readiness, as I believe did every other officer commanding a battalion, and the division could have assembled and marched in ten minutes had any order been given to that effect. However, the Light Division, after performing more than could have been expected, even from it, and doing so alone, without the aid which it looked for, and which might have been afforded it, held their ground, and sustained no disaster, but on the contrary inflicted a severe loss on the enemy, and covered itself with glory.

Craufurd, after his gallant fight, lay, with his division, in the different villages in our front, and a quiet calm succeeded the first outburst. There was an inactivity in the movements of the enemy, notwithstanding that the soldiers had been supplied with bread for many days; and a curious incident took place at the time that is worthy of mention. It shows the good terms upon which the British and French officers stood in regard to each other.

Colonel Napier of the 50th Regiment, who had been badly wounded at Corunna, and who had been treated with much attention by Soult and Ney after he was made prisoner at that battle, stopped at Pinhel. He was on his *parole*, and when asked by some of our officers, whom he knew, "where he was going?" replied, "I am going to pass some time with my friend Marshal Ney!" He did pass some time with him, and was an eye-witness to all that went on in his camp; but where such confidence was shown to any British officer, much less one of such high character and honour as Colonel Napier, it is needless to say that it was not forfeited.

Napier, after having stayed with his friend Ney for some weeks,[1] returned on his way to England, when *en passant* he found the ridge of Busaco was about to be contested, and the gallant Colonel, although not on duty, or in any way connected with the army, being in fact on his *parole*, wished to be a looker-on. It so happened that he was wounded, while standing near Lord Wellington. His name was returned, and the French official paper, the *Moniteur*, made some remarks upon the Colonel breaking his *parole*. It was, however, soon explained by the gallant officer, and, in return, the Paris papers did not let pass an occasion which afforded them amusement, and they quaintly remarked " that a man who was so fond of French fire, after what he had got of it before, ought to live in France!"

After a good deal of delay and vacillation, it appeared

[1] This story is true; but the visit was only for one day (see *Charles Napier's Life*, i. 133).

that Masséna had at last seriously resolved on his enterprise. He had, under his immediate command, nearly one hundred and twenty thousand bayonets and sabres, but from this force some deductions must be made, by which it would appear that at the utmost he did not bring more than sixty thousand fighting men across the Coa. Finally he passed that river, and our army retired towards the banks of the Mondego, and Lord Wellington was obliged to give battle. But this obligation did not emanate from him—quite the contrary.

It was necessary that he should do something, and the thing was forced upon him by the refractory spirit of the Portuguese councils. If then he was to fight, for the first time, with an army of Portuguese to back him, he judged that the ridge of Busaco was a good spot to try them, and he accordingly resolved to take his stand there. This ridge of mountain extends for about eight miles, and near its termination, and on a high point, stands a convent, inhabited by monks and friars. The face of the mountain is rugged, filled with dells and dykes, and the intervening space between its base and the top is one mass of rock and heath.

On the 26th of September, all the different corps were placed in the stations they should occupy, and the entire ridge of Busaco was fully manned; during the evening we could perceive the enemy occupying their different stations in our front, and the light troops of both armies were warmly engaged along the entire of the line.

At night we lay down to rest; each man, with his firelock in his grasp, remained at his post, anxiously waiting the arrival of the morrow, which was destined to be the last that many amongst us were to behold. We had no fires, and the death-like stillness that reigned throughout our army was

only interrupted by the occasional challenge of an advanced
sentry, or a random shot fired at some imaginary foe.

The night at length passed over, but long before the
dawn of day the warlike preparations of the enemy were to
be heard.   The trumpets sounded for the horsemen to pre-
pare for the fight, and the roll of the drums and shrill notes
of the fife gave notice to the French infantry that the hour
had arrived when its claim to be the best in Europe was to
be disputed.

On our side all was still as the grave.   Lord Wellington
lay amongst his soldiers, under no other covering than his
cloak, and as he passed through the ranks of the different
battalions already formed, his presence and manner gave
that confidence to his companions which had a magical effect.
All was now ready on our part; the men stood to their arms;
and as each soldier took his place in the line, his quiet demeanour, and orderly, but determined appearance, was a
strong contrast to the bustle and noise which prevailed
amongst our opposite neighbours; but those preparations
were of short continuance, and some straggling shots along
the brow of the mountain gave warning that we were about
to commence the battle of Busaco.[1]

---

[1] For the better comprehension of the ensuing narrative of the
doings of the 3rd Division at Busaco, it will be well to give its strength
and organisation on that day.   They were as follows :—

1st Brigade, General Mackinnon.
    1st Battalion 45th Foot: 74th Foot: 1st Battalion 88th Foot
    (Connaught Rangers).
2nd Brigade, General Lightburne.
    2nd Battalion 5th Foot: 2nd Battalion 83rd Foot : 3 companies
    of 5th Battalion 60th Foot.
Portuguese Brigade, Colonel Champlemond.
    9th and 21st Regiments of the Line (each two Battalions).

CHAPTER IV

Battle of Busaco—Daring advance of the French—The achievements of the 88th—Adventure of Captain Seton—Alcobaça—Remarks on the battle.

THIS battle, fought upon the 27th September 1810, was one in which the losses of the French, and of the British and Portuguese army, commanded by Lord Wellington, were not of that magnitude to give it a first-rate place on the battle list; [1] this same battle of Busaco was, nevertheless, one of the most serious ever fought in the Peninsula, and for this reason—it was the first in which the Portuguese levies were brought under fire, and upon their conduct in this, their maiden effort against their veteran opponents, depended the fate of Portugal, and the Peninsula also. Such being the case, it must ever be classed as a very important event, and one that should be recorded by the historian with great care and fidelity, yet, strange to say, there is not, that I have read, any faithful report of it in print. In vain do we turn even to Colonel Napier's splendid history of the war in

[1] The loss of the French being 4486 killed, wounded, and prisoners, including five generals, viz. General Graindorge killed, Generals Foy, Maucune, and Merle wounded, and General Simon made prisoner, while that of the allied army was no more than 1143, amongst which number not one general officer had fallen ; the total loss of the two armies, counting about one hundred thousand combatants, was under six thousand.

the Peninsula in expectation of finding a correct account; no such account is there to be found. In all, therefore, that I am going to relate as to the part which the 3rd Division took in it, I shall keep as close as I possibly can to what I know to be the facts.

On the morning of the 27th the haze was so thick that little could be seen at any great distance, but the fire of the light troops along the face of the hill put it beyond doubt that a battle would take place. Lord Wellington was close to the brigade of Lightburne, and from the bustle amongst his staff, it was manifest that the point held by Picton's division was about to be attacked. Two guns belonging to Captain Lane's troop of artillery were ordered upon the left of the 88th Regiment, and immediately opened their fire, while the Portuguese battery, under the German Major Arentschildt, passed at a trot towards the Saint Antonio Pass, in front of the 74th British.

A rolling fire of musketry, and some discharges of cannon, in the direction of Saint Antonio, announced what was taking place in that quarter, and the face of the hill immediately in front of the brigade of Lightburne, and to the left of the 88th Regiment, was beginning to show that the efforts of the enemy were about to be directed against this portion of the ground held by the 3rd Division.

The fog cleared away, and a bright sun enabled us to see what was passing before us. A vast crowd of *tirailleurs* were pressing onward with great ardour, and their fire, as well as their numbers, was so superior to that of our advance, that some men of the brigade of Lightburne, as also a few of the 88th Regiment, were killed while standing in line ; a colour-sergeant named Macnamara was shot through the head close beside myself and Ensign Owgan. Colonel King, commanding

the 5th Regiment, which was one of those belonging to
Lightburne's brigade, oppressed by a desultory fire he was
unable to reply to without disturbing the formation of his
battalion, brought his regiment a little out of its range,
while Colonel Alexander Wallace, of the 88th, took a file
of men from each company of his regiment, and placing
them under the command of Captain George Bury and
Lieutenant William Mackie, ordered them to advance to
the aid of our people, who were overmatched and roughly
handled at the moment. Our artillery still continued to
discharge showers of grape and canister at half range, but
the French light troops, fighting at open distance, heeded it
not, and continued to multiply in great force. Nevertheless,
in place of coming up direct in front of the 88th, they edged
off to their left, out of sight of that corps, and far away
from Lightburne's brigade, and from the nature of the
ground they could be neither seen nor their exact object
defined ; as they went to their left, our advance inclined to
the right, making a corresponding movement ; but though
nothing certain could be known, as we soon lost sight of
both parties, the roll of musketry never ceased, and many
of Bury's and Mackie's men returned wounded. Those two
officers greatly distinguished themselves, and Bury, though
badly wounded, refused to quit the field. A soldier of Bury's
company, of the name of Pollard, was shot through the
shoulder ; but seeing his captain, though wounded, continue
at the head of his men, he threw off his knapsack, and fought
beside his officer ; but this brave fellow's career of glory was
short, a bullet penetrated the plate of his cap, passed through
his brain, and he fell dead at Bury's feet. These were the
sort of materials the 88th were formed of, and these were
the sort of men that were unnoticed by their General !

Lord Wellington was no longer to be seen, and Wallace and his regiment, standing alone without orders, had to act for themselves. The Colonel sent his captain of Grenadiers (Dunne) to the right, where the rocks were highest, to ascertain how matters stood, for he did not wish, at his own peril, to quit the ground he had been ordered to occupy without some strong reason for so doing. All this time the brigade of Lightburne, as also the 88th, were standing at ordered arms.

In a few moments Dunne returned almost breathless; he said the rocks were filling fast with Frenchmen, that a heavy column was coming up the hill beyond the rocks, and that the four companies of the 45th were about to be attacked. Wallace asked if he thought half the 88th would be able to do the business. "You will want every man," was the reply.

Wallace, with a steady but cheerful countenance, turned to his men, and looking them full in the face, said, " Now, Connaught Rangers, mind what you are going to do; pay attention to what I have so often told you, and when I bring you face to face with those French rascals, drive them down the hill—don't give the false touch, but push home to the muzzle! I have nothing more to say, and if I had it would be of no use, for in a *minit* or two there'll be such an infernal noise about your ears that you won't be able to hear yourselves."

This address went home to the hearts of us all, but there was no cheering; a steady but determined calm had taken the place of any lighter feeling, and it seemed as if the men had made up their minds to go to their work unruffled and not too much excited.

Wallace then threw the battalion from line into column,

D

right in front, and moved on our side of the rocky point at a quick pace; on reaching the rocks, he soon found it manifest that Dunne's report was not exaggerated; a number of Frenchmen were in possession of this cluster, and so soon as we approached within range we were made to appreciate the effects of their fire, for our column was raked from front to rear. The moment was critical, but Wallace, without being in the least taken aback, filed out the Grenadiers and the first battalion-company, commanded by Captains Dunne and Dansey, and ordered them to storm the rocks, while he took the fifth battalion-company, commanded by Captain Oates, also out of the column, and ordered that officer to attack the rocks at the opposite side to that assailed by Dunne and Dansey. This done, Wallace placed himself at the head of the remainder of the 88th, and pressed on to meet the French column.

At this moment the four companies of the 45th, commanded by Major Gwynne, a little to the left of the 88th, and in front of that regiment, commenced their fire, but it in no way arrested the advance of the French column, as it, with much order and regularity, mounted the hill, which at this point is rather flat. But here, again, another awkward circumstance occurred. A battalion of the 8th Portuguese Infantry, under Colonel Douglas, posted on a rising ground on our right, and a little in our rear, in place of advancing with us, opened a distant and ill-directed fire, and one which would exactly cross the path of the 88th, as that corps was moving onward to meet the French column, which consisted of three splendid regiments, viz. the 2nd Light Infantry, the 36th, and the 70th of the line. Wallace, seeing the loss and confusion that would infallibly ensue, sent Lieutenant John Fitzpatrick, an officer of tried gallantry, with orders

to point out to this regiment the error into which it had
fallen; but Fitzpatrick had only time to take off his hat,
and call out " *Vamos commarades*," when he received two
bullets—one from the Portuguese, which passed through
his back, and the other in his left leg from the French,
which broke the bone, and caused a severe fracture; yet
this regiment continued to fire away, regardless of the consequences, and a battalion of militia, which was immediately
in rear of the 8th Portuguese, took to their heels the moment
the first volley was discharged by their own countrymen!

Wallace threw himself from his horse, and placing himself at the head of the 45th and 88th, with Gwynne of the
45th on the one side of him, and Captain Seton of the 88th
on the other, ran forward at a charging pace into the midst
of the terrible flame in his front. All was now confusion
and uproar, smoke, fire and bullets, officers and soldiers,
French drummers and French drums knocked down in every
direction; British, French, and Portuguese mixed together;
while in the midst of all was to be seen Wallace, fighting—
like his ancestor of old—at the head of his devoted
followers, and calling out to his soldiers to " press forward ! "
Never was defeat more complete, and it was a proud moment
for Wallace and Gwynne when they saw their gallant
comrades breaking down and trampling under their feet
this splendid division composed of some of the best troops
the world could boast of. The leading regiment, the 36th,
one of Napoleon's favourite battalions, was nearly destroyed ;
upwards of two hundred soldiers and their old colonel,
covered with orders, lay dead in a small space, and the face
of the hill was strewed with dead and wounded, which showed
evident marks of the rapid execution done at this point; for
Wallace never slackened his fire while a Frenchman was

within his reach. He followed them down the edge of the hill, and then he formed his men in line, waiting for any orders he might receive, or for any fresh body that might attack him. Our gallant companions, the 45th, had an equal share in the glory of this short but murderous fight—they suffered severely; and the 88th lost nine officers and one hundred and thirty-five men. The 8th Portuguese also suffered, but in a less degree than the other two regiments, because their advance was not so rapid, but that regiment never gave way nor was it ever broken; indeed there was nothing to break it, because the French were all in front of the 45th and 88th, and if they had broken the Portuguese they must have first broken the two British regiments, which it is well known they did not! The regiment of militia in their rear ran away most manfully; and if they were able to continue for any length of time the pace at which they commenced their flight, they might, I should say, have nearly reached Coimbra before all matters had been finally settled between us and the French. Two of their officers stood firm and reported themselves in person to Wallace on the field of battle; so there could be no mistake about them, no more than there was about the rest of their regiment.

Meanwhile, Captains Dunne, Dansey, and Oates had a severe struggle with the French troops that occupied the rocks. Dunne's sergeant (Brazil) killed a Frenchman by a push of his halbert, who had nearly overpowered his captain. Dansey was slightly wounded in four places, but it was said at the time that he killed three Frenchmen—for he used a firelock. Oates suffered less, as the men opposed to him were chiefly composed of those that fled from Dunne and Dansey. Dunne's company of Grenadiers, which at the onset counted about sixty, lost either two or three-and-thirty, and

Dansey's and Oates's companies also suffered, but not to the same amount. The French troops that defended those rocks were composed of the 4th Regiment and the Irish Brigade; several of the latter were left wounded in the rocks, but we could not discover one Irishman amongst them. [1]

Lord Wellington, surrounded by his staff and some general officers, was a close observer of this attack. He was standing on a rising ground in rear of the 88th Regiment, and so close to that corps that Colonel Napier of the 50th—who was on leave of absence—was wounded in the face by a musket shot quite close to Lord Wellington. His Lordship passed the warmest encomiums on the troops engaged, and noticed the conduct of Captain Dansey in his despatch. It has been said, and I believe truly, that Marshal Beresford, who was colonel of the 88th, expressed some uneasiness when he saw his regiment about to plunge into this unequal contest; but when they were mixed with Reynier's men and pushing them down the hill, Lord Wellington, tapping him on the shoulder, said, "Well, Beresford, look at them *now!*"

While these events which I have described were taking place, Picton in person took the command against the other division of Reynier's corps and had a sharp dispute with it at the pass of Saint Antonio; but General Mackinnon, who led on the troops, never allowed it to make any head. A shower of balls from Arentschildt's battery deranged its deployment, and a few volleys from the 74th British and the Portuguese brigade of Champlemond totally routed this column before it reached the top of the ridge. This attack was feeble in comparison with the one directed against Wallace, and, besides, Picton's force was vastly superior to

[1] There is an error here. The Irish Brigade were not engaged; they were in reserve, in the 8th corps.

that commanded by Wallace, while the troops opposed to him were little, if anything, more numerous.   Picton had at this point five companies of the 45th under Major Smyth, all the light companies of the 3rd Division, one company of the 60th Rifles, the 74th British and the Portuguese brigade of Champlemond, besides Arentschildt's battery of guns.   It is not, therefore, to be wondered at that Reynier made little or no impression on Picton's right.

The 5th Division, commanded by General Leith, was in movement towards the contested point, and reached it in time either to take the fugitives in flank or to drive back any fresh body destined to support their defeated comrades. It made great efforts to join Picton when he was attacked, but the advance was so rapid, the defeat so signal, and the distance—two miles across a rugged mountain—so great, that Leith and his gallant division could only effect in part what they intended.   The arrival of this force was, however, fully appreciated ; for although the brigade of Light-burne, belonging to Picton's division, had not fired a shot or been at all molested, and although the 74th Regiment was nearly at liberty, still, had another attack with fresh troops been made, Leith might have stood in Picton's shoes on the extreme right, while the latter could in a short time concentrate all his battalions, and either fight beside Leith or turn with vigour against any effort that might be made against his centre or left.   But it would seem that no reserve was in hand—at all events none was thrown into the fight ; and Masséna gave up without a second trial that in which he lost many men and much glory !

While Picton, Mackinnon, Wallace and Champlemond, and Leith's division, were occupied as I have described, the Light Division, under the gallant Robert Craufurd, maintained a severe struggle against a large proportion of Ney's corps. Those French troops were driven down the hill with great loss, and the general of brigade, Simon, who headed and led the attack, was taken prisoner by the 52nd Regiment, and between two and three hundred unwounded men shared the fate of their general. The leading brigade of Leith's division put to flight some of the enemy who kept a hold of a rocky point on Picton's right, and had Picton been aware of their being there he might have cut off their retreat, while Leith attacked them in front and flank; but their numbers were scanty, and they might not have been aware of the fate of their companions, otherwise they would in all probability have got out of Leith's clutches before his arrival, for their remaining in the rocks could be of no possible avail, and their force was too weak to hazard any serious attack on Picton's right. Indeed, they were routed by a battalion or two of Leith's division; and the entire British loss at this point did not count above forty or fifty. And thus ended a battle of which so many accounts have been given: all at variance with each other—and none more so than what I have just written.

It has been said that Picton directed the attack of the 45th under Major Gwynne, the 88th under Wallace, and the 8th Portuguese under Douglas. Not one syllable of this is true. The conception of this attack, its brilliant execution, which ended in the total overthrow of Reynier's column, all belong to Colonel Alexander Wallace of the 88th Regiment. At the time it was made Generals Picton and Mackinnon had their hands full at the pass of Saint Antonio, and were, in effect, as distant from Wallace as if they had been on the Rock of Lisbon; neither was General Lightburne to be seen. The nearest officer of rank to Wallace was Lord

Wellington, who saw all that was passing and never interfered *pro* or *con*, which is a tolerably strong proof that his
lordship thought no alteration for the better could be made;
and Wallace had scarcely reformed his line, a little in front
and below the contested ground, when Lord Wellington,
accompanied by Marshal Beresford and a number of other
officers, galloped up, and passing round the left of our line,
rode up to Wallace, and seizing him warmly by the hand,
said—

" Wallace, I never witnessed a more gallant charge than
that made just now by your regiment ! "

Wallace took off his hat—but his heart was too full to
speak. It was a proud moment for him; his fondest hopes
had been realised, and the trouble he had taken to bring the
88th to the splendid state of perfection in which that corps
then was, had been repaid in the space of a few minutes by
his gallant soldiers, many of whom shed tears of joy. Marshal
Beresford addressed several of the soldiers by name who had
served under him when he commanded the regiment; and
Picton, who at this time came up, expressed his satisfaction.
Lord Wellington then took leave of us; and Beresford,
shaking the officers by the hand, rode away with his lordship,
accompanied by the officers about him. We were once more
left to ourselves; the arms were piled, the wounded of all
nations collected and carried to the rear, and in a short time
the dead were left without a stitch of clothes to cover their
bodies. All firing had ceased, except a few shots low down
the hill on our right; and shortly after the picquets were
placed in front, a double allowance of spirits was served out
to Wallace's men.

We had now leisure to walk about and talk to each
other on the events of the morning, and look at the French

soldiers in our front. They appeared as leisurely employed
cooking their rations as if nothing serious had occurred to
them, which caused much amusement to our men, some of
whom remarked that they left a few behind them that had
got a "bellyful" already. The rocks which had been forced
by the three companies of the 88th presented a curious and
melancholy sight; one side of their base strewed with our
brave fellows, almost all of them shot through the head,
while in many of the niches were to be seen dead Frenchmen,
in the position they had fought; while on the other side,
and on the projecting crags, lay numbers who, in an effort
to escape the fury of our men, were dashed to pieces in their
fall!

Day at length began to close, and night found the two
armies occupying the ground they held on the preceding
evening; our army, as then, in utter darkness, that of the
enemy more brilliant than the preceding night, which
brought to our recollection the remark of a celebrated
general when he saw bonfires through France after a signal
defeat which the troops of that nation had sustained.
"Gad!" said the general, "those Frenchmen are like flint-
stones—the more you beat them the more fire they make!"

Captain Seton, Ensign Owgan, and myself, with one
hundred of the Connaught Rangers, formed the picquet in
advance of that regiment, and immediately facing the outposts of the enemy in our front. The sentries of each, as
is customary in civilised armies, although within half-shot
range of each other, never fired except upon occasions of
necessity. Towards midnight Seton, a good and steady
officer, went in front, for the third time, to see that the
sentinels which he himself had posted were on the alert.
He found all right; but upon his return to the main body

he missed his way, and happening in the dark to get too close to a French sharpshooter, he was immediately challenged, but not thinking it prudent to make any noise, in the shape of reply or otherwise, he held his peace. Not so with the Frenchman, who uttered a loud cry to alarm his companions, and discharged the contents of his musket at Seton; the ball passed through his hat, but did no other injury, and he might have rejoiced at his escape had the matter ended here; but the cry of the sentinel and the discharge of his musket alarmed the others, and one general volley from the line of outposts of both armies warned Seton that his best and safest evolution would be to sprawl flat on his face amongst the heath with which the hill was copiously garnished. He did so, and as soon as the tumult had in a great degree abated, he got up on his hands and knees and essayed to gain the ground which no doubt he regretted he had ever quit. He was nearing the picquet fast, when the rustling in the heath, increased by the awkward position in which he moved, put us on the *qui vive*. Owgan, who was a dead shot with a rifle, and who on this day carried one, called out, in a low but clear tone, " I see you, and if you don't answer you'll be a dead man in a second"; and he cocked his rifle, showing he meant to make good his promise.

Whether it was that Seton knew the temperament of the last speaker, or was flurried by the recollection of what he was near receiving from his obstinate taciturnity with the French soldier, is uncertain. But in this instance he completely changed his plan of tactics, and replied in a low and scarcely audible tone, " Owgan ! don't fire—it's me." So soon as he recovered his natural and more comfortable position—for he was still " all-fours "—we congratulated him on his lucky escape, and I placed my canteen of brandy to his mouth; it did not require much pressing to prevail upon him to take a hearty swig, which indeed he stood much in need of.

The night passed over without further adventure or annoyance, and in the morning the picquets on both sides were relieved. The dead were buried without much ceremony, and the soldiers occupied themselves cleaning their arms, arranging their accoutrements, and cooking their rations. The enemy showed no great disposition to renew his attack, and a few of us obtained leave to go down to the village of Busaco, in order to visit some of our officers, who were so badly wounded as to forbid their being removed further to the rear. Amongst the number was the gallant Major Silver of the 88th. He had been shot through the body, and though he did not think himself in danger, as he suffered no pain, it was manifest to the medical men he could not live many hours. He gave orders to his servant to leave him for a short time, and attend to his horses; the man did so, but on his return in about a quarter of an hour he found poor Silver lying on his right side as if he was asleep—but he was dead! Silver was one of the best soldiers in the army, and was thanked by Colonel Donkin, who commanded the brigade at the battle of Talavera, for his distinguished bravery in that action. He was laid in a deep grave in the uniform he had fought and died in.

The day after the action some English troops passed through the town of Alcobaça on their route to join the army; and this circumstance, coupled with our victory, led the inhabitants to suppose they, as well as their property, were perfectly safe; and the idea of removing the one or the other never once occurred to them. Their surprise and confusion was in consequence increased tenfold when they

beheld our troops enter the town. Alcobaça was at that
time a beautiful rich village, notwithstanding that it supported a magnificent convent and several hundred priests
and friars. Those gentlemen, although rigid in their mode
of living at times, know as well as any other class of people
how to live, and, having ample means of making out life
at their disposal, it is not to be wondered at that the
convent contained that which was far from unacceptable to
us, namely quantities of provisions.

On our arrival in the town the inhabitants, terrified at the
possibility of being captured by the French, fled, leaving, in
many instances, their houses in such haste as not to allow
themselves time to take away anything, not even their silver
forks and spoons—a luxury which almost the poorest family
in Portugal enjoys. These, and other articles, offered a
strong temptation to our men to do that which they should
not, *i.e.* possess themselves of whatever they found in those
uninhabited mansions. Their doing so, to be sure, was a
slight breach of discipline; but it was argued by the " friends
of the measure," that Lord Wellington having directed the
country parts as well as the towns to be laid waste, in order
to distress the enemy as much as possible, the Portuguese
were highly culpable in neither taking away their property
nor destroying it. It would be almost superfluous to add
that an argument of so sound a nature, and delivered in the
nick of time, had its due force; it in fact bore down all
opposition, and those whose consciences at first felt anything
like a *qualm*, in a little time became more at ease, so that by
the time the houses had been about half-sacked, there was
not one who, so far from thinking it improper to do what he
had done, would not have considered himself much to blame
had he pursued a different line of conduct.

The priests, more cautious, or perhaps better informed, removed their valuables; but in all their hurry they did not forget that hospitality for which they were proverbial. They left some of their brethren behind, who had a dinner prepared for our officers, and when their longer stay was useless to us, and might be attended with danger to themselves, they opened their different stores, and with a generous liberality invited us to take whatever we wished for. Poor men! Their doing so showed more their goodness of heart than their knowledge of the world. Had they been a little longer acquainted with the lads that were now about to stand in their places, they would not have thought such *congé* necessary. As soon as those good men left the dwelling in which they had passed so many tranquil years, we began to avail ourselves of the permission granted us, and which decency forbade our taking advantage of sooner. Every nook was searched with anatomical precision; not even a corner cupboard was allowed to escape the scrutiny of the present inmates of the convent, who certainly were as unlike the former in their demeanour as in their costume.

In taking a survey of the different commodities with which this place was supplied, I had the good fortune or, as it afterwards turned out, the *bad* fortune, to stumble upon several firkins of Irish butter. Unquestionably I never felt happier, because it was a luxury I had not tasted for months; but my servant, by a good-natured officiousness, so loaded my poor, half-starved, jaded mule with, not only butter, but everything else he could lay his paw upon, that, unable to sustain the shameful burden which had been imposed upon him, he fell exhausted in endeavouring to scramble through a quagmire, and I lost not only the cargo with which he was laden, but the animal himself; however,

I had the consolation to know that few of the articles cost me anything, and he himself was a sort of windfall, having been *found* by my servant on the retreat.

The army continued its march upon Torres Vedras with little interruption from the enemy, and early in October we occupied our entrenched camp. This formidable position had its right at Alhandra on the Tagus; its left rested on the part of the sea where the river Zizambre empties itself, and along its centre was a chain of redoubts armed with cannon of different calibre; between these forts was a double and, in some instances, triple row of breastworks for the infantry, and the position might be considered faultless.

On the night of the 29th the French army made that flank movement which obliged Lord Wellington to retire, and which is so well known as to render any detail from me unnecessary; and on that night we took our leave of the mountain of Busaco, and commenced our march to the Lines of Torres Vedras.

CHAPTER V

Occupation of the Lines of Torres Vedras—An army in motley—An
Irish interpreter—Death of the Marquis de la Romana—Retreat of
Masséna's army from Portugal—Indulgence of Lord Wellington—
The amenities of a subaltern's existence.

THE astonishment of the French general was great when he
beheld the reception prepared for him; and his friend the
Duke d'Abrantes must have been lowered in his estimation
not a little, because it is well known that, contrary to the
advice of several able officers, Masséna was overruled by
Junot, who assured him those heights could be easily
carried.

After numerous *reconnoissances*, the French Marshal came
to the resolution of renouncing any hope of success from an
assault; and his army formed a line blockade, with its right
at Otta, its centre at Alenquer, and its left at Villa Franca.
But it must have been a matter of deep regret to him to
have learned, when too late, that by this useless advance of
his, he exposed upwards of three thousand of his wounded
from the battle of Busaco, left at Coimbra, to be massacred
by the Portuguese militia and peasantry.

For the space of a month the French army remained
inactive in their wretched cantonments, their supply of
provisions growing every day more scanty; their horses,

reduced to the necessity of subsisting on the vine twigs, died by hundreds; and the soldiers, pining from disease, became discontented and discouraged. In consequence, the desertions increased with their increasing wants, and it appeared very evident that matters could not long continue in the state they had assumed at the beginning of November.

Although our situation was, in every respect, better than that of the enemy, we were far from comfortable. Our huts, from want of any good materials to construct them, were but a weak defence against the heavy rains which fell at this time. We had no straw to serve for thatch, and the heath which we were obliged to use as a substitute, though it looked well enough when in full leaf and blossom, and was a delightful shelter in fine weather, became a wretched protection against the torrents that soon after inundated us. The inside of our habitation presented an appearance as varied as it was uncomfortable; at one end might be seen a couple of officers, with their cloaks thrown about them, snoring on a truss of straw, while over their heads hung their blankets, which served as a kind of inner wall, and for a time stopped the flood that deluged the parts of the hut not so defended; but this, by degrees, becoming completely saturated with rain, not only lost its original appearance, but what was worse, its original usefulness; for the water, dripping down from the edges, gradually made its way towards the centre of the blanket, and thus, by degrees, it assumed a shape not unlike the parachute of a balloon. Finally the whole, being overpowered with its own weight, and either giving way at the point or bottom, or breaking its hold from the twigs which feebly held it at top, overwhelmed those it was intended to protect, and in the space of a minute more effectually drenched them than the heaviest fall of rain

would have accomplished in several hours. In another
corner lay some one else, who, for want of a better, substi-
tuted a sheet or an old tablecloth as a temporary defence;
but this was even more disastrous than the blanket, for from
the nature of its texture, and the imperfect manner in which
it was from necessity pitched, it made but a poor stand;
it soon performed the functions of a filtering machine, and
with equal effect, though less force, was to the full as un-
serviceable as the blanket. Others, more stout and convivial,
sat up smoking cigars and drinking brandy punch, waiting
for the signal to proceed to our alarm-post, a duty which
the army performed every morning two hours before day.
This was by no means a pleasant task; scrambling up a
hill of mud and standing shivering for a couple of hours in
the dark and wet was exceedingly uncomfortable, but I don't
remember to have heard one single murmur; we all saw the
necessity of such a line of conduct, and we obeyed it with
cheerfulness.

On the 14th of November Masséna broke up his camp,
and on that night his army was in full march upon Santarem;
ours made a corresponding movement, and the headquarters
were on the 18th established at Cartaxo.

It was the general opinion in the army that a battle in
the neighbourhood of Santarem would be the result of those
manœuvres, and this opinion was strengthened by Lord
Wellington making a *reconnoissance* on the 19th; but
although those expectations were disappointed, the situation
of the troops was much improved, and their comforts increased. Our division occupied the town of Torres Vedras,
while the other corps were in the villages of Alenquer,
Azambujo, and Alcoentre. The French army foraged the
country between Santarem and the river Zezere. Santarem

E

was much strengthened, and the two armies were thus circumstanced at the end of November 1810.

Our fatigues being for a time at an end, we occupied ourselves in such pursuits as each of us fancied. We had no unnecessary drilling, nor were we tormented with that greatest of all *bores* to an officer at any time, but particularly on service, uniformity of dress. The consequence was that every duty was performed with cheerfulness; the army was in the highest state of discipline; and those gentlemen who had, or fancied they had, a taste for leading the fashion, had now a fine opportunity of bringing their talents into play.

With such latitude it is not to be wondered at that our appearance was not *quite* as uniform as some general officers would approve of; but Lord Wellington was a most indulgent commander; he never harassed us with reviews, or petty annoyances, which so far from promoting discipline, or doing good in any way, have a contrary effect. A corporal's guard frequently did the duty at headquarters; and every officer who chose to purchase a horse might ride on a march. Provided we brought our men into the field well appointed, and with sixty rounds of good ammunition each, he never looked to see whether their trousers were black, blue, or grey; and as to ourselves, we might be rigged out in all the colours of the rainbow if we fancied it. The consequence was, that scarcely any two officers were dressed alike! Some with grey braided coats, others with brown; some again liked blue; while many from choice, or perhaps necessity, stuck to the "old red rag." Overalls, of all things, were in vogue, and the comical appearance of a number of infantry officers loaded with leather bottoms to their pantaloons, and huge chains suspended from the side buttons, like a parcel of troopers, was amusing enough. Quantities of hair, a regular brutus, a pair of mustachios, and screw brass spurs, were essential to a first-rate *Count,* for so were our dandies designated. The "cut-down" hat, exactly a span in height, was another *rage;* this burlesque on a *chapeau* was usually out-topped by some extraordinary-looking feather; while, again, others wore their hats without any feather at all— and indeed this was the most rational thing they did. In the paroxysm of a wish to be singularly singular, a friend of mine shaved all the hair off the crown of his head, and *he* was decidedly the most *outré*-looking man amongst us, and consequently the happiest. I myself had a hankering to be a *Count,* and had I half as much money to spare as time, I should not have been outdone by any man in the army, so I hit upon the expedient of cutting my hat down a couple of inches lower than any one else: *this* I thought would be better than nothing. Lieutenant Heppenstal, of the 88th Regiment, was nearly falling a sacrifice to the richness of his dress. He belonged to the light troops of our army at the battle of Busaco, and was warmly engaged with the advance of the enemy. He was a man of the most deter- mined bravery and gigantic strength, and more than once became personally engaged with the French riflemen. At one time, carried away by his daring impetuosity, he pursued his success so far as to be nearly mixed with the enemy; a number of Portuguese Caçadores, coming up at this moment, mistook him for a French general officer, and attempted to make him a prisoner; a scuffle ensued, in which he lost the skirts of his frockcoat; and it was not until an explanation took place that he was enabled to join his regiment in this laughable trim—his beautiful gold-tagged frock being con- verted into a regular spencer.

Poor Heppenstal! It was his first appearance under fire, and it was not difficult for those who witnessed his too gallant *début* to foresee that his career of glory would be short. He carried a rifle, and his unerring aim brought down many a man on the morning I am speaking of; but he did not long survive the praises so justly bestowed on him, and it will soon be my painful duty to record his death.

Dress, however, with its attractions, by no means engrossed all our thoughts; some were fond of shooting, and those whose tastes lay that way had plenty of sport, as the country abounded in game; others took to horse-racing, and here was a fine opportunity for the lovers of the turf and of dress to display their knowledge in both. Jockeys, adorned with all colours, were to be seen on the course, and the harlequin-like appearance of these equestrians was far from unpleasing. Some of the races were admirably contested, and afforded us as much gratification as those of Epsom and Doncaster do to the visitants of those receptacles of rank and fashion.

We had great inconvenience in making ourselves understood by our Portuguese allies, and a laughable circumstance of this sort took place between a friend of mine and a shoemaker, in the village of Rio Mayor. He left his boots, his only pair, to be mended, and understood they were to be put in serviceable condition for a *crusado novo*, less than three shillings of our money. Next day, on entering the shop, the man made two or three efforts to make the officer comprehend how well the work had been done; but it was all to no purpose, for my friend, not understanding one word of what was said, conceived the fellow wanted to impose a higher price upon him, and got into a violent rage. An Irish soldier, belonging to the 88th Regiment, of the name of Larracy, a shoemaker, who had been working for the Portuguese, a common indulgence allowed to the tradesmen of the army, came up to his officer and thus accosted him.

"Ah! your honour, I see you can't talk to him, but *lave* him to me; I've been working in his shop these three weeks, and, saving your presence, there isn't a bigger rascal in all Ireland; but I can *spake* as well as himself now, and I'm up to his ways."

Larracy thus became interpreter and *mediator,* and it would be difficult to say in which character he best acquitted himself. Possessing no knowledge whatever of the language, notwithstanding his repeated assurances that he could talk it *nately,* he brought that happy talent for invention, for which the Irish most undeniably stand unrivalled, into play. Seizing one of the boots, he approached his employer, and suiting the word to the action, addressed him in the following words :—

"Si, senhor! Quanto the munnee, for the solee, the heelee, and the nailee ?"

The astonishment portrayed in the countenance of the Portuguese baffles all description; he surveyed Larracy from head to foot, and with much gravity of manner replied, "*En não entendo-o que vós me dizeis.*"[1]—"And sure I'm telling him so," rejoined Larracy. "What does the fellow say?" demanded my friend. "What does he say?—What does he say, is it? He says he put a fine pair of welts to your boots, sir (and it's true for him!); and that your honour will have to give him a dollar [*about two shillings more than was demanded by the Portuguese!*], but just only *lave* him to me, and give *me* the dollar, and if I don't *bate* him down in the

[1] "I do not understand a word you are saying to me."

price, never believe a word that I'll tell your honour again; and I'll carry home your boots for you, and bring you the account in *rotation* (by which he meant in writing), and the change of the dollar."—"Oh! never mind, you are an honest fellow, Larracy, and keep the change for your trouble; but you may tell your employer it is the last job he shall ever do for me."—"Och! sure I told your honour he was a blackguard," grinned Larracy, escorting his officer to the door, and putting the dollar in his pocket.

While in the other parts of the Peninsula much activity prevailed, with us all was quiet; and although the season was advancing towards spring, there was no appearance of our commencing the offensive, and conjectures innumerable were the consequence. Promotion, that great planet whose influence more or less affected us all, was perpetually on the tapis. There were some among us of a desponding cast; they would say, "Have we not lost Almeida, Rodrigo, and now, though last not least, Badajoz? And should we be obliged to evacuate the Peninsula, good-bye to promotion." Others there were who held a different opinion, and, resting their hopes on some fortunate " turn-up," expected ere long to have the enviable title of captain attached to their name. To this class I belonged, and as it was the most numerous in the army, it was in consequence the most clamorous on this head.

The life of a subaltern, in what Miss Mac-Tab would call a marching regiment, where many of us, and I myself for one, had little except our pay, is a perpetual scene of irritating calculation from the 24th of one month to the 24th of the next. No matter under what circumstances, or in what quarter of the globe the subaltern is placed, his *first* thought points towards that powerful magnet the *twenty-fourth*—his *next* to promotion.

The 24th has scarcely passed when the same routine is pursued, every hour increasing in interest according to the immediate wants of the calculator; and time rolls on, either rapidly or slowly, in the exact ratio with the strength or weakness of his purse. The moment he receives his pay he discharges his bills, and by the time he has got about half-way into the first week of the next month, he has little occasion for a knowledge of Cocker to enable him to calculate his money.

The period generally reckoned on by a subaltern to get his company, in a good fighting regiment—that is to say, one that had the good luck to be in the thick and thin of what was going on, for all regiments fight alike for that matter—was from five to six years. The "extra shilling" was rarely heard of, and never thought of but with disgust.[1]

[1] The extra shilling was given to lieutenants who had served in that rank seven years or more, and had not obtained a company.

CHAPTER VI

Excesses and sufferings of the French during their retreat—Combats of Foz d'Aronce and Sabugal—Battle of Fuentes d'Oñoro—Sir E. Pakenham, Colonel Wallace, and the 88th Regiment.

THE retreat of the French army from Portugal commenced on the night of the 5th of March 1811, and was marked by acts more suited to a horde of barbarians than a European army. On the fact being ascertained at our headquarters, we were put in their track, which, when once found, it would have been a difficult matter to lose, the whole country through which they passed being a vast extent of burning ruins. Not a town, not a village, and rarely a cottage escaped the general conflagration. The beautiful town of Leyria was left a heap of ruins; Pombal shared the same fate; and the magnificent convent of Alcobaça was burned to the ground. Two of the finest organs in Europe were destroyed by this wanton act; and a century will be insufficient to repair the evils which a few months inflicted on this unfortunate country.

Scenes of the most revolting nature were the natural attendants on such a barbarous mode of warfare, and scarcely a league was traversed by our army, in its advance, without our eyes being shocked by some frightful spectacle. The French army was doubtless much exasperated against

56

the Portuguese nation, in consequence of the manner in which
they destroyed what would have contributed to the comforts
of men who had been half-starved for six months.   And now,
after so many privations, having a long retreat before them,
with a scanty allowance of provisions in their haversacks, it
is more to be lamented than wondered at, that the march of
the French troops was accompanied by many circumstances
which were disgraceful to them.

On the 9th of March our advance-guard came up with
the rear of the enemy, commanded by Marshal Ney, in the
neighbourhood of Pombal.   The Light Division was warmly
engaged, and some charges of cavalry took place on the high
ground near the castle; but the infantry of our division
(the 3rd) arrived too late to support the Light, and no
decisive result was the consequence.   Masséna continued
his retreat that night and next day; but on the 11th we
found him posted on a rising ground near the village of
Redinha; our army formed in line on the plain, and an
action of some consequence was expected; but the French
marshal was so pressed in front, while his left was vigorously
attacked, that it was not without sustaining a severe loss he
effected his passage across the river Redinha.

On the 15th we surprised their covering division while in
the act of cooking near the village of Foz d'Aronce.   They
retreated in the greatest hurry, leaving several camp kettles
full of meat behind them.   As we approached the town, the
road leading to it was covered with a number of horses,
mules, and asses, all maimed; but the most disgusting sight
was about fifty of the asses floundering in the mud, some
with their throats half cut, while others were barbarously
houghed or otherwise injured.   What the object of this
proceeding meant I never could guess; the poor brutes

could have been of no use to us, or indeed any one else, as I believe they were unable to have travelled another league. The meagre appearance of these creatures, with their backbones and hips protruding through their hides, and their mangled and bleeding throats, produced a general feeling of disgust and commiseration.

The village of Foz d'Aronce was warmly contested, and more than once taken and retaken. Night put a stop to this affair, in which we sustained a loss of about four hundred men. The enemy lost nearly a thousand *hors de combat;*[1] and, as usual, taking advantage of the night, got off, and continued their retreat upon Guarda, having destroyed the bridge on the river Ceira as they retired.

The army did not lose any officer of rank in the affair of Foz d'Aronce, but the service sustained a loss in Lieutenant Heppenstal—a young man who, had he lived, would have been an ornament to a profession for which Nature seemed to have destined him. He was known to be one of the bravest men in the army, but on this occasion his usual spirits deserted him. He moved along silent, inattentive, and abstracted—a brisk firing in our front soon roused all his wonted energy, and he advanced with his men apparently cheerful as ever; turning to a brother officer he said, "You will laugh at what I am going to say; you know I am not afraid to die, but I have a certain feeling that my race is nearly run."—"You jest," said his friend. "No, I don't," was his reply; they shook hands, the light troops advanced, and in a few minutes the brave Heppenstal was a corpse. His presentiment was too just, and though I had heard of

---

[1] These figures are very wild. The English lost 4 officers and 60 men, the French 456 killed and wounded only, according to the official accounts.

instances of the kind before, this was the first that came
under my immediate observation. I ran up to the spot
where he lay; he was bleeding profusely; his breast was
penetrated by two bullets, and a third passed through his
forehead. His death was singular, and it appeared as if he
was resolved to fulfil the destiny that he had marked out
for himself. Our light troops were gradually retreating on
their reinforcements, and were within a few paces of the
columns of infantry; his men repeatedly called out to him
to retire with the rest, but he, either not hearing, or not
attending to what they said, remained, with his back against
a pine-tree, dealing out death at every shot. Pressed as we
were for time, we dug him a deep grave at the foot of the
tree where he so gallantly lost his life, and we laid him in it
without form or ceremony.

Nothing particular occurred after the action of Foz
d'Aronce until our arrival at Guarda. As usual, we met
with groups of murdered peasantry and of French soldiers.
At the entrance of a cave, amidst these rocky mountains, lay
an old man, a woman, and two young men, all dead. This
cave, no doubt, had served them as an asylum the preceding
winter, and appearances warranted the supposition that
these poor creatures, in a vain effort to save their little
store of provisions, fell victims to the ferocity of their
murderers. The clothes of the two young peasants were
torn to atoms, and bore ample testimony that they did not
lose their lives without a struggle to preserve them; the
hands of one were dreadfully mangled, as if in a last effort
to save his life he had grasped the sword which ultimately
despatched him. Beside him lay his companion, his brother
perhaps, covered with wounds; and a little to the right was
the old man. He lay on his back with his breast bare; two

large gashes were over his heart, and the back part of his head was beaten to pieces. Near him lay an old rusty bayonet fixed on a pole, which formerly served as a goad for oxen, and one of his hands grasped a bunch of hair, torn, no doubt, from the head of the assassin; the old woman was in all probability strangled, as no wound appeared on her body.

At some distance from this spot were two French soldiers belonging to the 4th Léger; their appearance was frightful. They had been wounded by our advance, and their companions either being too much occupied in providing for their own safety to think of them, or their situation being too hopeless to entertain an idea of their surviving, they were abandoned to the fury of the peasants, who invariably dodged on the flanks or in the rear of our troops. These poor wretches were surrounded by half a dozen Portuguese, who, after having plundered them, were taking that horrible vengeance too common during this contest. On the approach of our men they dispersed, but, as we passed on, we could perceive them returning like vultures that have been scared away from their prey for the moment, but who return to it again with redoubled voraciousness. Both the Frenchmen were alive, and entreated us to put an end to their sufferings. I thought it would have been humane to do so, but Napoleon and Jaffa flashed across me, and I turned away from the spot.[1]

On the 30th of March General Picton arrived before Guarda. His approach to that town was not only unperceived, but seemed unexpected, having advanced to within two gun-shots of the town without meeting a vedette. Such conduct

[1] The reference is to the discredited story that Napoleon poisoned all his non-transportable wounded at Jaffa, during his retreat to Egypt, in order to prevent them from being massacred by the Turks.

on the part of the French general was not only culpable in
the extreme, but showed the greatest presumption and
confidence, because, had we a brigade of guns with us, and
a few hundred cavalry, the five thousand men that occupied
Guarda would have been forced to lay down their arms.
Fortunately for them, we had neither the one nor the other ;
and instead of being in a condition to attack the town, we
had the mortification to witness the French getting out of
it, bag and baggage, as quick as they could. The scene of
confusion that the streets presented was great ; infantry,
artillery, and baggage, men, women, and children, all mixed
pell-mell together, hurrying to the high road leading to
Sabugal. Our cavalry came up shortly after the enemy had
evacuated the place, but too late to do much good. Some
prisoners and baggage and a few head of cattle were captured, and we took up our quarters in the town for the
night.

On the 3rd of April we again, and for the last time in
Portugal, encountered the enemy at Sabugal. The Light
Division had a gallant affair with the corps of General
Reynier, and though greatly outnumbered, they not only
succeeded in forcing the position, but captured a howitzer
and several prisoners. The 3rd Division soon after reached
the ground, and its leading battalions, especially the 5th
Regiment, had deployed, and having thrown in a heavy fire,
were advancing with the bayonet, when a violent hail-storm
came on and completely hid the two armies from each other.
Reynier hurried his divisions off the field ; and this unlooked-
for event snatched a brilliant exploit from us, as the total
overthrow of this corps would have been in all probability
the result.

The French suffered severely, but they never fought

better; so rapidly did they fire that, instead of returning their ramrods, they stuck them in the ground for expedition, and continued to fight until overpowered by our men, who are certainly better at close fighting than long shot.

The enemy fought their howitzer well, and almost all the gunners lay dead about it. A young artillery officer was the first I took notice of—his uniform was still on him, an unusual thing; he wore a blue frock-coat; across his shoulder hung his cartouche-box; and the middle of his forehead was pierced by a musket ball. His features, which were beautiful, showed, nevertheless, a painful distortion, and it was evident that the shock which deprived him of life, though momentary, was one of excruciating agony. Beside him lay one of the gunners, whose appearance was altogether different from that of his officer. A round shot had taken off his thigh a few inches below the groin, and his death, though not as instantaneous, seemed to be void of pain. The bare stump exhibited a shocking sight—the muscles, arteries, and flesh, all hanging in frightful confusion, presented the eye with a horrid sample of the effects of those means made use of by man for his own destruction; the ramrod of the gun was near him; his back rested against one of the wheels; and there was that placid look in his countenance which would lead you to think he had sat himself down to rest.

The wounded having been all removed, and the enemy continuing their retreat, we bivouacked on the ground they had occupied at the commencement of the action, and the next day we went into cantonments. The French recrossed the Agueda, and Portugal was, with the exception of Almeida, freed from their presence, after they had occupied it for nearly eight months, and had inflicted on the inhabitants every misery it is possible to conceive.

Four weeks had scarcely elapsed when we were again called into action. On the 2nd of May Marshal Masséna passed the river Agueda at Rodrigo, and moved upon Almeida in order to supply it with provisions. He had left a garrison of three thousand men in that fortress, commanded by General Brennier, in whom he placed much confidence. The French Marshal stationed his army on the river Azava, in the neighbourhood of Carpio, Espeja, and Gallegos; and next day (the 3rd) made a movement on Almeida. Lord Wellington made a corresponding movement, and our army occupied a fine line of battle—its right at Nava d'Aver, the centre at Fuentes d'Oñoro, and the left resting on the ruins of the Fort de la Conception; in our front ran the little stream of Oñoro. General Pack's brigade of Portuguese invested Almeida.

Without waiting to ascertain the strength or weakness of the position, Marshal Masséna, with that impetuosity which had formerly characterised him, ordered the village of Fuentes d'Oñoro to be carried; and to make his success certain the entire of the sixth corps was employed in the attack. The town was at this time occupied by some of our 1st Division, consisting of the Highland regiments, supported by others of the line, and the light companies of the 1st and 3rd Divisions, commanded by Major Dick of the 42nd Highlanders, and Colonel Williams of the 60th. The village was taken and retaken several times, and night found both armies occupying a part each.

Masséna, perceiving that the obstacles opposed to his carrying this point, which he considered the key of our position, were too great for him to surmount, employed himself during the 4th of May in reconnoitring our line, and in making preparations for the battle which was to take

place the following day.   On our side we were not inactive :
the avenues leading to Pozobello and Fuentes were barricaded in the best manner the moment would allow ;
temporary defences were constructed at the heads of the
different streets, and trenches dug here and there as a protection against the impetuous attacks expected from the
cavalry of General Montbrun. We lay down to rest perfectly assured that every necessary precaution had been
taken by our General ; and as to the result of the battle,
we looked upon that as certain, a series of engagements with
the enemy having taught us to estimate our own prowess ;
and being a good deal overcome with the heat of the weather,
we lay down to rest and slept soundly.

Day had scarcely dawned when the roar of artillery and
musketry announced the attack of Fuentes d'Oñoro and
Pozobello.   Five thousand men filled the latter village, and
after a desperate conflict carried it with the bayonet.
General Montbrun, at the head of the French cavalry,
vigorously attacked the right of our army ; but he was
received with much steadiness by our 7th Division, which,
though it fought in line, repulsed the efforts made to break
it, and drove back the cavalry in confusion.   The light
troops, immediately in front of the 1st and 3rd Divisions,
were in like manner charged by bodies of the enemy's horse,
but by manœuvres well executed, in proper time, these
attacks were rendered as fruitless as the main one against
the right of our army.   The officer who commanded this
advance,[1] either too much elated with his success, or holding
the efforts of the enemy in too light a point of view, unfortunately extended his men once more to the distance at
which light troops usually fight ; the consequence was fatal.

[1] Colonel Hill of the Guards : he was taken prisoner.

The enemy, though defeated in his principal attack, was still powerful as a minor antagonist; and seeing the impossibility of success against the main body, redoubled his efforts against those which were detached; accordingly he charged with impetuosity the troops most exposed, amongst whom were those I have been describing.   The bugle sounded to close, but whether to the centre, right, or left, I know not; certain it is, however, that the men attempted to close to the right, when to the centre would have been more desirable, and before they could complete their movement the French cavalry were *mixed with them.*

Our division was posted on the high ground just above this plain; a small rugged ravine separated us from our comrades; but although the distance between us was short, we were, in effect, as far from them as if we were placed upon the Rock of Lisbon.   We felt much for their situation, but could not afford them the least assistance, and we saw them rode down and cut to pieces without being able to rescue them, or even discharge one musket in their defence.

Our heavy horse and the 16th Light Dragoons executed some brilliant charges, in each of which they overthrew the French cavalry.   An officer of our staff, who led on one of those attacks, unhorsed and made prisoner Colonel La Motte of the 15th French Chasseurs; but Don Julian Sanchez, the Guerilla chief, impelled more by valour than prudence, attacked with his Guerillas a first-rate French regiment; the consequence was the total overthrow of the Spanish hero; and as I believe this was the first attempt this species of troops ever made at a regular charge against a French regiment, so I hope, for their own sakes, it was their last.

All the avenues leading to the town of Fuentes d'Oñoro

F

were in a moment filled with French troops; it was occupied by our 71st and 79th Highlanders, the 83rd, the light companies of the 1st and 3rd Divisions, and some German and Portuguese battalions, supported by the 24th, 45th, 74th, and 88th British Regiments, and the 9th and 21st Portuguese.

The sixth corps, which formed the centre of the French army, advanced with the characteristic impetuosity of their nation, and forcing down the barriers, which we had hastily constructed as a temporary defence, came rushing on, and, torrent-like, threatened to overwhelm all that opposed them. Every street, and every angle of a street, were the different theatres for the combatants; inch by inch was gained and lost in turn. Whenever the enemy were forced back, fresh troops, and fresh energy on the part of their officers, impelled them on again, and towards mid-day the town presented a shocking sight; our Highlanders lay dead in heaps, while the other regiments, though less remarkable in dress, were scarcely so in the numbers of their slain. The French Grenadiers, with their immense caps and gaudy plumes, in piles of twenty and thirty together—some dead, others wounded, with barely strength sufficient to move; their exhausted state, and the weight of their cumbrous appointments, making it impossible for them to crawl out of the range of the dreadful fire of grape and round shot which the enemy poured into the town. Great numbers perished in this way, and many were pressed to death in the streets.

·It was now half-past twelve o'clock, and although the French troops which formed this attack had been several times reinforced, ours never had; nevertheless the town was still in dispute. Masséna, aware of its importance, and mortified at the pertinacity with which it was defended, ordered a fresh column of the ninth corps to reinforce those already engaged. Such a series of attacks, constantly supported by fresh troops, required exertions more than human to withstand; every effort was made to sustain the post, but efforts, no matter how great, must have their limits. Our soldiers had been engaged in this unequal contest for upwards of eight hours; the heat was moreover excessive, and their ammunition was nearly expended. The Highlanders were driven to the churchyard at the top of the village, and were fighting with the French Grenadiers across the tomb-stones and graves; while the ninth French Light Infantry had penetrated as far as the chapel, distant but a few yards from our line, and were preparing to *debouche* upon our centre. Wallace with his regiment, the 88th, was in reserve on the high ground which overlooked the churchyard, and he was attentively looking on at the combat which raged below, when Sir Edward Pakenham galloped up to him, and said, " Do you see that, Wallace?"—"I do," replied the Colonel, " and I would rather drive the French out of the town than cover a retreat across the Coa."—" Perhaps," said Sir Edward, " his lordship don't think it tenable." Wallace answering said, " I shall take it with my regiment, and keep it too."—" Will you?" was the reply; " I'll go and tell Lord Wellington so; see, here he comes." In a moment or two Pakenham returned at a gallop, and, waving his hat, called out, " He says you may go—come along, Wallace."

At this moment General Mackinnon came up, and placing himself beside Wallace and Pakenham, led the attack of the 88th Regiment, which soon changed the state of affairs. This battalion advanced with fixed bayonets in column of sections, left in front, in double quick time, their firelocks at the trail. As it passed down the road leading to the chapel, it was warmly cheered by the troops that lay at each side of the wall, but the soldiers made no reply to this greeting. They were placed in a situation of great distinction, and they felt it; they were going to fight, not only under the eye of their own army and general, but also in the view of every soldier in the French army; but although their feelings were wrought up to the highest pitch of enthusiasm, not one hurrah responded to the shouts that welcomed their advance. There was no noise or talking in the ranks; the men stepped together at a smart trot, as if on a parade, headed by their brave colonel.

It so happened that the command of the company which led this attack devolved upon me. When we came within sight of the French 9th Regiment, which were drawn up at the corner of the chapel, waiting for us, I turned round to look at the men of my company; they gave me a cheer that a lapse of many years has not made me forget, and I thought that that moment was the proudest of my life. The soldiers did not look as men usually do going into close fight—pale; the trot down the road had heightened their complexions, and they were the picture of everything that a chosen body of troops ought to be.

The enemy were not idle spectators of this movement; they witnessed its commencement, and the regularity with which the advance was conducted made them fearful of the result. A battery of eight-pounders advanced at a gallop to an olive-grove on the opposite bank of the river, hoping by the effects of its fire to annihilate the 88th Regiment, or, at all events, embarrass its movements as much as possible; but this battalion continued to press on, joined by its exhausted comrades, and the battery did little execution.

On reaching the head of the village, the 88th Regiment

was vigorously opposed by the French 9th Regiment, supported by some hundred of the Imperial Guard, but it soon closed in with them, and, aided by the brave fellows that had so gallantly fought in the town all the morning, drove the enemy through the different streets at the point of the bayonet, and at length forced them into the river that separated the two armies. Several of our men fell on the French side of the water. About one hundred and fifty of the grenadiers of the Guard, in their flight, ran down a street that had been barricaded by us the day before, and which was one of the few that escaped the fury of the morning's assault; but their disappointment was great, upon arriving at the bottom, to find themselves shut in. Mistakes of this kind will sometimes occur, and when they do, the result is easily imagined; troops advancing to assault a town, uncertain of success, or flushed with victory, have no great time to deliberate as to what they will do; the thing is generally done in half the time the deliberation would occupy. In the present instance, every man was put to death; but our soldiers, as soon as they had leisure, paid the enemy that respect which is due to brave men. This part of the attack was led by Lieutenant George Johnston, of the 88th Regiment.

CHAPTER VII

As soon as the town of Fuentes d'Oñoro was completely
cleared of the enemy, we sheltered ourselves in the best
manner we could behind the walls, and at the angles of the
different streets; but this was a task not easy to be accomplished, the French batteries continuing to fire with much
effect. Nevertheless, Sir Edward Pakenham remained on
horseback, riding through the streets with that daring bravery
for which he was remarkable; if he stood still for a moment,
the ground about him was ploughed up with round shot.

About this time Colonel Cameron, of the 79th Highlanders, fell, as did also Captain Irwin of the 88th Regiment.
The death of the latter officer was singular. He had been
many years in the army, but this was his first appearance in
action. He was short-sighted, and the firing having in some
degree slackened, he was anxious to take a view of the scene
that was passing; he put his head above the wall behind
which his men were stationed, but had scarcely placed his
glass to his eye, when a bullet struck him in the forehead—
he sprang from the earth and fell dead.

General Mackinnon and a group of mounted officers were

behind the chapel wall, which was the highest point in the village, and consequently much exposed to the enemy's view. This ill-built wall was but a feeble defence against round shot, and it was knocked down in several places, and some wide gaps were made in it. The general stood at one of these breaches giving his directions; he attracted the enemy's notice, and they redoubled their fire on this point. Salvos of artillery astounded our ears, at each of which some part of the old wall was knocked about us; at one of these discharges, five or six feet of it was beaten down, and several men were crushed. Colonel Wallace, of the 88th, was covered with the rubbish, his hat was knocked off, and we thought he was killed, but fortunately he escaped unhurt.

By two o'clock the town was comparatively tranquil. The cannonading on the right of the line had ceased, but the enemy continued to fire on the town; this proceeding was attended with little loss to us, and was fatal to many of their wounded, who lay in a helpless state in the different streets, and could not be moved from their situation without great peril to our men—and they were torn to pieces by the shot of their own army. Several of these poor wretches were saved by the humane exertions of our soldiers, but still it was not possible to attend to all, and, consequently, the havoc made was great. Towards evening the firing ceased altogether, and it was a gratifying sight to behold the soldiers of both armies, who but a few hours before were massacring each other, mutually assisting to remove the wounded to their respective sides of the river. The town too, as was usual in such cases, was not passed unnoticed; it contained little, it is true, yet even that little was better than nothing; and it was laughable to see the scrupulous observation of *etiquette* practised by our men, when any windfall, such as a chest of bread or bacon, happened to fall to the lot of a group of individuals in their foraging excursions. The following was the method taken to divide the spoil, and as no national distinction was thought of, the French as well as the British shared in whatever was acquired. An old experienced stager or two took upon themselves the responsibility of making a division of the plunder according to the number that were present at the capture. This done, one of the party was placed with his back to the booty, when one of those who had partitioned it called out with an audible voice, "Who is to have this?" at the same time pointing to the parcel about to be transferred, while he that was appealed to without hesitation particularised some one of the number, who immediately seized on his portion, put it into his haversack, and proceeded in search of fresh adventures.

We had now leisure to walk through the town and observe the effects of the morning's affray. The two armies lost about five thousand men, and as the chief of this loss was sustained by the troops engaged in the town, the streets were much crowded with the dead and wounded. French and British lay in heaps together, and it would be difficult to say which were most numerous. Some of the houses were also crowded with dead Frenchmen, who either crawled there after being wounded, in order to escape the incessant fire which cleared the streets, or who, in a vain effort to save their lives, were overpowered by our men in their last place of refuge; and several were thrust half-way up the large Spanish chimneys.

General Mackinnon, who directed the attack of the 88th Regiment, and accompanied it in its advance, ordered it to retire to the position it had previously occupied, and as he was unwilling to attract the notice of the enemy too much, he desired that this operation should be performed by companies. My company, or at least the one I commanded, was the first to quit the town. As I approached the spot where Sir Edward Pakenham was on horseback, he said, "Where are you going, sir?" not at the moment recognising the regiment. I told him that General Mackinnon had desired me to retire, but of course if he wished me to stay I would. "Oh no," said he, "the 88th have done enough for this day; but the regiment that replaces you would do well to bring a keg of ammunition, *each man*, in addition to his sixty rounds, for, while I have life, the town shall not be taken." He was in a violent perspiration and covered with dust, his left hand bound round with his pocket-handkerchief as if he had been wounded; he was ever in the hottest of the fire, and if the whole fate of the battle depended upon his own personal exertions he could not have fought with more devotion.

Lord Wellington caused the village of Fuentes d'Oñoro to be occupied by five thousand fresh troops. The Light Division was selected for this service, and it passed us about five o'clock on the evening of the 5th. General Craufurd took the command of this post, and every precaution was resorted to to strengthen the town; temporary walls were thrown up at the bottom of the streets, carts and doors were put into requisition to barricade every pass, but, as it turned out, those observances were unnecessary, for Marshal Masséna, giving up all idea of success, declined any further contest. Thus was the object of his movement frustrated—a battle lost, and Almeida left to its fate.

Our wounded were removed to Villa Formosa, and Lord Wellington decided upon diminishing his front. By this movement we lost our communication with Sabugal, but we effectually covered Almeida, and still possessed the pass of Castello Bom. At half-past nine o'clock at night, the regiments which had so bravely defended Fuentes d'Oñoro passed us, as we were about to lie down to rest; they were much fatigued, and we were struck with their diminished appearance. The 79th Highlanders, in particular, attracted our notice. We asked them what their loss had been; they said, thirteen officers, including their colonel, Cameron, and more than three hundred rank and file; and the soldiers were nearly correct in their estimate.[1]

The next day, the 6th, we had no fighting; each army kept its position, and Villa Formosa continued to be the receptacle for the wounded. This village is beautifully situated on a craggy hill, at the foot of which runs the little stream of Oñoro. Its healthful and tranquil situation, added to its proximity to the scene of action, rendered it a most desirable place for our wounded; the perfume of several groves of fruit-trees was a delightful contrast to the smell that was accumulating on the plain below; and the change of scene, added to a strong desire to see a brother officer, who had been wounded in the action of the 5th, led me thither.

On reaching the village, I had little difficulty in finding out the hospitals, as every house might be considered one, but it was some time before I discovered *that* which I wished for. At last I found it. It consisted of four rooms; in it were pent up twelve officers, all badly wounded. The largest room was twelve feet by eight, and this apartment had for its occupants four officers. Next the door, on a bundle of

---

[1] The 79th, by the official return, lost 32 killed, 152 wounded, and 94 missing—a total of 278.

straw, lay two of the 79th Highlanders, one of them shot
through the spine. He told me he had been wounded in
the streets of Fuentes on the 5th, and that although he had
felt a good deal of pain before, he was now perfectly easy
and free from suffering. I was but ill skilled in surgery,
but, nevertheless, I disliked the account he gave of himself.
I passed on to my friend; he was sitting on a table, his
back resting against a wall. A musket-ball had penetrated
his right breast, and passing through his lungs came out at
his back, and he owed his life to the great skill and attention of Doctors Stewart and Bell, of the 3rd Division.
The quantity of blood taken from him was astonishing;
three, and sometimes four, times a day they would bleed
him, and his recovery was one of those extraordinary instances seldom witnessed. In an inner room was a young
officer shot through the head. His was a hopeless case. He
was quite delirious and obliged to be held down by two men;
his strength was astonishing, and more than once, while
I remained, he succeeded in escaping from the grasp of his
attendants. The Scotch officer's servant soon after came in,
and, stooping down, inquired of his master how he felt, but
received no reply; he had half turned on his face; the man
took hold of his master's hand, it was still warm, but the
pulse had ceased—he was dead. The suddenness of this
young man's death sensibly affected his companions; and
I took leave of my friend and companion, Owgan, fully
impressed with the idea that I should never see him again.

I was on my return to the army when my attention was
arrested by an extraordinary degree of bustle, and a kind of
half-stifled moaning, in the yard of a *quinta*, or nobleman's
house. I looked through the grating, and saw about two
hundred wounded soldiers waiting to have their limbs

amputated, while others were arriving every moment. It would be difficult to convey an idea of the frightful appearance of these men : they had been wounded on the 5th, and this was the 7th ; their limbs were swollen to an enormous size. Some were sitting upright against a wall, under the shade of a number of chestnut-trees, and many of these were wounded in the head as well as limbs. The ghastly countenances of these poor fellows presented a dismal sight. The streams of gore, which had trickled down their cheeks, were quite hardened with the sun, and gave their faces a glazed and copper-coloured hue ; their eyes were sunk and fixed, and what between the effects of the sun, of exhaustion, and despair, they resembled more a group of bronze figures than anything human—there they sat, silent and statue-like, waiting for their turn to be carried to the amputating tables. At the other side of the yard lay several whose state was too helpless for them to sit up ; a feeble cry from them occasionally, to those who were passing, for a drink of water, was all that we heard.

A little farther on, in an inner court, were the surgeons. They were stripped to their shirts and bloody. Curiosity led me forward ; a number of doors, placed on barrels, served as temporary tables, and on these lay the different subjects upon whom the surgeons were operating ; to the right and left were arms and legs, flung here and there, without distinction, and the ground was dyed with blood.

Dr. Bell was going to take off the thigh of a soldier of the 50th, and he requested I would hold down the man for him. He was one of the best-hearted men I ever met with, but, such is the force of habit, he seemed insensible to the scene that was passing around him, and with much composure was eating almonds out of his waistcoat-pockets, which he offered to share with me, but, if I got the universe for it, I could not have swallowed a morsel of anything. The operation upon the man of the 50th was the most shocking sight I ever witnessed ; it lasted nearly half an hour, but his life was saved.

Turning out of this place towards the street, I passed hastily on. Near the gate an assistant-surgeon was taking off the leg of an old German sergeant of the 60th. The doctor was evidently a young practitioner, and Bell, our staff-surgeon, took much trouble in instructing him. It is a tolerably general received opinion, that when the saw passes through the marrow the patient suffers most pain ; but such is not the case. The first cut and taking up the arteries is the worst. While the old German was undergoing the operation, he seemed insensible of pain when the saw was at work ; now and then he would exclaim in broken English, as if wearied, " Oh ! mine Got, is she off still ? " but he, as well as all those I noticed, felt much when the knife was first introduced, and all thought that red-hot iron was applied to them when the arteries were taken up. The young doctor seemed much pleased when he had the sergeant fairly out of his hands, and it would be difficult to decide whether he or his patient was most happy ; but, from every- thing I could observe, I was of opinion that the doctor made his *début* on the old German's stump. I offered up a few words—prayers they could not be called—that, if ever it fell to my lot to lose any of my members, the young fellow who essayed on the sergeant should not be the person to operate on me.

Outside of this place was an immense pit to receive the dead from the general hospital, which was close by. Twelve or fifteen bodies were flung in at a time, and covered with a layer of earth, and so on, in succession, until the pit was filled. Flocks of vultures already began to hover over this spot, and Villa Formosa was now beginning to be as disagreeable as it was the contrary a few days before. This was my first and last visit to an amputating hospital, and I advise young gentlemen, such as I was then, to avoid going near a place of the kind, unless obliged to do so—mine was an accidental visit.

Masséna, renouncing all hope of gaining any advantage by a fresh attack upon our position, recrossed the river Agueda with his army, and left the governor of Almeida to shift for himself. On the 8th and 9th we heard several explosions in that direction, but although we guessed that the governor was destroying some of the magazines previous to his surrender, it never for a moment occurred to us that he meditated what he afterwards executed with too much success. On the morning of the 11th we heard, with the greatest astonishment, that the garrison, after having successfully passed through our lines that encompassed the place, had escaped, with trifling loss, by the pass of San-Felices, and succeeded in reaching the French lines on the Agueda. This was certainly the most extraordinary event that took place during the campaign, and the regiments that formed the blockade afforded amusement for several days to our men; the soldiers used to say that the regiment nearest the town *was asleep*, and that the others were *watching them*.

The command of the army of Portugal was now transferred to Marshal Marmont, Duke of Ragusa. Masséna returned to France in ill-health and ill-humour, in consequence of the bad success of his combinations since his elevation to the command of this army, which, it was confidently stated, was to drive the English from the Peninsula.

With the qualifications of our new antagonist we were unacquainted, except that having been for a considerable time aide-de-camp to the Emperor Napoleon, we looked upon him as something out of the common way—a kind of *rara avis*. However, we found him out before we parted with him.

For six days we had not seen our baggage, and were in consequence without a change of linen. We lay among dirty straw for those six days.

I had no nightcap, and my socks scarcely deserved the name. But this was not all; those who had beards—at this epoch I had not—suffered them to grow to a hideous length, and their faces were so altered as to be scarcely recognisable even by themselves. They might be compared to old Madame Rendau, who, not having consulted her glass since her husband's death, on seeing her own face in the mirror of another lady, exclaimed, "Who is this?" We all agreed that it would be delightful to bathe ourselves in the river, and half a dozen of us walked out to the banks of the Dos Casas. Having washed ourselves, we had a hankering for clean linen, and as none of us could be brought to the opinion of the Irishman, who said it was a charming thing when he *turned* his shirt, we proceeded to *wash* ours, and as this was the first appearance of any of us in the character of a *blanchisseur*, we all acquitted ourselves badly, but I worst of all. In an unguarded moment I flung my unfortunate shirt a little farther than the others did, and, not being quite as light as the day it came out of the fold, it sank to the bottom, and I never saw it afterwards. I soon discovered the cause of my mishap; a small whirlpool (which at the moment appeared in my eyes little inferior to Charybdis) carried it into its vortex, and left me shivering and shaking like a solitary heron watching for a fish by the bank of a river. This accident, however, happened at rather a lucky time; our men had ransacked the French knapsacks with tolerable effect, and as soon as my mishap was known to the men of the company, I was not long wanting the means to supply my loss. At another time this might not have been a matter of easy accomplishment, because it is well known in the army that the men in my regiment were never remarkable for carrying *too great a kit.*

The soldiers, as was their custom, made a display of the different articles they had picked up: some had watches, others rings, and almost all money. There cannot be a stronger contrast between the soldiers of any two nations than between those of France and England: the former, cautious, temperate, and frugal, ever with something valuable about him; the latter the most unthinking, least cautious, and intemperate animal in existence, with seldom a farthing in his pocket, although his pay is three times greater than the others. A French soldier was quite a prize to one of our fellows, and the produce of the plunder gained served him for drink for a week, and sometimes for a fortnight!

I knew a soldier once make a capture of *thirteen hundred dollars,* which having squandered, this same man, in less than a year afterwards, was tried for his life for a highway robbery, and he would have been hanged had not a Portuguese woman proved an *alibi* in his favour. The booty taken by him (for I am convinced the woman swore falsely to save his life) amounted to six vintems, or about *eightpence* sterling! Under similar circumstances a French soldier would have hoarded up his treasure, and, on his return home, dressed like a gentleman, and gone to all the dancing-houses in his neighbourhood.

CHAPTER VIII

Guerilla warfare; its true character—The 3rd Division marches for the Alemtejo—Frenchmen and Irishmen on a march—English regiments—Colonel Wallace—Severe drilling—Maurice Quill and Doctor O'Reily—Taking a rise.

WE occupied our old quarters at Nava d'Aver, and were well received by the inhabitants, who preferred taking a quiet view of the combats of the 3rd and 5th to taking a part in both or either; their plan of operations was of a far different sort, and although unattended with any danger to themselves, was fraught with the most disastrous consequences to their foes, which is, no matter what may be urged against it, the very essence of the art of war.

It may, perhaps, be asked what their method was? or why I, a mere subaltern, should take upon myself the censorship of the art of war? My answer to the former shall be plain and I hope conclusive. To the latter, that having served during part of the year 1809, the entire of 1810-11-12, and part of 1813, in the 3rd Division (commonly designated the "fighting division") of the Peninsular army, and the division never having, during the period alluded to, squibbed off as much as one cartridge without my being in every place, I had opportunities of gaining, and I think I did gain, a little insight into military tactics. If, however, the view I have taken of the subject upon which I am speaking be an erroneous one, I fear my readers will come to the conclusion that I have lost some time which might have been better employed — or, to speak more plainly, that I have mistaken my profession. Marshal Saxe used to say that a mule which had made twenty campaigns under Cæsar would still be but a mule.

I have digressed thus far before touching on a subject that, no doubt (although I have not seen any work of the kind), has been written upon, and upon which much diversity of opinion did exist at one time in England; whether it still exists or not I shall not pretend to say, not having been in the United Kingdom for some years; but certain it is that a very general opinion was prevalent that the war in the Peninsula was carried on, on the part of the peasantry, in a spirit bordering more on a crusade than the ordinary exertions of a brave people struggling for liberty, and that those heroes fought more like a parcel of devils incarnate than mortal men. Indeed, the engravings struck off at Lisbon in commemoration of those days certainly represented them as a gigantic, ferocious people, while the few British that were thrown into the background looked like so many dwarfs who were afraid to come to close quarters with the French. I have ever combated this mistaken opinion, nor does the recollection of the hundreds of those heroes that I have seen marched to the different depôts, handcuffed like a gang of criminals, weaken the view I have taken of the *voluntary* part the Peninsular people took in the contest. In a word, their plan was this :—

The moment our troops had completely routed a body of the enemy's infantry, strewing the ground with dead and wounded, disorganised a park of artillery, or unhorsed some squadrons of dragoons, *then*, and *then* only, would these *gallant fellows* sally forth from their lurking places, and (first taking the precaution to put a stop to any sort of parley from their unfortunate victims by knocking them on the head) completely rifle them of everything they possessed. On the contrary, if our troops met with any reverse, as in the case of Don Julian Sanchez and his ragged band, our allies would take advantage of every incident of ground, and make one of their rapid retrograde movements, sufficient to baffle the evolutions of the most redoubtable *légère* regiments in the French army. This I say is the true harassing system, and the one suited to the genius of the Peninsular nations. It weakens your enemy, and is attended with no risk to yourselves or your friends, which is the same thing; but in England many think that the Portuguese and Spaniards did as much, if not more, during the Peninsular contest than the British army.

Matters remained tranquil in our neighbourhood after the battle of Fuentes d'Oñoro, and the retreat of the army of Portugal across the Agueda, and Lord Wellington employed himself in giving directions for the repairs of the injury inflicted by Brennier upon Almeida previous to his evacuation of that fortress. The troops had recovered from their fatigues and were fresh again and ready for anything, when accounts reached us from the Alemtejo that General Beresford was carrying on the siege of Badajoz, in which operation he was likely to be disturbed by Marshal Soult, who was on his march from Seville. Our division broke up from its cantonments on the 16th of May, and Lord Wellington, who rode at a rapid pace, reached Elvas in three days. There he received the report of the battle of Albuera.

The weather was fine and we continued our route without any forced marches, taking the old beaten track through Castello Branco, Niza, and Portalegre. Our march was uninterrupted by any particular incident; we had no enemy near us, and were therefore left to ourselves.

The French army have the character of being the best marchers in Europe, and I know from experience that no men, to use a phrase of the *Fancy*, understand better than they do how to "hit and get away"; nevertheless I would say, that an army composed exclusively of Irishmen would outmarch any French army as much as I know they would outfight them. The quality which carries a Frenchman through, and enables him to overcome obstacles truly formidable in themselves, is his gaiety, and his facility of accommodating, not only his demeanour, but his *stomach* also, to circumstances as they require it. An Irishman is to the full as gay as a Frenchman; if he does not possess his *piquant* wit—and I don't say that he does not—he has in a paramount degree the rich humour of his own country, which is nowhere else to be found. He can live on as little nourishment as a Frenchman; give him his pipe of tobacco and he will march for two days without food and without *grumbling*; give him, in addition, a little spirits and a biscuit, and he will work for a week. This will not be a task so easy of accomplishment to the English soldier; early habits have given him a relish for good eating, and plenty of it too; if he has not a regular allowance of solid food, it is certain he will not do his work well for any great length of time. But an Irish fellow has been accustomed all his life to be what an Englishman would consider half-starved; therefore quantity or quality is no great consideration with him; his stomach is like a corner cupboard—*you might throw anything into it.* Neither do you find elsewhere the lively thought, the cheerful song or pleasant story, to be met *only* in an Irish regiment. We had a few Englishmen in my corps, and I do not remember ever to have heard one of them attempt a joke. But there are those who think an Irish regiment more difficult to manage than that of any other nation. Never was there a more erroneous idea. The English soldier is to the full as drunken as the Irish, and not half so pleasant in his liquor.

These opinions are, however, mere matter of fancy. Some of our best regiments were English, and one, to please me, decidedly the finest in the Peninsular army, the 43rd, was principally composed of Englishmen. Then there was that first-rate battle regiment, the 45th, a parcel of Nottingham weavers, whose sedentary habits would lead you to suppose they could not be prime marchers; but the contrary was the fact, and they marched to the full as well as my own corps, which were all Irish save three or four. But if it come to a hard tug, and that we had neither rations nor shoes, then, indeed, the Connaught Rangers would be in their element, and outmarch almost any battalion in the service; and for this plain reason, that scarcely one of them wore many pairs of shoes prior to the date of his enlistment, and as to the rations (the most part of them at all events), a dozen times had been in all probability the *outside* of their acquaintance with such delicacies.

But the grand secret in a good marching, good fighting, or loyal regiment, one not given to a habit of deserting, is being *well commanded;* because the finest body of men may be ruined, the efforts of the bravest regiment paralysed, and the best disposed corps become marauders and deserters, from having an inefficient man at their head.

Colonel Alexander Wallace, who commanded us for so many years, and under whom the regiment repeatedly covered itself with glory, was the very chief we wanted. Although a Scotchman himself, he was intimately acquainted with the sort of men he had under him, and he dealt with them and addressed their feelings in a way that was peculiar to himself and suited to them. In action he was the same as on parade, and in either case he was as he should be. If we were placed (as we often were) in any critical situation, he would explain to the soldiers what he expected them to do ; if in danger of being charged by cavalry he would say, " Mind the square ; you know I often told you that if ever you had to form it from line, in face of an enemy, you'd be in a d——d ugly way, and have plenty of noise about you ; mind the tellings off, and don't give the *false touch* to your right or left hand man ; for by G—d, if you are once broken, you'll be running here and there like a parcel of *frightened pullets !* " But Colonel Wallace was out of his place as a mere commander of a regiment ; he was eminently calculated to head a division, because he not only possessed that intrepidity of mind which would brave any danger, but genius to discover the means of overcoming it. It was by his foresight that our brave companions, the 45th, were sustained in their unequal contest with Reynier's division at Busaco ; and Lord Wellington, who saw and fully appreciated the manœuvre, rode up to the 88th Regiment, and seizing Colonel Wallace by the hand, said : " Upon my honour, Wallace, I never witnessed a more gallant charge than that just now made by your regiment." The dead and wounded of the 2nd and 4th Léger, the 15th and 36th (four French regiments which were opposed to the 88th singly), lay thick on the face of the hill, and their numbers gave ample testimony that we deserved the praises bestowed upon us by our General. The 45th also came in for their share of praise, and no battalion ever merited it better than they did;—at one time they were engaged with nearly ten times their own number.

It was the fashion with some to think that the 88th were a parcel of wild rattling rascals, ready for a row, but loosely officered. The direct contrary was the fact. Perhaps in the whole British army there was not one regiment so severely drilled. If a man coughed in the ranks, he was punished; if the sling of the firelock, for an instant, left the hollow of the shoulder when it should not, he was punished; and if he moved his knapsack when standing at ease, he was punished—more or less of course, according to the offence. The consequence of this system, exclusively Colonel Wallace's, was that the men never had the appearance of being fatigued upon a march; and when they halted, you did not see them thrusting their firelocks against their packs to support them. Poor Bob Hardyman of the 45th said the reason the Connaught Rangers carried their packs better than any other regiment was "that they never had anything in them"! and, to speak candidly, we never had more than was necessary, and in truth it was very little that satisfied our fellows.

At drill our manœuvres were chiefly confined to line marching, echelon movements, and formation of the square in every possible way; and in all these we excelled. Colonel Wallace was very unlike an old Major who, having once got his battalion *into* square, totally forgot how to get it *out* of it. Having tried several ways, each time more effectually clubbing the sections, he thus addressed his officers and soldiers: "Gentlemen! I can clearly discern that there is a *something wanting*, and I strongly recommend you, when you reach your barracks, to peruse Dundas![1]—Men, you may go home," and he thus dismissed them.

I never remember our having as much as one adjutant's drill; all was done by the commanding officer himself. Our adjutant was left ill at Lisbon, and he that acted was more of a good penman (an essential point) than a drill. I forget now how the circumstance of our having been sent an adjutant from the Guards occurred, but one of their sergeant-majors did reach us in the capacity of adjutant. On his arrival at headquarters he dined with the Colonel, who invited him to attend parade the next morning. We were under arms at ten, and never once ordered arms until two! Not a man fell out of the ranks, not a man coughed, and not a man moved his pack. When the drill was over, "Well," said Colonel Wallace, "what do you think of the state of the battalion?"—"Very steady indeed, sir," replied the Guardsman. He left us that night, *and we never saw him afterwards.*

On the 24th of May we reached Campo Mayor, and here I became acquainted with Maurice Quill. It would be quite idle in me to attempt giving any very detailed account of a character so well known; one who, whenever he opened his mouth, was sure to raise a laugh, and often before he had time to speak; and he by whom I was introduced (Dr. O'Reily) was little, if anything, inferior to Quill in either eccentricity or humour.

The first question Quill asked O'Reily was, if we all slept soundly the night Brennier got away from Almeida. O'Reily replied, "that some of our army certainly slept sounder than

---

[1] "Dundas" is the famous drill-book of Sir David Dundas, who succeeded the Duke of York as Commander-in-Chief.

was desirable; but that in their affair at Albuera they did seem to have had their eyes perfectly open, not only during the action, but after it." At this moment, a couple of hundred of those troops that had been broken by the Polish horse, having escaped from the enemy, passed us.

During our conversation, O'Reily, as was customary with him, became quite abstracted, and apparently absorbed in his own reflections, and upon our turning round we discovered him in one of Mendoza's attitudes! "What are you squaring at?" demanded Maurice. "My good friend Quill," replied O'Reily, " I have long felt the difficulty of coming to a satisfactory conclusion as to the probability of science being eventually able to overcome savage strength. There is much, sir, to be said on both sides of the question, and I have great doubts concerning the battle about to be decided."—" What battle? why, sure, we are not going to fight another so soon?" said Quill. "The fight to which I allude, sir," said O'Reily, with Quixote-like gravity—for he paused between every word—" is the one pending between Crib and the black man Molineux; it will be a contest of science against brute strength "—and he threw himself into one of the finest defensive attitudes I ever saw; "there," said he, "there is the true science for you; nevertheless, it might be overcome by savage strength, and there is the rub, sir. I have devoted much time in endeavouring to come to a satisfactory conclusion on this point, but hitherto without effect, so I must await the issue of this fearful encounter; and, my dear Quill, having said so much on the subject, allow me to wish you a very good morning." It was evident that, although Quill was no novice, O'Reily had taken "a rise out of him," and it afforded us matter of amusement for many a day after.

We remained in Campo Mayor until the 27th of May (in order to allow the stores and battering train from Elvas to arrive), on which day we passed the Guadiana at a ford, distant from San Christoval about three cannon-shots'; we received no interruption in our passage of the river, and the operation was performed without loss. The 28th, 29th, and 30th were taken up in marking out our camp, and constructing huts; and as the weather was beautiful, and our camp abundantly supplied by the peasantry, we passed a very agreeable time of it.

The river ran within a few yards of us; its marshy banks being thickly covered with plantations of olives, afforded a delightful shade to us when we either went to fish or bathe. Its breadth at this point might be about sixty toises, and it is well stocked with fine mullet. We had several expert fishermen amongst us, and they contrived not only to supply their own tables with fish, but also to increase the comforts of their friends.

CHAPTER IX

Second siege of Badajoz—A *reconnoissance*—Death of Captain Patten—
Attacks on Fort San Christoval—Their failure—Causes of their
failure—Gallant conduct of Ensign Dyas, 51st Regiment—His
promotion by the Duke of York.

BADAJOZ was laid siege to for the second time on the 30th of
May 1811; on that day the investment of the town on the
left bank of the Guadiana was completed, as was also that
of the fort of San Christoval on the right bank; and the
trenches before both were opened that night.

This was my first siege, and the novelty of the thing
compensated me in some degree for the sleepless nights I
used to pass at its commencement; but habit soon reconciled
me, and I could sleep soundly in a battery for a couple of
hours at a time. Nothing astonished me so much as the noise
made by the engineers; I expected that their loud talking
would bring the enemy's attention towards the sound of our
pick-axes, and that all the cannon in the town would be
turned against us—and, in short, I thought every moment
would be my last. I scarcely ventured to breathe until we
had completed a respectable first parallel, and when it was
fairly finished, just as morning began to dawn, I felt
inexpressibly relieved. The 7th Division was equally
fortunate before San Christoval.

As soon as the enemy had a distinct view of what we had been doing, he opened a battery or two against us, with, however, but little effect, and I began to think a siege was not that tremendous thing I had been taught to expect; but at this moment a thirty-two pound shot passed through a mound of earth in front of that part of the parallel in which I was standing (which was but imperfectly finished), and taking two poor fellows of the 83rd (who were carrying a hand-barrow) across their bellies, cut them in two, and whirled their remnants through the air. I had never before so close a view of the execution a round shot was capable of performing, and it was of essential service to me during this and my other sieges. It was full a week afterwards before I held myself as upright as before.

By ten o'clock in the morning our line of batteries presented a very disorganised appearance; sand-bags, gabions, and fascines knocked here and there; guns flung off their carriages, and carriages beaten down under their guns. The boarded platforms of the batteries, damp with the blood of our artillery-men, or the headless trunks of our devoted engineers, bore testimony to the murderous fire opposed to us, but nevertheless everything went on with alacrity and spirit; the damage done to the embrasures was speedily repaired, and many a fine fellow lost his life endeavouring to vie with the men of the Engineers in braving dangers, unknown to any but those who have been placed in a similar situation.

It was on a morning such as I am talking of that Colonel Fletcher, chief officer of Engineers, came into the battery where I was employed; he wished to observe some work that had been thrown up by the enemy near the foot of the castle the preceding night. The battery was more than usually full of workmen repairing the effects of the morning's fire, and the efforts of the enemy against this part of our works were excessively animated. A number of men had fallen and were falling, but Colonel Fletcher, apparently disregarding the circumstance, walked out to the right of the battery, and, taking his stand upon the level ground, put his glass to his eye, and commenced his observations with much composure. Shot and shell flew thickly about him, and one of the former tore up the ground by his side and covered him with clay; but not in the least regarding this, he remained steadily observing the enemy. When at length he had satisfied himself, he quietly put up his glass, and turning to a man of my party who was sitting on the outside of an embrasure, pegging in a fascine, said, " My fine fellow, you are too much exposed; get inside the embrasure, and you will do your work nearly as well."—" I'm almost finished, Colonel," replied the soldier, "and it isn't worth while to move now; those fellows can't hit me, for they've been trying it these fifteen minutes." They were the last words he ever spoke! He had scarcely uttered the last syllable when a round shot cut him in two, and knocked half of his body across the breech of the gun. The name of this soldier was Edmund Man; he was an Englishman, although he belonged to the 88th Regiment. When he fell, the French cannoniers, as was usual with them, set up a shout, denoting how well satisfied they were with their practice!

One evening, while we were occupied in the usual way in the trenches, a number of us stood talking together; several shells fell in the works, and we were on the alert a good deal in order to escape from them. A shell on a fine night at a distance is a pretty sight enough, but I, for one, never liked too near a view of it. We were on this night kept tolerably busy in avoiding those that fell amongst us; one, however, took us by surprise, and before we could escape, fell in the middle of the trench; every one made the best of his way to the nearest *traverse*, and the confusion was much increased by some of the sappers passing at the moment with a parcel of gabions on their backs. Colonel Trench of the 74th, in getting away, ran against one of these men, and not only threw him down, but fell headlong over him, and sticking fast in one of the gabions was unable to move. As soon as the shell exploded, we all sallied forth from our respective nooks, and relieved Colonel Trench from his awkward position. "Well," said Colonel King, of the 5th, "I often saw a *gabion* in a *trench*, but this is the first time I ever saw a *Trench* in a *gabion*." Considering the time and place the pun was not a bad one, and made us all laugh heartily, in which Colonel Trench good-humouredly joined.

Not long after this a round shot carried away the arm of a soldier of the 94th. Dr. O'Reily of my corps, happening to be the nearest medical man, was awoke out of a sound sleep by his orderly sergeant, and having examined the stump, amputated the fractured part. O'Reily was one of the most eccentric, and at the same time one of the pleasantest fellows in the world. He delighted in saying extraordinary things in extraordinary places, and it was amusing to those who knew him well to see his countenance after saying something out of the common way before a stranger. In the present instance, after having wrapped his boat-cloak about him, and settled himself in the same position he had been in before he performed the operation on the 94th man, he, with the most profound gravity of manner, asked the sergeant if he recollected the state in which he had found him? "Indeed, sir," replied the orderly with a broad grin, "your honour was fast asleep, *snorin'* mighty loud."—"Well then, sir, if you return here in five minutes, in all human probability you will find me in precisely the same situation," and he immediately fell asleep, or feigned to do so.

On the evening of the 5th I was sent in advance with a covering party of forty men; we were placed some distance in front of the works, and as usual received directions to beware of a surprise. Our batteries were all armed, and a sortie from the garrison was not improbable; the night was unusually dark, and except an occasional shell from our mortars, the striking of the clocks in the town, or the challenge of the French sentinels along the battlements of the castle, everything was still.

A man of a fanciful disposition, or indeed of an ordinary way of thinking, is seldom placed in a situation more likely to cause him to give free scope to his imagination than when lying before an enemy on a dark night; every sound, the very rustling of a leaf, gives him cause for speculation; figures will appear, or seem to appear, in different shapes; sometimes the branch of a tree passes for a tremendous fellow with extended arms, and the waving of a bush is mistaken for a party crouching on their hands and knees.

I don't know why it was, but I could not divest myself of the idea that an attack upon our lines was meditated. I cast a look at my men as they lay on the ground, and saw that each held his firelock in his grasp and was as he should be; half an hour passed away in this manner, but no sound gave warning that my suspicions were well founded. The noise of the workmen in the trenches lessened by degrees, and as the hour of midnight approached there was, comparatively speaking, a death-like silence. I went forward a short distance, but it was a short distance, for in truth—to say the least of it—I was a little "hipped." I even wished the enemy would throw a shot or two against our works to give a fillip to my thoughts. Heavens! how I envied the soldiers, who slept like so many *tops* and snored so loud. I went forward again, but had not proceeded more than about one hundred paces when I heard voices whispering in my front, and upon observing more minutely in the direction from whence the sounds proceeded, I saw distinctly two men. The uniform of one was dark ; the other wore a large cloak, and I could hear his sabre clinking by his side as he approached me.

At the instant I do not know *what* sum I would have considered too great to have purchased my ransom and placed me once more at the head of my men. I need scarcely say that I regretted the step I had taken, but it was too late. The figures continued to advance towards the spot where I was crouched, and were already within a few paces of me. I did not know what to do; I dreaded remaining stationary, and I was ashamed to run away— there was not a moment to be lost, and I made up my mind to sell my life dearly. I sprang up with my drawn sabre in my hand, and called out as loud as I was able (and it was but a so-so effort), "Who goes there?" My delight was great to find, in place of two Frenchmen (the advance, as I expected, of several hundred), Captain Patten of the Engineers attended by a sergeant of his corps ; he held a dark lantern under his cloak, and told me he had been on his way to reconnoitre the breach in the castle wall, but that he thought it as well to return to the first covering party he should meet with in order to get a file of men which he proposed taking with him to within a short distance of the breach. I was just then in that frame of mind from my own little adventure to approve highly of his precaution, and I gave him a couple of what our fellows (the Connaught Rangers) used to call lads *that weren't easy*, or, to speak without a metaphor, two fellows that would walk into the mouth of a cannon if they were bid to do it.

Previous to this I had passed an uneasy night, but I was now filled with much anxiety for the fate of Captain Patten and my own two men. They had left me about a quarter of an hour when a few musket-shots from the bastion nearest the breach announced that the *reconnoissance* had not been made unnoticed by the enemy; and shortly after, the return of my soldiers confirmed the fact.

It appeared that upon arriving within pistol-shot of the wall Captain Patten motioned to the men to lie down, while he crept forward to the breach; he had succeeded in ascertaining its state, and was about to return to the soldiers, when some inequality in the ground caused him to stumble a little, and the noise attracted the notice of the nearest sentinel, whose fire gave the alarm to the others. One of their shots struck Captain Patten in the back, a little below the shoulder, and he survived its effects but a few hours. Thus fell a fine young man, an ornament to that branch of the service to which he belonged, and a branch which in point of men of highly cultivated scientific information, as well as the most chivalrous bravery, may challenge the world to show its superior.

The fire against the castle was continued on the following day, the 6th, with much effect, and the batteries in front of San Christóval had not only overcome the fire of that outwork, but towards midday the breach was judged assailable.

H

At nine o'clock at night one hundred men of the 7th Division, commanded by Major Macintosh of the 85th Regiment, advanced to the assault; the forlorn hope, consisting of six volunteers, and led on by Ensign Joseph Dyas of the 51st Regiment, who solicited this honour, headed the attack.

The troops advanced with much order, although opposed to a heavy fire.   Arrived upon the glacis, they speedily descended the ditch, and the forlorn hope, accompanied by an officer of Engineers, pressed on to the breach.   They had scarcely arrived at its foot when the officer of Engineers was mortally wounded, and Ensign Dyas was in consequence the only person to direct the men at the breach; for the main body, including the commanding officer, attempted to mount what appeared to them to be the breach, but what was in reality nothing more than an embrasure which had been a good deal injured by the fire of our batteries.   Some of the foremost succeeded in planting ladders against its rugged face, but their efforts were baffled by the exertions of the French engineers who, notwithstanding our fire of grape and musketry, had contrived to clear away the rubbish from the base of the wall; and the ladders were in consequence not of a sufficient length to enable the men to make a lodgment.   A quarter of an hour had now elapsed, during which time several fruitless attempts had been made to enter the fort; and Major Macintosh, with his few remaining men, succeeded with difficulty in reaching their own lines, which they had left but a short time before with feelings of a very different description.   None of the party could give any account of Ensign Dyas—indeed, how could they? for the storming party had never seen the forlorn hope from the moment they descended the ditch!   As is common in such cases, there were many who said they believed that he, individually, was the last living man in the ditch, and it was a generally received opinion that Dyas had fallen. Major Macintosh, in company with a few friends, was sitting in his tent talking over the failure of the attack, and regretting, amongst others, the loss of this officer, when to his amazement he entered the tent not only alive but unhurt. This brave young fellow, after having lost the greater part of his men, and finding himself unsupported by the storming party, at length quitted the ditch, but not until he heard the enemy entering it by the sally-port.

On the 7th, 8th, and 9th the fire against San Christoval was continued with increased vigour, and on the latter day it was resolved that the attack of it should be a second time made that night. A superior number of troops to those which failed on the 6th, but still *inferior* to the garrison of the fort, were selected for the attack, and the command given to Major Mac Geechy, an English officer in the service of Portugal, who volunteered this duty—Dyas again leading the forlorn hope. As before, the troops advanced under the fire of every gun that could be brought to bear upon them, and with much spirit descended the ditch. A little disorder amongst the men who carried the ladders caused some delay, but the detachment pressed on to the breach without waiting for the reorganisation of the ladder men. The soldiers posted on the glacis, by their determined fire, notwithstanding their exposed situation, forced the enemy to waver, and if ever there was a chance of success, it was at this moment. Dyas and his companions did as much as men could do, but in vain. Their efforts were heroic, though unavailing; the spot was strewed with the dead and dying; the breach was packed with Frenchmen, and the glacis and ditch covered with our dead and disabled soldiers. Major Mac Geechy fell pierced with bullets, and almost all the party shared his fate. Ensign Dyas was struck by a pellet [1] in the forehead, and fell upon his face, but, undismayed by this, he sprang up and rallied his few remaining followers, but in vain. This heroic intrepidity deserved a better fate, but his efforts were paralysed by the obstacles opposed to him, and Dyas was at length reluctantly obliged to abandon an enterprise, on the issue of which he had a second time chivalrously, though unsuccessfully, staked his life. As before, he was the last to leave the ditch, and with much difficulty reached our lines. His mode of escape was as curious as it was novel. One of the ladders that could not be placed upright still hung from the glacis on the pallisadoes; this he sprang up, and in an instant he was upon the glacis, where he flung himself upon his face. The Frenchmen upon the walls, seeing him fall at the moment of their fire, shouted out "*Il est tué, en voila le dernier!*"

Dyas, perfectly collected, saw that his only chance of escape was by remaining quiet for a short time, which he did, and then seizing a favourable moment when the garrison were thrown off their guard by the silence that prevailed, he jumped up, and reached our batteries in safety. He and *nineteen* privates were all that escaped out of *two hundred*, which was the original strength of the storming party and forlorn hope.[2]

It may, perhaps, be asked by persons unacquainted with these details, what became of Ensign Dyas; and they no

---

[1] A small bullet, larger than a swan drop. Four of them were enclosed in a piece of wood, three inches long, and at the top was placed the musket-ball. This shrapnel in miniature did considerable execution.

[2] An exaggeration: 114 out of 200, not 180, were killed or wounded.

doubt will say what a lucky young man he was to gain
promotion in so short a time; but such was not the case,
although he was duly recommended by Lord Wellington.
This was no doubt an oversight, as it afterwards appeared,
but the consequences have been of material injury to Ensign,
now Captain, Dyas.   This officer, like most brave men, was
too modest to press his claim, and after having served
through the entire of the Peninsular war, and afterwards at
the memorable battle of Waterloo, he, in the year 1820—
ten years after his gallant conduct—was, by *a mere chance*,
promoted to a company, in consequence of the representation
of Colonel Gurwood (another, but more lucky, forlorn-hope
man) to Sir Henry Torrens.

Colonel Gurwood was a perfect stranger (except by
character) to Dyas, and was with his regiment, the 10th
Hussars, at Hampton Court, where Sir Henry Torrens
inspected the 51st Regiment.   Colonel Ponsonby and Lord
Wiltshire (not one of whom Dyas had ever seen) also
interested themselves in his behalf; and immediately on Sir
Henry Torrens arriving in London, he overhauled the
documents connected with the affair of San Christoval, and
finding all that had been reported to him to be perfectly
correct, he drew the attention of His Royal Highness the
Duke of York to the claims of Lieutenant Dyas.

His Royal Highness, with that consideration for which
he was remarkable, immediately caused Lieutenant Dyas to
be gazetted to a company in the 1st Ceylon Regiment.

Captain Dyas lost no time in waiting upon Sir Henry
Torrens and His Royal Highness the Duke of York.   The
Duke received him with his accustomed affability, and after
regretting that his promotion had been so long overlooked,
asked him what leave of absence he would require before he

joined his regiment. Captain Dyas said, "Six months, if His Royal Highness did not think it too long."—"Perhaps," replied the Duke, "you would prefer two years." Captain Dyas was overpowered by this considerate condescension on the part of the Duke, and after having thanked him, took a respectful leave; but the number of campaigns he had served in had materially injured his health, and he was obliged to retire on the half-pay of his company.

CHAPTER X

We withdraw from Badajoz—Dislike of the British soldier for siege-work—Affair of El Bodon—Gallant conduct of the 5th and 77th Regiments—Narrow escape of the 88th from being made prisoners—Picton's conduct on the retreat of Guinaldo.

At eleven o'clock at night, on the 9th of June 1811, the siege of Badajoz virtually ceased. From the moment the second attack against San Christoval was repulsed, Lord Wellington resolved to make the best of a bad business, and he converted the siege into a blockade. On the 10th, the battering train and stores were removed from the trenches, and by the 13th our works were clear. The town was closely blockaded until the 17th, on which day we broke up from before the place, and crossing the Guadiana by the ford above San Christoval, reached the banks of the Caya, in the neighbourhood of Aronches, a little after noon.

It appeared from the different reports of our spies that the whole disposable force, not only of Soult's army of the South, but also of that of Portugal, were in march against us; and Lord Wellington accordingly took up a defensive position near Elvas, with his vanguard at Campo Mayor, consisting of the 3rd and 7th Divisions of infantry. The Dukes of Dalmatia and Ragusa formed their junction at Badajoz on the 28th, and the two Marshals dined there together on that day. Great praise was bestowed upon General

Phillipon for his fine defence of the place, and, as a matter of course, much bombastic stuff was trumpeted forth in the papers about the valour displayed by the Imperial soldiers on the occasion. Our losses were rated at more than four times their real amount; and though no blame was attached by the enemy to our troops, the Engineers were attacked with a severity that I have reason to think was unjust. One writer speaking on the subject says:—

"Had the Engineers followed the rules of fortification with as much ability as his lordship displayed in the application of the principles of the higher branches of tactics, Badajoz would, no doubt, have surrendered about the 14th or 15th of June. It scarcely would be believed, were it not expressly mentioned in the official reports, that in the beginning of the nineteenth century, troops should have been sent to the assault with ladders after the breach had been judged practicable."

I shall leave it to the gentlemen of the Engineers to answer these remarks; but as far as I have been able to collect the facts, and I have received my information from good, I might say the best, authority, our defeat before San Christoval arose from three causes: first, the want of knowledge displayed by the officer commanding the first attack of the real situation of the breach, owing to the unfortunate circumstance of the engineer being killed at the onset; secondly, the shortness of the ladders, and the smallness of the storming party each night; and thirdly, the conduct of the men who were entrusted with the charge of the ladders —a foreign corps, it is true;[1] but why employ troops of this description upon a service so desperate?

[1] The battalion of Brunswick Oels, largely composed of German deserters from the French army.

There is no duty which a British soldier performs before an enemy that he does with so much reluctance—a retreat always excepted—as working in trenches.   Although essentially necessary to the accomplishment of the most gallant achievement a soldier can aspire to—the storming a breach —it is an inglorious calling; one full of danger, attended with great labour, and, what is even worse, with a deal of annoyance; and for this reason, that the soldiers are not only taken quite out of their natural line of action, but they are, if not entirely, at least partially, commanded by officers, those of the Engineers, whose habits are totally different from what they have been accustomed to.

No two animals ever differed more completely in their propensities than the British engineer and the British infantry soldier.   The latter delights in an open field, and a fair "stand-up fight," where he meets his man or men (for numbers, when it comes to a hand-to-hand business, are of little weight with the British soldier); if he falls there, he does so, in the opinion of his comrades, with credit to himself; but a life lost in the trenches is looked upon as one thrown away and lost ingloriously.   The engineer, on the contrary, braves all the dangers of a siege with a cheerful countenance; he even courts them, and no mole ever took greater delight in burrowing through a sandhill than an engineer does in mining a covered way, or blowing up a counterscarp.   Not so with the infantry soldier, who is obliged to stand to be shot at, with a pick-axe or shovel in his hand instead of his firelock and bayonet.   If, then, this is a trying situation, as it unquestionably is for a soldier, where death by round-shot and shell in the works is comparatively less than it is at the moment of the assault of a breach, how much more care should there be taken in the selection of the ladder men than appears to have been the case at San Christoval ?

On the 22nd of June, the two French Marshals moved a large body of troops towards Elvas and Campo Mayor, in order to cover their *reconnoissance* of our position. Our army at this time counted about sixty-six thousand men, of which number only six thousand were cavalry. The combined French army exceeded us by about ten thousand, and in the arm of horse they were upwards of three thousand our superiors. Notwithstanding this disproportion of force, Lord Wellington had made able dispositions to beat the French Marshals in detail, and there is little or no doubt but that he would have succeeded, had Marmont been acting in concert with a man as presumptuous as himself; but Soult was too good a judge not to see the sort of adversary he was opposed to, and it was not possible to entrap him. Albuera taught him a lesson.

After the *reconnoissance* of the 22nd, and after supplies had been thrown into Badajoz, the enemy took up the quarters he had occupied previous to the junction of the armies of Portugal and the South—the army of Soult in the neighbourhood of Seville, that of Marmont at Placentia. The 7th and 3rd Divisions of our army occupied Campo Mayor : and having got ourselves and our appointments into good order, we began to have all the annoyances of garrison duty, which was not lessened by the presence of three or four general officers. The mounting of guard, the salute, and all the minutiæ of our profession, were attended to with a painful particularity ; and poor old General Sontag was near falling a sacrifice to his zeal on this particular point of duty. This officer was by birth either a German or Prussian, I don't know which, but, from his costume, I should myself say that he was a disciple of the Grand Frederick; he was a great Martinet, and had all the appearance of one brought up in the school of that celebrated warrior, and might have passed, and deservedly so, for aught I know to the contrary, for one who had served in the "Seven Years' War." His dress was singular, though plain; he usually wore a cocked hat and jacket, tight blue pantaloons, and brown top hunting-boots.

One day, when it came to my tour of duty, General Sontag was the senior officer on the parade. Mounted on a spirited horse, he took his station in front to receive the "salute," when the band of my regiment, much more celebrated for its harshness and noise than its sweetness, struck up as discordant a jumble of sounds as ever proceeded from the same number of wind instruments. The animal, a German horse, and no doubt with a good ear for music, took fright, and standing upright on his hinder legs, commenced pawing and snorting in a manner that astounded every one present, the old General alone excepted; he continued immovably steady in his saddle, from which a less skilful or an inexperienced rider must inevitably have been flung, and sawed his horse's mouth with such effect as to compel him to resume his former and more natural position. But, unfortunately, at this moment the drum-major, who justly estimated the cause of the refractory movements of the brute, made a flourish with his mace as a token for the band—music I can't call it—to desist, and so terrified the animal that he made a sudden plunge to get away, but was so firmly held by the grip of his rider, that his feet came from under him, and both the General and his charger were prostrate on the ground in a second.

It was an alarming, as well as a ludicrous exhibition. For

a moment the General was unable to disentangle his foot
from one of the stirrups, and when he got rid, after much
exertion, of this encumbrance, he lost not only his hat but
his wig also; providentially he sustained no injury, and
every one was glad of it. He was a man much esteemed in
his brigade, and had, perhaps, the largest nose in the world!
He was humorously styled by some Marshal (Nez) Ney!
His nose hung in two huge flaps under his cheek-bone, and
their colour and size were like two red mogul plums. Joe
Kelly said that he would be a capital *gardener*, "because he
always had his fruit under his eye"!

A few weeks terminated our sojourn here, and the day of
our leaving it was a delightful one to us all. We marched
to the northern frontier, which we considered as our own
natural element; for in Estremadura we witnessed nothing
but reverses, and our division had no opportunity of keeping up its established name. The country between the
river Coa and the Agueda was filled with troops. The 3rd
Division occupied Aldea de Ponte, Albergaria, and the
neighbouring villages. Gallegos, Espeja, Carpio, El Bodon,
and Pastores, were likewise occupied; and Ciudad Rodrigo
might be said to be invested; the garrison were, at all events,
much circumscribed in the extent of country for their
foragers, but, nevertheless, they made some successful excursions to the nearest villages, such as Pastores and El
Bodon. The 11th Light Dragoons, stationed at the latter,
were considerably annoyed by the nocturnal visits of the
garrison. A regiment of infantry was, therefore, thought
necessary to co-operate with the cavalry, and mine (the 88th)
was the one selected. General Picton, no matter what his
other faults might be (and who is there amongst us without
one?), knew well what he was about when he sent "the

Rangers of Connaught " to support the 11th; he was aware
that before many hours after their arrival in their quarters
they would be tolerably well acquainted with the resources
of the country about them; and that though now and then,
perhaps, in a case of emergency, they might enlist an odd
sheep or goat into their own corps, they would not allow
the French to do it.   The General was right, and thought it
better that a few sheep should be lost than an entire pen of
them carried off in triumph, and our dragoons (the worst of
it!) bearded to the edge (almost) of their sabres.

We were not long unemployed.   On the tenth night
after our arrival the enemy made a formidable attack on
our outposts at the village of Pastores.   The advanced
sentry, Jack Walsh, passed the word to the next, who communicated with the picket, and in an instant every man was
on his legs.   Walsh waited quietly until the French officer
who headed the advance approached to within a few paces
of where he was standing, when he deliberately took aim at
him, and shot him dead.   The remainder retired for a
moment, panic-struck, no doubt, at the fate of their leader;
they, however, rallied—for they were not only brave, but,
what is almost as great a stimulus, hungry—and they
forced our advance to give way; but Colonel Alexander
Wallace, placing himself at the head of his men, drove back
this band of cormorants, and they never molested us afterwards.

Notwithstanding that we were thus placed with respect
to Rodrigo, the army of Portugal maintained its position;
the army of the North, commanded by Count Dorsenne,
remained in its cantonments on the Douro, and Rodrigo was
thus abandoned to its own resources.

Lord Wellington was not an idle spectator of this supineness on the part of the two French generals. As early as the month of August he directed that a large number of the tradesmen [1] of our army, with a proportion of officers, should be attached to the Engineers, in which branch we were deficient in point of numbers; and these men in less than six weeks gained much useful information, and besides, made a quantity of fascines and gabions sufficient for the intended operations. By the 5th of September the town of Ciudad Rodrigo was completely blockaded, and we were employed in making arrangements for its siege when the two generals, Dorsenne and Marmont, made theirs to drive us back on Portugal.

On the 22nd of September they formed their junction at Tamames, which is about three leagues distant from Rodrigo. Their united force amounted to sixty thousand men, including six thousand horse; ours to not quite fifty thousand, including the force necessary to observe the garrison. We could not, therefore—taking it for granted, as a matter of course, that we wished to maintain the blockade—have brought forty thousand bayonets and sabres into the field, with an inferiority, too, in cavalry of two thousand! This, in a country so well calculated for the operations of that arm, at once decided Lord Wellington, and he raised the blockade on the 24th.

Early on the morning of the 25th the French army were in motion; the cavalry, under General Montbrun, supported by several battalions of infantry, advanced upon the position held by our 3rd Division; but the over-zeal of Montbrun, and the impetuosity of his cavalry, would not allow them to keep pace with the infantry, who were in consequence com-

[1] *I.e.* the men who in civil life had been smiths, carpenters, joiners, etc.

pletely distanced at the onset, and never regained their place during the day.

The ground occupied by the 3rd Division was of considerable extent, and might, to an ordinary observer, appear to be such as to place that corps in some peril of being defeated in detail : for instance, the 5th Regiment, supported by the 77th, two weak battalions, barely reckoning seven hundred men, were considerably to the left, and in advance of El Bodon, and were distant upwards of one mile from the 45th, 74th, and 88th ; while the 83rd and 94th British, and the 9th and 21st Portuguese were little, if anything, closer to those two battalions.   Some squadrons of the 1st German Hussars and 11th Light Dragoons supported the advance, and a brigade of nine-pounders, drawn by mules, and served by Portuguese gunners, under the command of a German major, named Arentschildt, crowned the causeway occupied by the 5th and 77th.

These dispositions were barely completed when Montbrun, at the head of his veteran host, came thundering over the plain at a sweeping pace ; ten of his squadrons dashed across the ravine that separated them from Arentschildt's battery, which opened a frightful fire of grape and canister at point blank distance.   But although the havoc made by those guns was great, it in no way damped the ardour of the French horse ; they panted for glory, and nothing of this kind could check their impetuosity ; once fairly over the ravine, they speedily mounted the face of the causeway, and desperately, but heroically, charged the battery.   Nothing could resist the torrent—the battery was captured and the cannoniers massacred at their guns.

In an instant the 5th, commanded by the gallant Major Ridge, formed line, threw in an effective running fire, steadily ascended the height, charged the astonished French Dragoons, and having repulsed and poured a volley into the latter, as they rushed down the opposite face of the hill, recaptured the guns, with which, joined by the 77th, they deliberately retired across the open plain after a long and determined stand against the enemy's cavalry and artillery, and only retreating when the approach of a strong body of French infantry rendered such a movement imperative.

Flushed with his first success, Montbrun, at the head of his victorious squadrons, now thought to ride through the 5th and 77th, but this handful of heroes threw themselves into square, and received the attack with unflinching steadiness. Nothing but the greatest discipline, the most undaunted bravery, and a firm reliance on their officers, could have saved these devoted soldiers from total annihilation; they were attacked with a fury unexampled on three faces of the square. The French horsemen rode upon their bayonets, but, unshaken by the desperate position in which they were placed, they poured in their fire with such quickness and precision that the cavalry retired in disorder.

While this was taking place on the left, the regiments of the right brigade were posted on a height parallel to that occupied by the 5th and 77th. We had a clear and painful view of all that was passing, and we shuddered for our companions; the glittering of the countless sabres that were about to assail them, and the blaze of light which the reflection of the sun threw across the brazen helmets of the French horsemen, might be likened to the flash of lightning that preceded the thunder of Arentschildt's artillery—but we could do nothing. A few seconds passed away; we saw the smoke of the musketry—it did not recede, and we were assured that the attack had failed; in a moment or two

more we could discern the brave 5th and 77th following
their beaten adversaries, and a spontaneous shout of joy
burst from the brigade.   What would we have given at that
moment to have been near them?   They were not only our
companions in arms, but our intimate friends (I mean the
5th, for the 77th had but just joined the army, and were,
comparatively, strangers to us).   But we were now menaced
ourselves.   From the great space that intervened between
the regiments that had been engaged and those that had
hitherto been unoccupied, it was not easy, taking into
account the mass of French cavalry that covered the plain,
to reunite the 3rd Division.   Lord Wellington, it is true,
was on the spot, but the *spot* was a large one, with but
few troops to cover it, and had the French cavalry done
their duty on that day, I doubt much if the 3rd Division
would not have ceased to exist!   Meanwhile the time was
passing away without the enemy undertaking anything
serious; but the 5th and 77th, and the other troops under
General Colville, seeing the danger of their position, and
profiting by the inaction of the French troopers, who seemed
to be paralysed after their failure, made one of the most
memorable retreats on record, across the plain, surrounded
by three times their own number of horse, and exposed to
the fire of a battery of eight-pounders.   But the 45th, 74th,
and 88th had not yet been able to disentangle themselves
from the rugged ground and vineyards to the rear of El
Bodon, and their junction with the remainder of the division
might be said to be at this moment (three o'clock) rather
problematical, because the French Light Horse and Polish
Lancers, not meeting with a force of our cavalry sufficient to
stop their progress, spread themselves over the face of the
country, capturing our baggage and stores, and threatening

I

to prevent the junction of the right brigade with the other two.

While the French might be said to have the undisputed possession of the entire field of battle, over which they were pouring an immense mass of dragoons, followed by infantry and artillery, the regiments of our division which were in column continued their retrograde movement upon Fuente-Guinaldo. The 45th and 74th had by this time cleared the rugged ground and enclosures, and were in march to join the remainder of the column; but the 88th were most unaccountably left in a vineyard, which was enclosed by a loose stone wall. In the hurry of the moment they might, and I believe would, have been forgotten, had not the soldiers, who became impatient upon hearing the clashing of weapons outside the enclosure, burst down several openings in the wall, by which means they not only saw the danger of the position in which their comrades were placed, but also the hopelessness of their own, if they did not speedily break down the walls that incarcerated them; for our 1st Hussars and 11th Light Dragoons were giving way before the over-powering weight of the enemy's horse, while the bulk of the 3rd Division were marching in a line parallel to the enclosure occupied by the 88th; so it was manifest that if this regiment did not at the instant break from its prison, a few moments would have decided its fate, and left the 3rd Division *minus* the Connaught Rangers.

Each moment that we remained was of consequence, and the delay of five minutes would have been fatal; we were without orders, and were at a loss how to act; but nothing tends more to bring the energies of men into action than their seeing clearly the danger that they are placed in, and the consciousness that their only means of escaping it depends

upon their firm reliance on themselves. Some officers called
out to have the wall broken down, and in a second several
openings were made in it. Every officer made the greatest
efforts to supply, by his own particular dispositions, such as
were on the whole necessary; but an operation of so delicate
a nature, made in the face of a powerful antagonist, could
not be performed with as much order and regularity as was
desirable. From the great coolness of the men, and the
intelligence and gallantry of the officers, the regiment was at
last extricated from its dangerous position, but it was far,
very far, from being safe yet; and had the French dragoons,
at the close of the day, shown the same determination they
did at its commencement, not one man of the 88th would
have escaped.

We had scarcely cleared the enclosure when we witnessed
a series of petty combats between our horse and that of the
enemy, some of whom had posted themselves directly between
us and our entrenched camp at Fuente-Guinaldo. Immediately in our front, some of Lord Wellington's staff were
personally engaged with the French troopers; and one of
them, either Captain Burgh or the young Prince of Orange,
owed his life to the excellence of his horse. Lieutenant
King, of the 11th Dragoons, lost one arm by a sabre cut;
Prior, of the same regiment, had all his front teeth knocked
out by a musket shot, and Mrs. Howley, the black cymbal-
man's wife, of the 88th, was captured by a lancer. The fate
of the officers I have mentioned was deplored, but the loss
of Mrs. Howley was a source of grief to the entire division.
The officers so maimed might be replaced by others, but
perhaps in the entire army such another woman, take her
for all and all, as Mrs. Howley could not be found. The
88th at length took its place in the column at quarter

distance, and the 3rd Division continued its retrograde movement.

Montbrun, at the head of fifteen squadrons of light horse, pressed closely on our right flank, and made every demonstration of attacking us with the view of engaging our attention until the arrival of his infantry and artillery, of which latter only one battery was in the field; but General Picton saw the critical situation in which he was placed, and that nothing but the most rapid, and at the same time most regular, movement upon Guinaldo could save his division from being cut off to a man. For six miles across a perfect flat, without the slightest protection from any incident of ground, without artillery, and I might say without cavalry (for what were four or five squadrons to twenty or thirty?) did the 3rd Division continue its march. During the whole time the enemy's cavalry never quitted them; a park of six guns advanced with the cavalry, and taking the 3rd Division in flank and rear, poured in a frightful fire of round-shot, grape, and canister. Many men fell in this way, and those whose wounds rendered them unable to march were obliged to be abandoned to the enemy.

This was a trying and pitiable situation for troops to be placed in, but it in no way shook the courage or confidence of the soldiers; so far from being dispirited or cast down, the men were cheerful and gay, the soldiers of my corps (the 88th) telling their officers that if the French dared to charge, every officer should have a *nate* horse to ride upon.

General Picton conducted himself with his accustomed coolness; he remained on the left flank of the column, and repeatedly cautioned the different battalions to mind the quarter distance and the "tellings off." "Your safety," added he, "my credit, and the honour of the army, is at stake : all rests with you at this moment." We had reached to within a mile of our entrenched camp, when Montbrun, impatient lest we should escape from his grasp, ordered his troopers to bring up their right shoulders and incline towards our column : the movement was not exactly bringing his squadrons into line, but it was the next thing to it, and at this time they were within half pistol-shot of us. Picton took off his hat, and holding it over his eyes as a shade from the sun, looked sternly, but anxiously at the French. The clatter of the horses and the clanking of the scabbards were so great when the right half squadron moved up, that many thought it the forerunner of a general charge ; some mounted officer called out, " Had we not better form square ? "—" No," replied Picton ; " it is but a *ruse* to frighten us, but it won't do."

At this moment a cloud of dust was discernible in the direction of Guinaldo ; it was a cheering sight ; it covered the 3rd Dragoon Guards, who came up at a slinging trot to our relief. When this fine regiment approached to within a short distance of us they dismounted, tightened their girths, and prepared for battle ; but the French horse slackened their pace, and in half an hour more we were safe within our lines. The Light Division, which were also critically circumstanced on this memorable day, joined us in the morning, and thus the whole army was re-united.

CHAPTER XI

THE Duke of Ragusa and the Count Dorsenne employed
themselves the whole of the day (the 26th of September)
in reconnoitring the ground we occupied, and everything
announced that a battle would be fought the next day
(which, had it taken place, would have been the anniversary
of the battle of Busaco, gained by us the preceding year),
but Lord Wellington observing a considerable body of
troops moving upon his left, apparently with the intention
of turning it, withdrew from his entrenched camp in the
course of the night to the neighbourhood of Alfayates,
leaving the 4th Division, commanded by General Cole, at
Aldea-de-Ponte.

At break of day on the 27th the French army were in
motion, but their surprise seemed great on finding our lines
unoccupied. Marmont pushed his advance upon the village
of Aldea-de-Ponte, and a gallant affair for our 4th Division
took place there. The two regiments of Fusileers [1] particularly distinguished themselves, and repulsed the enemy at

[1] The 7th and 23rd Royal Welsh.

the point of the bayonet.   Night put an end to this affair,
which cost us a couple of hundred men, and nearly double
that number fell on the side of the French.

The enemy being but ill supplied with provisions, and
the country in which they now were (Portugal) being quite
unsuited to their operations, as well as unable to supply
their wants, the French Marshal, having provisioned Rodrigo,
which was the object sought for when he formed his junction
with the army of the north, resolved upon retracing his steps,
which he did on the following day, the 28th.

Lord Wellington issued a most flattering order to the
troops engaged on the 25th, and so delighted was he with
the conduct of the 5th and 77th that he held them up as
an example to the army.   On the 29th we went into
cantonments, our division occupying Aldea-de-Ponte; and
until our arrival there, I had no idea the loss of men and
horses on the 27th had been so great.   The ground was
thickly covered with both, and immense numbers of vultures
had already established themselves in the neighbourhood.
These birds, the sure harbinger of a disputed field, crowded
around us in vast flocks: whether this was owing to the
lateness of the season, or to a scantiness in the supply of
their accustomed food, I know not; but the voracity of
these birds, and consequently their boldness, was beyond
anything I had ever before witnessed.   In many instances
they would throw off their ordinary wariness, and strut
before the carcase they were devouring, as if they supposed
we were about to dispute their pretensions to it; but it is
astonishing what birds of this description will do when
really pressed by hunger.

Fuente-Guinaldo was occupied by our Light Division, who
made that town agreeable both to themselves and also to

their brothers in arms, not only by their hospitality, but by
the attraction of their theatrical performances, which were
got up in a style quite astonishing, considering the place
and the difficulties which they must have found in supplying
themselves with suitable costume ; but the Light Division had
an *esprit de corps* among them, whether in the field or
quarters, that must be seen to be understood. Their *dramatis
personæ* were admirable, and Captain Kent of the Rifles, by
his great abilities, rendered every performance in which he
took a part doubly attractive. The 3rd Division, although
unable to cope with the Light in this species of amusement,
got up races, which, though inferior to those of the former
year at Torres Vedras, were far from bad ; amongst the
jockeys was one, an officer in the Portuguese service, who,
though an excellent horseman, was, without exception, the
ugliest man in the division, or perhaps in the army. Major
Leckie of the 45th took the greatest dislike to him on this
account, and gave him the name of " Ugly Mug"—by which
cognomen he was after known.

Just as the horses were about to start for a tolerably
heavy stake, I went up to Leckie, who was one of the most
knowing men on our turf. " Well, Leckie," said I, " who's
the winning jockey to-day ? "—" Why look," replied he,
" I've laid it on thick myself upon Wilde's horse, Albuquer-
que, and tortured as I am with this infernal attack of
gout (to which he was a great martyr), I have hobbled out
to witness the race ; but, my dear fellow, I don't care one
rush who wins, provided *Mug* loses." However, *Mug* won
his race easily, and poor Leckie went home quite out of
sorts. Whether from the effect of his favourite horse losing,
or " Mug's" winning, or that the exertion was too much for
him, I know not, but upon his return to Aldea-de-Ponte, he

was seized with a violent attack of gout; towards midnight he was a little more composed, and had just sunk into a gentle slumber, when he was awoke by a young Ensign who had lately joined, and who occupied an apartment in the house where Leckie was quartered. This officer played a little on the violin, and had a very good voice; he began to practise both, and commenced singing the little air in *Paul and Virginia* of

> Tell her I love her while the clouds drop rain,
> Or while there's water in the pathless main;

but whether from being imperfect in the song, or that those particular lines struck his fancy, he never got beyond them. Leckie became very fidgety—every scrape of the violin touched his heart, but in a far different manner from that in which it seemed to affect the performer; a quarter of an hour passed on, and the same lines were repeated; at last the accompaniment grew fainter and fainter, until it died away altogether.

Leckie became composed: "Well!" exclaimed he, "that young fellow is at rest for the night, and so I hope shall I be," and he was beginning to settle himself in a more easy posture when the same sounds reassailed him. This was too bad! He sprang out of bed, the perspiration rolling in large drops down his forehead; he rushed to the door of the Ensign's apartment, which he forced at one push, and in a second was standing before the astonished musician in his shirt. The fatal words, "Tell her I love her," had just been uttered, and he was preparing to add, "while the clouds drop rain," when Leckie exclaimed, "By God, sir, I'll tell her anything you wish, if you'll only allow me to sleep for half an hour." It would be impossible to convey an idea of the confusion of

the young man upon finding his commanding officer before
him at such a time and upon such an occasion; he made a
thousand apologies, and poor Leckie, who was one of the
pleasantest fellows in the world, in spite of his pain, could
not avoid laughing at the occurrence, which amused him to
the hour of his death.

Matters being in the state I have described in the month
of October 1811, and as there was no likelihood of any active
operations taking place, we began to make ourselves as comfortable as the wretched village of Aldea-de-Ponte would
admit of. Any person acquainted with a Portuguese cottage
will readily acknowledge that a good chimney is not its forte;
we therefore turned all the skill our masons possessed to the
construction of fire-places that would not smoke, and it
required all their knowledge in the arcana of their profession
to succeed even in part. However, they did succeed, partially,
I must admit; but it was easy to satisfy us, and we made
up for the badness of our fire-places by stocking them
abundantly with wood, of which article there was no lack,—
but we had barely sufficient straw to keep our horses and
mules alive, much less afford ourselves a bed. In the entire
village, I believe, there were not a dozen mattresses. Provisions were but ill supplied us, and we were reduced to
subsist upon half allowance of bad biscuit. As to money, we
had scarcely a sou; for although there was plenty of specie in
Lisbon for our use, the want of animals to convey it to the
army left us as ill off as if there had not been a dollar in
the chest of the Paymaster-General. So that between smoky
houses, no beds, little to eat, and less money, we were in
anything but what might be termed " good winter-quarters."

This state of privation was sadly annoying to the soldiers,
and the men of my corps, or, as I am more in the habit of

calling them, "the boys," were much perplexed as to what they would do. Several desertions had taken place in the army, but our fellows did not like that at-all-at-all. "Why, then, by my sowl," said Owen Mackguekin, of the Grenadiers, "I think Misther Strahan, the commissary, is grately to blame to keep us poor boys without mate to ate, when those *pizanos* have plenty of good sheep and goats; and sure if they'd ate them themselves, a man wouldn't say anything; but they'll neither ate them, nor give us lave to do so, and sure a'tanny rate, *baccallâo* and *azete*[1] is good enough for them." I need scarcely remark that an argument so full of sound sense was not likely to be thrown away upon the hearers of Owen Mackguekin. From this moment our fellows determined to be their own commissaries.

For some weeks there had been a general defalcation amongst the different neighbouring flocks, and the Portuguese shepherds, confounded to know what had become of them, armed themselves, and kept watch with a degree of vigilance that they were heretofore unaccustomed to. Wolves, they remarked, were not sufficiently numerous in that part of the country to effect such havoc, even in the depth of winter; but, said they, it is impossible at this early stage of the season that it could be them; and they were right, for it would be difficult to point out one regiment that did not take something in the shape of tithe from the sheep-holders.

One night in November, 1811, three of the "boys" walked out of their quarters with nothing at all—but their bayonets; Mackguekin headed them. The sheep-fold they assailed was defended by five armed Portuguese; but what did the "boys" care for that? After nearly sending the unfortunate men to the other world, they very deliberately

[1] Salt fish and vinegar.

tied their arms and legs together " to keep them aisy," as they afterwards said, and then performing the same office to three sheep, they left their owners to look after the remainder.

As may be supposed, this affair made a great noise. The Provost-Marshal was directed to search, with the utmost care, the quarters and premises of all the regiments; but the fellow instinctively, I believe, turned towards those of my corps; and here, I am sorry to confess, he found that which he wanted, namely, the three sheep, part of them in a camp-kettle on the fire, and the remainder in an outhouse. This was enough. The three men were identified by the Portuguese, tried, flogged, and had to pay for the sheep, which (the worst of it!) they had not the pleasure of even tasting. But this example by no means put a stop to the evil. The sheep-folds were plundered, the shepherds pummelled, and our fellows flogged without mercy. General Picton at length issued orders, directing the rolls of the regiment to be called over by an officer of each company at different periods during the night, and by this measure the evil was remedied. But we did not get credit for even this. That pleasantest of all pleasant fellows, Bob Hardyman of the 45th, used to say, in jest, that instead of the officers going round the quarters, we entrusted the duty to a sergeant; and, according to Bob's account, the manner of his performing the duty was as follows :—

Arrived at the door, he gave a gentle tap, when voices from within called out, " Who's there ? "

Ser. " It's me, boys ! "

Sol. " And who are you ? "

Ser. " Why then, blur 'an ouns, boys, don't yees know my voice ? "

Sol. " Och ! and to be sure we do now."

Ser. " Well, boys, yees know what I'me come about."

Sol. " Sure we do, sergeant."

Ser. " Well, boys, are yees all within ? "

Sol. " Within, is it ! to be sure we are ; why, where else would we be ? "

Ser. " That's right, boys ! but boys, take care, are yees all in bed ? "

Sol. " In bed ! sure we are, and all asleep too ! ! "

Ser. " Och ! that's right, honies, it's myself that's proud to find yees grown so regular ! "

And having thus performed his duty, he wished them good-night. But poor Bob Hardyman was one of those sort of fellows that could say a thing (and make you laugh at it too, although at your own expense) that if another person attempted, he would get his teeth knocked down his throat ; he verified a saying in his own county (Galway), that one man in that country might steal a horse with impunity, when another darn't look over the hedge where he was grazing.

At Aldea-de-Ponte, the headquarters of our division, all was quiet ; and although our allowance of provisions was scanty, and our supply of money scarcely sufficient to procure us salt and rice for our soup, the division, nevertheless, was in high order ; we had a good deal of drill, and regular examinations of the men's kits—a very necessary precaution with all regiments, and with my corps as well as another. At an inspection of this kind by General Mackinnon he found fault—and deservedly so, I must confess—with the scanty manner in which some of the men of my company were supplied. The General was too much the gentleman to row, or call names, but it was clear from his manner that he was far from satisfied with the wardrobe displayed by these fellows; indeed, if he was, it would have been easy to please him! At last coming to a "boy" of the name of Darby Rooney, whose knapsack was what a Frenchman would term *vide*, or, to speak more intelligibly, one that contained nothing whatever but his watch-coat, a piece of pipe-clay and button-brush! he seemed thunderstruck, as well he might, for I believe "he ne'er had looked upon its like before"!

With more asperity of manner than I ever observed him to make use of, he asked "Darby" to whose squad he belonged. Darby Rooney understood about as much English as enabled him to get over a parade tolerably, but a conversation such as the General was about to hold with him was beyond his capacity, and he began to feel a little confused at the prospect of a *tête-à-tête* with his General: "Squidha —squodha—cad-dershe-vourneen?"[1] said he, turning to the orderly-sergeant, Pat Gafney, who did not himself speak the English language quite as correctly as Lindley Murray. "Whist, ye Bostoon,"[2] said Gafney, "and don't make a baste of yourself before the General."—"Why," said General Mackinnon, "I believe he don't understand me."—"No, sir," replied Gafney, "he don't know what your honour manes."

The General passed on, taking it for granted that the man had never heard of a squad, and making some gentlemanlike observations on the utility of such partitions of a company, expressed himself satisfied with the fine appearance of the regiment, and our inspection ended with credit to us, this solitary instance excepted. This was, however, enough. Ill-nature and scandal seldom lack arguments. They are ever ready to take a hint, and it is

[1] "What does he say, honey?"
[2] "Hold your tongue, you booby."

unnecessary that a report should be as true as the gospel to
form a foundation for their belief of it. An hour had not
elapsed when the entire division were made acquainted
(through some of our friends!) with the story. Groups of
officers might be seen together (God forgive them!) laughing
at our expense. " Well!" cried one, "did you hear what
happened with the Connaughts to-day?"—"No," replied a
second, "but I'll bet twenty dollars I guess; another sheep
or goat found in their quarters?"—"No. But when
General Mackinnon inspected them just now, there was not
one man in the regiment who knew what a squad was!"—
"I would have sworn it," replied a third. An old crone of
a major now joined the group, and shaking his head said,
"Ah! they are a sad set!" Poor idiot! The 88th was a
more really *efficient* regiment than almost any *two* corps in
the 3rd Division.

CHAPTER XII

THE joke about Darby Rooney's wardrobe, and the conversation that took place between him and General Mackinnon, was circulated throughout the army, and I believe there was not one regiment unacquainted with the circumstance; indeed, so general was its circulation, that it reached the headquarters of Lord Wellington himself, and, if report spoke truly (which it doesn't always do), it caused his lordship to laugh heartily.

I have myself—before and since I wrote the story—often been asked if it was really a fact that we had no squads in the companies of my regiment, and I have invariably answered that we had not, and that every iota told by Bob Hardyman was true, for I think Bob's description of the Connaught Rangers altogether too rich to be contradicted or even altered. But were I myself to give a " full and true account" of the " boys," I would set them down as a parcel of lads that took the world easy—or, as they themselves would say, " aisy "—with a proper share of that nonchalance which is only to be acquired on service—real service ; but I cannot bring myself to think them, as many did, a parcel of devils,

128

neither will I by any manner of means try to pass them off for so many saints! But the fact is (and I have before said so) that there was not one regiment in the Peninsular army more severely—perhaps so severely—drilled as mine was; but I also say, without the slightest fear of contradiction, that the officers never tormented themselves or their men with too much fuss. We approached their quarters as seldom as we possibly could—I mean as seldom as was necessary—and thereby kept up that distance between officers and privates so essential to discipline; this we considered the proper line of conduct to chalk out, and we ever acted up to it. We were amused to see some regiments whose commanding officers obliged every subaltern to parade his men at bedtime in their blankets!—why, they looked like so many hobgoblins! But if such an observance were necessary as far as concerned the soldiers, surely a sergeant ought to be able to do this much.

If a selection of good sergeants and corporals be made by the officer at the head of a regiment, and if that officer will only allow those individuals to do their duty, there is not the least doubt but that they will do it—I peril myself upon the assertion, and I bet a sovereign that the "Guards" agree with me. I well remember some regiments managed in the opposite way during the Peninsular War. Those poor fellows were much to be pitied, for they were not only obliged to fag, but to dress also, with as much scrupulous exactness as the time and place would admit of. What folly! But was Lord Wellington to blame for this? Unquestionably not. He never troubled his head about such trifles, and had the commanding officers of corps followed the example set them (of not paying too much respect to minutiæ) by the Commander-in-Chief, the

K

situation of the junior officers in the army would have been far different from what it was.

Another custom prevailed in many regiments, which was attempted to be got up in mine, but we crushed it in its infancy; it was the sending a surgeon or his assistant to ascertain the state of an officer's health, should he think himself not well enough to attend an early drill.

We had in my old corps, amongst other "characters," one that, at the period I am writing about, was well known in the army to be as jovial a fellow as ever put his foot under a mess-table. His name was Fairfield; and though there were few who could sing as good a song, there was not in the whole British army a worse duty officer. Indeed, it was next to impossible to catch hold of him for any duty whatever; and so well known was his dislike to all military etiquette, that the officer next to him on the roster, the moment Fairfield's name appeared for guard-mounting or court-martial, considered himself as the person meant, and he was right nine times out of ten. The frequent absence of Fairfield from drill, at a time too when the regiment was in expectation of being inspected by the general of division, obliged the officer commanding to send the surgeon to ascertain the nature of his malady, which from its long continuance (on occasions of duty!) strongly savoured of a chronic complaint. The doctor found the invalid traversing his chamber rather lightly clad for an indisposed person; he was singing one of Moore's melodies, and accompanying himself with his violin, which instrument he touched with great taste. The doctor told him the nature of his visit, and offered to feel his pulse, but Fairfield turned from him, repeating the lines of Shakespeare, " Canst thou minister," etc. etc. " Well," replied the surgeon, " I am sorry for it, but

I cannot avoid reporting you fit for duty."—"I'm sorry you cannot," rejoined Fairfield; "but my complaint is best known to myself! and I feel that were I to rise as early as is necessary, I should be lost to the service in a month." "Why," said the doctor, "Major Thompson says you have been lost to it ever since he first knew you, and that is now something about six years," and he took his leave for the purpose of making his report.

The Major's orderly was soon at Fairfield's quarters with a message to say that his presence was required by his commanding officer. Fairfield was immediately in attendance. "Mr. Fairfield," said the Major, "your constant habit of being absent from early drill has obliged me to send the surgeon to ascertain the state of your health, and he reports that you are perfectly well, and I must say that your appearance is anything but that of an invalid—how is this?" "Don't mind him, sir," replied Fairfield; "I am, thank God! very well *now*, but when the bugle sounded this morning at four o'clock a cold shivering came over me—I think it was a touch of ague!—and besides, Dr. Gregg is too short a time in the Connaught Rangers to know my *habit*."—"Is he?" rejoined the old Major, "he must be d——d stupid then. But that is a charge you surely can't make against me. I have been now about nineteen years in the regiment, during six of which I have had the pleasure of knowing you, and you will allow me to tell you, that I am not only well acquainted with 'your habit,' but to request you will, from this moment, *change it*"—and with this gentle rebuke he good-humouredly dismissed him. He was an excellent duty officer ever after.

A regiment is a piece of mechanism, and requires as much care as any other machine whose parts are obliged to act in unison to keep it going as it ought. If a screw or two be loose, a skilful hand will easily right them without injuring the machine; but if it falls into the hands of a self-sufficient ignorant bungler, it is sure to be injured, if not destroyed altogether; and as certain as the daylight, if it is ever placed in a situation where it must from necessity be allowed to act for itself—where the main spring cannot control the lesser ones much less the great body of the machine—it will be worse than useless—worse than a log—not only in the way, but not to be depended upon!

It must not, however, be supposed that these observations are meant to favour a too little regard to that system of discipline which is so essential to be observed in the army, and without which any army—but particularly a British one—would be inefficient. Extremes should be avoided, and too much familiarity is as bad as too much severity. I once heard of a commanding officer of a first-rate regiment who was in the habit of allowing the junior officers of his corps to make too free with him; he at length found it necessary to send his adjutant to inquire the reason why a young ensign, who was in the habit of absenting himself from parade, did so on one of those days which was allotted as a garrison parade? The adjutant informed the ensign that the colonel awaited his reply. "Shall I say you are unwell?" demanded he. "Oh no," replied the ensign, "I'll settle the matter with the commanding officer myself." The hour of dinner approached, yet no communication was received from the ensign. Passing from his quarters to the mess-room, the commanding officer met the ensign, and was about to accost him when the latter turned his head aside and declined recognising his colonel, who, upon arriving at the mess-room, was so dejected as to attract the notice of all the officers. Upon being asked why he was so out of spirits, the colonel, "good easy man," told a "round unvarnished tale," and in conclusion added, "I thought nothing of his not answering my message, but I cannot express how much I am hurt at the idea of his cutting me as he did when I wished to speak with him!" This was *un peu trop fort;* and had the regiment in question been much longer under the command of the good-natured personage I have described, there is little doubt but that it would have become rather relaxed in its discipline.

The different movements amongst the contending armies in the end of 1811 caused it to be presumed that the campaign the following year would open with much spirit; and so it did, although earlier than was anticipated. Marmont, thinking himself safe till the spring, had not only quartered his army in very extensive cantonments, but also detached General Montbrun, with three divisions, to co-operate with Marshal Suchet in the kingdom of Valencia. Intimately acquainted with these details, Lord Wellington redoubled his efforts in the arrangement of all that was necessary to carry on the siege of Ciudad-Rodrigo with vigour. The 3rd Division, which was one of those destined to take a part in the attack, broke up from its cantonments on the morning of the 4th of January 1812. Carpio, Espeja, and Pastores were occupied by our troops, and the greatest activity prevailed throughout every department, but more especially in that of the Engineers. All the cars in the country were put into requisition for the purpose of conveying fascines, gabions, and the different materials necessary to the Convent of La Caridad, distant a league and half from Rodrigo. The guns were at Gallegos, and everything was in that state of preparation which announced that a vigorous attack was about to be made, in the depth of a severe winter, against a fortress that had withstood for twenty-five days all the efforts of Marshal Masséna in the summer of 1810, when it was only occupied by a weak garrison of Spaniards. Yet, nevertheless, every one felt confident, and the soldiers burned with impatience to wipe away the blot of the former year in the unfortunate siege of San Christoval and Badajoz.

I have before mentioned that we had not an effective corps of engineers—I mean in point of numbers. To remedy this defect a proportion of the most intelligent officers and soldiers of the infantry were selected during the autumn months and placed under the direction of Colonel Fletcher, the Chief Engineer. They were soon taught how to make fascines and gabions, and what was of equal consequence—how to use them. They likewise learned the manner of working by sap, and by this means that branch of our army, which was before the weakest, had now become very efficient.

The morning of the 4th of January was dreadfully in-auspicious. The order for marching arrived at three o'clock, and we were under arms at five. The rain fell in torrents, and the village of Aldea-de-Ponte, which the brigade of General Mackinnon occupied, was a sea of filth; the snow on the surrounding hills drifted down with the flood and nearly choked up the roads, and the appearance of the morning was anything but a favourable omen for us, who had a march of nine leagues to make ere we reached the town of Robleda on the river Agueda, which was destined to be our resting-place for the night.

At half-past six the brigade was in motion, and I scarcely remember a more disagreeable day; the rain which had fallen in the morning was succeeded by snow and sleet, and some soldiers, who sunk from cold and fatigue, fell down exhausted, soon became insensible, and perished ; yet, strange to say, an Irishwoman of my regiment was delivered of a child upon the road, and continued the march with her infant in her arms.

Notwithstanding the severity of the day, it was impossible to avoid occasionally smiling at the *outré* appearance of some of the officers. The total disregard which the Commander-in-Chief paid to uniformity of dress is well known, and there were many on this day who were obliged to acknowledge that they showed more taste than judgment in their selection. Captain Adair of my corps nearly fell a victim to the choice he had made on this our first day of opening the campaign of 1812. He wore a pair of boots that fitted him with a degree of exactness that would not disgrace a " Hoby "; the heels were high and the toes sharply pointed ; his pantaloons were of blue web ; his frock-coat and waistcoat were tastefully and fashionably chosen, the former light blue richly frogged with lace, the latter of green velvet with large silver Spanish buttons ; but he forgot the most essential part of all—and that was his boat-cloak. For the first ten or twelve miles he rode, but the cold was so intense that he was obliged to dismount, and unquestionably his dress was but ill calculated for walking. The rain with which his pantaloons were saturated was by this time nearly frozen (for the day had begun to change), and he became so dreadfully chafed that he was necessitated to give up the march, and we left him at a village half way from Robleda, resembling more one of those which composed " the army of martyrs " than that commanded by Lord Wellington. I myself was nearly in as bad a state, but being a few years younger, and more serviceably clad, I made an effort to get on.

We had by this time (eight o'clock at night) proceeded a considerable way in the dark, and, as may be supposed, it was a difficult matter to keep the men together as compactly as could be wished. Whenever an opportunity occurred a jaded soldier or two of my regiment used to look in on our Spanish friends, and if they found them at supper, they could not bring themselves to refuse an offer to "take share of what was going," and, to say the truth, this was no more than might be expected from a set of fellows who belonged to a country so proverbial for its hospitality to strangers as theirs (Ireland) was! Besides this, the men of the Connaught Rangers had a way of making themselves "at home" that was peculiar to them, and for which—whatever else might be denied them!—they got full credit. Bob Hardyman used to say "they had a *taking way* with them."

Passing a hamlet a short distance from Robleda we saw a number of Spaniards, women as well as men, outside the door of a good-looking house; much altercation was apparently taking place; at length a soldier (named Ody Brophy) rushed out with half a flitch of bacon under his arm; a scuffle ensued, and Lieutenant D'Arcy, to whose company the soldier belonged, ran up to inquire the cause of the outcry, but it was soon too manifest to be misunderstood; the war-whoop was raised against our man, who, on his part, as stoutly defended himself, not by words alone but by blows, which had nearly silenced his opponents, when he was seized by my friend D'Arcy. *Piccaroon, Ladrone,* and other opprobrious epithets were poured with much volubility against him, but he, with the greatest *sang froid*, turned to his officer and said, "Be aisy now, and don't be vexing yourself with them or the likes of them. Wasn't it for you I was making a bargain? and didn't I offer the value of it?

Don't I see the way you're lost with the hunger, and the
divil a bit iv rations you'll get ate to-night.   Och! you
cratur, iv your poor mother, that's dead! was to see you
after such a condition, it's she that id be leev'd iv herself
for letting you away from her at-all-at-all."—" Well," said
D'Arcy (softened, no doubt, and who would not at such a
speech?), "what did you offer for it?"—" What did I offer
for it, is it?   Fait, then, I offered enough, but they made
such a noise that I don't think they heard me, for, upon my
sowl, I hardly heard myself with the uproar they made; and
sure I told them iv I hadn't money enough to pay for it
(and it was true for me I hadn't, unless I got it dog cheap!)
you had; but they don't like a bone in my skin, or in yours
either, and that is the raison they are afther offinding me
afther such a manner.   And didn't one of the women get
my left thumb into her mouth, and grunch it like a bit of
mate?   Look at it," said he in conclusion, at the same time
thrusting his bleeding hand nearly into D'Arcy's face, " fait
and iv your honour hadn't come up, it's my belief she would
have bit it clane off at the knuckle."   This speech, delivered
with a rapidity and force that was sufficient to overwhelm
the most practised rhetorician, carried away everything along
with it, like chaff before a whirlwind, and D'Arcy made all
matters smooth by paying the price demanded (two dollars),
and the piece of bacon was carried away by Ody, who was a
townsman of D'Arcy's, and who repeatedly assured him " he
would do more than that to sarve him."

It was impossible to avoid paying a tribute of praise to
Ody Brophy for the tact with which he avoided the storm
with which he was threatened; and upon this occasion he
proved himself as good a pilot as ever guided a vessel, and
to the full equal to one I once heard of in the harbour of

Cork. A captain of a man-of-war, newly appointed to a ship on the Irish station, took the precaution, in "beating out" of harbour, to apprise the pilot that he was totally unacquainted with the coast, and therefore he must rely on the pilot's local knowledge for the safety of his ship.

"You are perfectly sure, pilot," said the captain, "you are well acquainted with the coast?"

"Do I know my own name, sir."

"Well, mind, I warn you not to approach too near the shore."

"Now make yourself aisy, sir; in troth you may go to bed iv you plaise."

"Then shall we stand on?"

"Why—what else would we do?"

"Yes, but there may be hidden dangers which you know nothing about."

"Dangers! I'd like to see the dangers dare hide themselves from Mick—sure, don't I tell you I know every rock on the coast" (here the ship strikes), "*and that's one of 'em.*"

CHAPTER XIII

Spanish village accommodation—The siege of Ciudad Rodrigo—Picton's address to the Connaught Rangers in front of the breach—Lieutenant William Mackie and the forlorn hope.

THE brigade reached Robleda at nine o'clock at night, and our quarters there, which at any time would have been considered good, appeared to us, after our wretched billets at Aldea-de-Ponte, and the fatigue of a harassing march, sumptuous. The villages in Spain, like those of France, are well supplied with beds, and the house allotted to me, D'Arcy, and Captain Peshall, was far from deficient in those essentials. A loud knocking at the door of the cottage announced the arrival of Peshall, who, like some others, had been "thrown out" on the march, and who sought for his billet in the best manner he could. He was a man who might boast of as well-stocked a canteen as any other captain in the army; and upon this occasion it made a proud display. The fireplace was abundantly supplied with wood, and at each side of the chimney there was a profusion of that kind of furniture which I ever considered as indispensable to complete the garniture of a well-regulated cuisine, no matter whether in a cottage or château—I mean hams, sausages, and flitches of well-cured bacon.

While I contemplated all the luxuries with which I was

189

surrounded, I felt exceedingly happy, and I am inclined to think that the evening of the 4th of January 1812 was, if not one of the pleasantest of my life, unquestionably one of the most rational I ever passed. Our baggage had by this time arrived, and having got on dry clothes, we began to attack the contents of Peshall's canteen, which was ever at the service of his friends; it contained, among other good things, a Lamego ham, and a cold roast leg of mountain mutton, "morsels which may take rank, notwithstanding their Spartan plainness, with the most disguised of foreign manufacture." It is scarcely necessary to add that we did ample justice to the viands placed before us, and having taken a sufficient libation of brandy punch, in which the Spaniard joined us, we turned our thoughts to our beds.

We arose early the following morning, the 5th, and the brigade reached the small village of Atalaya, distant three leagues from Rodrigo, a little before noon. That fortress was completely invested on the evening of the 7th, and dispositions were made to commence operations against it on the night following.

Ciudad Rodrigo stands upon an eminence, on the right bank of the river Agueda, and is difficult of access; it had been, since its occupation by the French, much strengthened by the construction of a redoubt on the hill above St. Francisco; some old convents in the suburbs were also turned into defences, and these places no longer presented their original peaceful appearance, but were, in fact, very respectable outworks, and tended much to our annoyance and loss at the commencement of the siege.

To be safe against a *coup-de-main*, Rodrigo would require a force of from five to six thousand troops, and its present garrison did not reckon anything like three thousand bayonets; it was therefore manifest that, notwithstanding the unfavourable time of the year, it must fall if not speedily succoured; yet it would seem that Marshal Marmont took no measures to make a diversion in its favour. Strongly impressed with this state of the matter, our commander saw the advantage he would have over his opponent, by acting with as little delay as possible. Protected by a strong escort, Lord Wellington carefully reconnoitred the town on the 8th; and shortly after dark, three hundred men of the Light Division, headed by Colonel Colborne of the 52nd, were formed for the attack of St. Francisco. They were followed by a working party, composed also of men of the Light Division. The storming party, led on by Colonel Colborne, advanced under cover of the night, and were not discovered until they had reached to within a few yards of the redoubt, and our troops rushed on with such impetuosity that the outwork was carried, and the soldiers that defended it put to the sword, before the garrison of Rodrigo thought it in danger; and profiting by the panic with which the enemy were seized, Colonel Colborne caused the works of the redoubt to be razed, completed the first parallel, and rendered our future approaches secure.

The duty in the trenches was carried on by the 1st, 3rd, 4th, and Light Divisions, each taking its separate tour every twenty-four hours. We had no tents or huts of any description, and the ground was covered with snow, nevertheless the soldiers were cheerful, and everything went on well. The fortified convents in the suburbs were respectively carried, and each sortie made by the garrison was immediately repulsed; in some instances our men pursued them to the very *glacis*, and many a fine fellow, carried away by his enthusiasm, died at the muzzles of their cannon.

Every exertion was made to forward the work, so fully were all impressed with its necessity; but notwithstanding the animated exertions of the engineers, and the ready co-operation of the infantry, their progress was at times unavoidably slower than was anticipated. In some instances the soil was so unfavourable, it was next to an impossibility to make head against it; instead of clay or gravel, we frequently met with a vein of rock, and invariably when this occurred our losses were severe, for the pick-axes, coming in contact with the stone, caused sparks to issue that plainly told the enemy where we were, and, as a matter of course, they redoubled their efforts on these points; nevertheless, on the 14th, in the afternoon, we were enabled to open our fire from twenty-two pieces of cannon, superior to those which armed our batteries at Badajoz the year before, inasmuch as the former guns were of brass, while those which we now used were of metal. On this night we established the second parallel, distant only one hundred and fifty yards from the body of the place.

On the 15th the second parallel was in a forward state, and the approach by sap to the glacis was considerably advanced; the effect also of our fire was such as made us perceive a material alteration in the enemy's mode of replying to it; and it was apparent, that although but seven days before the place, our labours were soon likely to be brought to a termination. The cannonade of the enemy, however, if not as great as at first, was more effective, and our casualties more numerous, for their guns and mortars were directed with a scientific precision that did credit to the men who served them. But every hour proved the visible superiority of our fire over that of the enemy, which at times seemed to be altogether extinguished; and whenever it shone

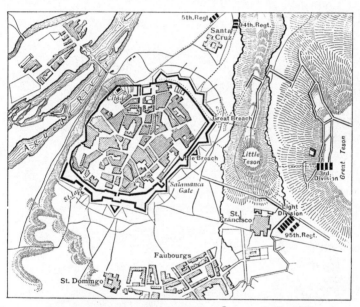

PLAN OF SIEGE OF CIUDAD RODRIGO.   January 8–19, 1812.

forth with anything like brilliancy, it was but momentary, and might be well likened to some spark of combustible matter, issuing from the interior of a nearly consumed ruin. Wherever danger was greatest, there were our engineers, and it was painful to see their devotedness; on horseback or on foot, under cover or exposed to fire, was to them the same, and their example was followed by the soldiers with an enthusiasm unequalled; in short, it was plain that a few hours would suffice to decide the fate of Ciudad Rodrigo. At this period (the 18th) the 4th Division occupied and performed the duty in the trenches.

Early on the morning of the 19th, the 3rd Division (although not for duty that day) received orders to march to the Convent of La Caridad; and as Lord Wellington was not in the habit of giving us unnecessary marches, we concluded that he intended us the honour of forming one of the corps destined to carry the place. On our march we perceived our old friends and companions, the Light Division, debouching from their cantonments, and the joy expressed by our men when they saw them is not to be described; we were long acquainted, and like horses accustomed to the same harness, we pulled well together. At two o'clock in the afternoon we left La Caridad, and, passing to the rear of the first parallel, formed in column about two gun-shots distant from the main breach. The 4th Division still occupied the works, and it was the general opinion that ours (the 3rd) were to be in reserve. The number of Spaniards, Portuguese, and soldiers' wives in the character of sutlers, was immense, and the neighbourhood, which but a few days before was only an empty plain, now presented the appearance of a vast camp. Wretches of the poorest description hovered round us, in hopes of getting a morsel of food, or of plundering some dead or wounded soldier: their cadaverous countenances expressed a living picture of the greatest want; and it required all our precaution to prevent these miscreants from robbing us the instant we turned our backs from our scanty store of baggage or provisions.

Our bivouac, as may be supposed, presented an animated appearance—groups of soldiers cooking in one place; in another, some dozens collected together, listening to accounts brought from the works by some of their companions whom curiosity had led thither; others relating their past battles to any of the young soldiers who had not as yet come hand-to-hand with a Frenchman; others dancing and singing; officers' servants preparing dinner for their masters; and officers themselves, dressed in whatever way best suited their taste or convenience, mixed with the men, without any distinguishing mark of uniform to denote their rank. The only thing uniform to be discovered amongst a group of between four and five thousand was good conduct and confidence in themselves and their general.

It was now five o'clock in the afternoon, and darkness was approaching fast, yet no order had arrived intimating that we were to take a part in the contest about to be decided. We were in this state of suspense when our attention was attracted by the sound of music; we all stood up, and pressed forward to a ridge, a little in our front, and which separated us from the cause of our movement, but it would be impossible for me to convey an adequate idea of our feelings when we beheld the 43rd Regiment, preceded by their band, going to storm the left breach; they were in the highest spirits, but without the slightest appearance of levity in their demeanour—on the contrary, there was a cast of determined severity thrown over their countenances that expressed in legible characters that they knew the sort of service they were about to perform, and had made up their minds to the issue. They had no knapsacks—their firelocks were slung over their shoulders—their shirt-collars were open, and there was an indescribable *something* about them that at one and the same moment impressed the lookers-on with admiration and awe. In passing us, each officer and soldier stepped out of the ranks for an instant, as he recognised a friend, to press his hand—many for the last time; yet, notwithstanding this animating scene, there was no shouting or huzzaing, no boisterous bravadoing, no unbecoming language; in short, every one seemed to be impressed with the seriousness of the affair entrusted to his charge, and any interchange of words was to this effect: "Well, lads, mind what you're about to-night"; or, "We'll meet in the town by and by"; and other little familiar phrases, all expressive of confidence. The regiment at length passed us, and we stood gazing after it as long as the rear platoon continued in sight: the music grew fainter every moment, until at last it died away altogether; they had no drums, and there was a melting sweetness in the sounds that touched the heart.

The first syllable uttered after this scene was, "And are we to be left behind?" The interrogatory was scarcely put, when the word "Stand to your arms!" answered it. The order was promptly obeyed, and a breathless silence prevailed when our commanding officer, in a few words, announced to us that Lord Wellington had directed our division to carry the grand breach. The soldiers listened to the communication with silent earnestness, and immediately began to disencumber themselves of their knapsacks, which were placed in order by companies and a guard set over them. Each man

L

then began to arrange himself for the combat in such manner as his fancy or the moment would admit of—some by lowering their cartridge-boxes, others by turning theirs to the front in order that they might the more conveniently make use of them; others unclasping their stocks or opening their shirt-collars, and others oiling their bayonets; and more taking leave of their wives and children. This last was an affecting sight, but not so much so as might be expected, because the women, from long habit, were accustomed to scenes of danger, and the order for their husbands to march against the enemy was in their eyes tantamount to a victory; and as the soldier seldom returned without plunder of some sort, the painful suspense which his absence caused was made up by the gaiety which his return was certain to be productive of; or if, unfortunately, he happened to fall, his place was sure to be supplied by some one of the company to which he belonged, so that the women of our army had little cause of alarm on this head. The worst that could happen to them was the chance of being in a state of widowhood for a week.

It was by this time half-past six o'clock, the evening was piercingly cold, and the frost was crisp on the grass; there was a keenness in the air that braced our nerves at least as high as *concert pitch*. We stood quietly to our arms, and told our companies off by files, sections, and sub-divisions; the sergeants called over the rolls—not a man was absent.

It appears it was the wish of General Mackinnon to confer a mark of distinction upon the 88th Regiment, and as it was one of the last acts of his life, I shall mention it. He sent for Major Thompson, who commanded the battalion, and told him it was his wish to have the forlorn hope of the grand breach led on by a subaltern of the 88th Regiment, adding at the same time that, in the event of his surviving, he should be recommended for a company. The Major acknowledged this mark of the General's favour, and left him folding up some letters he had been writing to his friends in England—this was about twenty minutes before the attack of the breaches. Major Thompson, having called his officers together, briefly told them the wishes of their General ; he was about to proceed, when Lieutenant William Mackie (*then senior Lieutenant*) immediately stepped forward, and dropping his sword said, " Major Thompson, I am ready for that service." For once in his life poor old Thompson was affected—Mackie was his own townsman, they had fought together for many years, and when he took hold of his hand and pronounced the words, " God bless you, my boy," his eye filled, his lip quivered, and there was a faltering in his voice which was evidently perceptible to himself, for he instantly resumed his former composure, drew himself up, and gave the word, " Gentlemen, fall in," and at this moment Generals Picton and Mackinnon, accompanied by their respective staffs, made their appearance amongst us.

Long harangues are not necessary to British soldiers, and on this occasion but few words were made use of. Picton said something animating to the different regiments as he passed them, and those of my readers who recollect his deliberate and strong utterance will say with me, that his mode of speaking was indeed very impressive. The address to each was nearly the same, but that delivered by him to the 88th was so characteristic of the General, and so applicable to the men he spoke to, that I shall give it word for word ; it was this :—

" Rangers of Connaught ! it is not my intention to expend

any powder this evening.   We'll do this business with the could iron."

I before said the soldiers were silent—so they were, but the man who could be silent after such an address, made in such a way, and in such a place, had better have stayed at home.   It may be asked what did they do?   Why, what would they do, or would any one do, but give the loudest hurrah he was able.

CHAPTER XIV

Storm of Ciudad Rodrigo—Gallant conduct of three soldiers of the 88th
—Desperate struggle and capture of a gun—Combat between
Lieutenant Faris and the French grenadier—A Connaught
Ranger transformed into a sweep—Anecdote of Captain Robert
Hardyman of the 45th—Death of General Mackinnon—Plunder of
Ciudad Rodrigo—Excesses of the soldiers.

THE burst of enthusiasm caused by Picton's address to the
Connaught Rangers had scarcely ceased, when the signal-
gun announced that the attack was to commence. Generals
Picton and Mackinnon dismounted from their horses, and
placing themselves at the head of the right brigade, the
troops rapidly entered the trenches by sections right in
front; the storming party under the command of Major
Russell Manners of the 74th heading it, while the forlorn
hope, commanded by Lieutenant William Mackie of the
88th, and composed of twenty volunteers from the Connaught Rangers, led the van, followed closely by the 45th,
88th, and 74th British, and the 9th and 21st Portuguese; the
77th and 83rd British, belonging to the left brigade, brought
up the rear and completed the dispositions.

While these arrangements were effecting opposite the
grand breach, the 5th and 94th, belonging to the left
brigade of the 3rd Division, were directed to clear the
ramparts and Fausse Braye wall, and the 2nd Regiment of

Portuguese Caçadores, commanded by an Irish colonel of the name of O'Toole, was to escalade the curtain to the left of the lesser breach, which was attacked by the Light Division under the command of General Robert Craufurd.

It wanted ten minutes to seven o'clock when these dispositions were completed; the moon occasionally, as the clouds which overcast it passed away, shed a faint ray of light upon the battlements of the fortress, and presented to our view the glittering of the enemy's bayonets as their soldiers stood arrayed upon the ramparts and breach, awaiting our attack; yet, nevertheless, their batteries were silent, and might warrant the supposition to an unobservant spectator that the defence would be but feeble.

The two divisions got clear of the covered way at the same moment, and each advanced to the attack of their respective points with the utmost regularity. The obstacles which presented themselves to both were nearly the same, but every difficulty, no matter how great, merged into insignificance when placed in the scale of the prize about to be contested. The soldiers were full of ardour, but altogether devoid of that blustering and bravadoing which is truly unworthy of men at such a moment; and it would be difficult to convey an adequate idea of the enthusiastic bravery which animated the troops. A cloud that had for some time before obscured the moon, which was at its full, disappeared altogether, and the countenances of the soldiers were for the first time, since Picton addressed them, visible —they presented a material change. In place of that joyous animation which his fervid and impressive address called forth, a look of severity, bordering on ferocity, had taken its place; and although ferocity is by no means one of the characteristics of the British soldier, there was, most

unquestionably, a savage expression in the faces of the men
that I had never before witnessed. Such is the difference
between the storm of a breach and the fighting a pitched
battle.

Once clear of the covered way, and fairly on the plain
that separated it from the fortress, the enemy had a full
view of all that was passing; their batteries, charged to the
muzzle with case-shot, opened a murderous fire upon the
columns as they advanced, but nothing could shake the
intrepid bravery of the troops. The Light Division soon
descended the ditch and gained, although not without a
serious struggle, the top of the narrow and difficult breach
allotted to them; their gallant General, Robert Craufurd,
fell at the head of the 43rd, and his second in command,
General Vandeleur, was severely wounded, but there were
not wanting others to supply their place; yet these losses,
trying as they were to the feelings of the soldiers, in no way
damped their ardour, and the brave Light Division carried
the left breach at the point of the bayonet. Once established upon the ramparts, they made all the dispositions
necessary to ensure their own conquest, as also to render
every assistance in their power to the 3rd Division in their
attack. They cleared the rampart which separated the lesser
from the grand breach, and relieved Picton's division from
any anxiety it might have as to its safety on its left flank.

The right brigade, consisting of the 45th, 88th, and 74th,
forming the van of the 3rd Division, upon reaching the
ditch, to its astonishment, found Major Ridge and Colonel
Campbell at the head of the 5th and 94th mounting the
Fausse Braye wall. These two regiments, after having performed their task of silencing the fire of the French troops
upon the ramparts, with a noble emulation resolved to

precede their comrades in the attack of the grand breach. Both parties greeted each other with a cheer, only to be understood by those who have been placed in a similar situation; yet the enemy were in no way daunted by the shout raised by our soldiers—they crowded the breach, and defended it with a bravery that would have made any but troops accustomed to conquer, waver. But the "fighting division" were not the men to be easily turned from their purpose; the breach was speedily mounted, yet, nevertheless, a serious affray took place ere it was gained. A considerable mass of infantry crowned its summit, while in the rear and at each side were stationed men, so placed that they could render every assistance to their comrades at the breach without any great risk to themselves; besides this, two guns of heavy calibre, separated from the breach by a ditch of considerable depth and width, enfiladed it, and as soon as the French infantry were forced from the summit, these guns opened their fire on our troops.

The head of the column had scarcely gained the top, when a discharge of grape cleared the ranks of the three leading battalions, and caused a momentary wavering; at the same instant a frightful explosion near the gun to the left of the breach, which shook the bastion to its foundation, completed the disorder. Mackinnon, at the head of his brigade, was blown into the air. His aide-de-camp, Lieutenant Beresford of the 88th, shared the same fate, and every man on the breach at the moment of the explosion perished. This was unavoidable, because those of the advance, being either killed or wounded, were necessarily flung back upon the troops that followed close upon their footsteps, and there was not a sufficient space for the men who were ready to sustain those placed *hors de combat* to rally. For an instant all was confusion; the blaze of light caused by the explosion resembled a huge meteor, and presented to our sight the havoc which the enemy's fire had caused in our ranks; while from afar the astonished Spaniard viewed for an instant, with horror and dismay, the soldiers of the two nations grappling with each other on the top of the rugged breach which trembled beneath their feet, while the fire of the French artillery played upon our columns with irresistible fury, sweeping from the spot the living and the dead. Amongst the latter was Captain Robert Hardyman and Lieutenant Pearse of the 45th, and many more whose names I cannot recollect. Others were so stunned by the shock, or wounded by the stones which were hurled forth by the explosion, that they were insensible to their situation; of this number I was one, for being close to the magazine when it blew up, I was quite overpowered, and I owed my life to the Sergeant-Major of my regiment, Thorp, who saved me from being trampled to death by our soldiers in their advance, ere I could recover strength sufficient to move forward or protect myself.

The French, animated by this accidental success, hastened once more to the breach which they had abandoned, but the leading regiments of Picton's division, which had been disorganised for the moment by the explosion, rallied, and soon regained its summit, when another discharge from the two flank guns swept away the foremost of those battalions.

There was at this time but one officer alive upon the breach (Major Thomson, of the 74th, acting engineer); he called out to those next to him to seize the gun to the left, which had been so fatal to his companions—but this was a desperate service. The gun was completely cut off from the breach by a deep trench, and soldiers, encumbered with their firelocks, could not pass it in sufficient time to anticipate the next discharge—yet to deliberate was certain death. The French cannoniers, five in number, stood to, and served their gun with as much *sang froid* as if on a parade, and the light which their torches threw forth showed to our men the peril they would have to encounter if they dared to attack a gun so defended; but this was of no avail. Men going to storm a breach generally make up their minds that there is no great probability of their ever returning from it to tell their adventures to their friends; and whether they die at the bottom or top of it, or at the muzzle, or upon the breech of a cannon, is to them pretty nearly the same!

The first who reached the top, after the last discharge, were three of the 88th. Sergeant Pat Brazil—the brave Brazil of the Grenadier company, who saved his captain's life at Busaco—called out to his two companions, Swan and Kelly, to unscrew their bayonets and follow him; the three men passed the trench in a moment, and engaged the French cannoniers hand to hand; a terrific but short combat was the consequence. Swan was the first, and was met by the two gunners on the right of the gun, but, no way daunted, he engaged them, and plunged his bayonet into the breast of one; he was about to repeat the blow upon the other, but before he could disentangle the weapon from his bleeding adversary, the second Frenchman closed upon him, and by a *coup de sabre* severed his left arm from his body a little above the elbow; he fell from the shock, and was on the eve of being massacred, when Kelly, after having scrambled under the gun, rushed onward to succour his comrade. He bayoneted two Frenchmen on the spot, and at this instant Brazil came up; three of the five gunners lay lifeless, while Swan, resting against an ammunition chest,

was bleeding to death.   It was now equal numbers, two
against two, but Brazil in his over-anxiety to engage was
near losing his life at the onset; in making a lunge at the
man next to him, his foot slipped upon the bloody platform,
and he fell forward against his antagonist, but as both rolled
under the gun, Brazil felt the socket of his bayonet strike
hard against the buttons of the Frenchman's coat.   The
remaining gunner, in attempting to escape under the carriage
from Kelly, was killed by some soldiers of the 5th, who just
now reached the top of the breach, and seeing the serious
dispute at the gun, pressed forward to the assistance of the
three men of the Connaught Rangers.

While this was taking place on the left, the head of the
column remounted the breach, and regardless of the cries
of their wounded companions, whom they indiscriminately
trampled to death, pressed forward in one irregular but
heroic mass, and putting every man to death who opposed
their progress, forced the enemy from the ramparts at the
bayonet's point.   Yet the garrison still rallied, and defended
the several streets with the most unflinching bravery; nor
was it until the musketry of the Light Division was heard in
the direction of the Plaza Mayor, that they gave up the
contest! but from this moment all regular resistance ceased,
and they fled in disorder to the Citadel.   There were, nevertheless, several minor combats in the streets, and in many
instances the inhabitants fired from the windows, but whether
their efforts were directed against us or the French is a point
that I do not feel myself competent to decide; be this as it
may, many lives were lost on both sides by this circumstance,
for the Spaniards, firing without much attention to regularity,
killed or wounded indiscriminately all who came within their
range.

During a contest of such a nature, kept up in the night, as may be supposed, much was of necessity left to the guidance of the subordinate officers, if not to the soldiers themselves. Each affray in the streets was conducted in the best manner the moment would admit of, and decided more by personal valour than discipline, and in some instances officers as well as privates had to combat with the imperial troops. In one of these encounters Lieutenant George Faris, of the 88th, by an accident so likely to occur in an affair of this kind, separated a little too far from a dozen or so of his regiment, and found himself opposed to a French soldier who, apparently, was similarly placed. It was a curious coincidence, and it would seem as if each felt that he individually was the representative of the country to which he belonged; and had the fate of the two nations hung upon the issue of the combat I am about to describe, it could not have been more heroically contested. The Frenchman fired at and wounded Faris in the thigh, and made a desperate push with his bayonet at his body, but Faris parried the thrust, and the bayonet only lodged in his leg. He saw at a glance the peril of his situation, and that nothing short of a miracle could save him; the odds against him were too great, and if he continued a scientific fight he must inevitably be vanquished. He sprang forward, and, seizing hold of the Frenchman by the collar, a struggle of a most nervous kind took place; in their mutual efforts to gain an advantage they lost their caps, and as they were men of nearly equal strength, it was doubtful what the issue would be. They were so entangled with each other their weapons were of no avail, but Faris at length disengaged himself from the grasp which held him, and he was able to use his sabre; he pushed the Frenchman from him, and ere he could recover himself he laid his head open nearly to the chin. His sword-blade, a heavy, soft, ill-made Portuguese one, was doubled up with the force of the blow, and retained some pieces of the skull and clotted hair! At this moment I reached the spot with about twenty men, composed of different regiments, all being by this time mixed *pell mell* with each other. I ran up to Faris—he was nearly exhausted, but he was safe. The French grenadier lay upon the pavement, while Faris, though tottering from fatigue, held his sword firmly in his grasp, and it was crimson to the hilt. The appearance of the two combatants was frightful!—one lying dead on the ground, the other faint from agitation and loss of blood; but the soldiers loudly applauded him, and the feeling uppermost with them was, that our man had the best of it! It was a shocking sight, but it would be rather a hazardous experiment to begin moralising at such a moment and in such a place.

Those of the garrison who escaped death were made prisoners, and the necessary guards being placed, and everything secured, the troops not selected for duty commenced a very diligent search for those articles which they most fancied, and which they considered themselves entitled to by "right of conquest." I believe on a service such as the present, there is a sort of tacit acknowledgment of this "right"; but be this as it may, a good deal of property most indubitably changed owners on the night of the 19th of January 1812. The conduct of the soldiers, too, within the last hour, had undergone a complete change; before, it was all order and regularity, now it was nothing but licentiousness and confusion—subordination was at an end; plunder and blood was the order of the day, and many an officer on this night was compelled to show that he carried a sabre.

The doors of the houses in a large Spanish town are remarkable for their strength, and resemble those of a prison more than anything else; their locks are of huge dimensions, and it is a most difficult task to force them. The mode adopted by the men of my regiment (the 88th) in this dilemma was as effective as it was novel; the muzzles of a couple of muskets were applied to each side of the keyhole, while a third soldier, fulfilling the functions of an officer, deliberately gave the word, "make ready"—"present"— "fire!" and in an instant the ponderous lock gave way before the combined operations of the three individuals, and doors that rarely opened to the knock of a stranger in Rodrigo, now flew off their hinges to receive the Rangers of Connaught.

The chapels and chandlers' houses were the first captured, in both of which was found a most essential ingredient in the shape of large wax candles; these the soldiers lighted, and commenced their perambulations in search of plunder, and the glare of light which they threw across the faces of the men, as they carried them through the streets, displayed their countenances, which were of that cast that might well terrify the unfortunate inhabitants. Many of the soldiers with their faces scorched by the explosion of the magazine at the grand breach; others with their lips blackened from biting off the ends of their cartridges, more covered with blood, and all looking ferocious, presented a combination sufficient to appal the stoutest heart.

Scenes of the greatest outrage now took place, and it was pitiable to see groups of the inhabitants half naked in the streets—the females clinging to the officers for protection— while their respective houses were undergoing the strictest scrutiny. Some of the soldiers turned to the wine and spirit

houses, where, having drunk sufficiently, they again sallied
out in quest of more plunder; others got so intoxicated
that they lay in a helpless state in different parts of the
town, and lost what they had previously gained, either by
the hands of any passing Spaniard, who could venture
unobserved to stoop down, or by those of their own companions, who in their wandering surveys happened to recognise a comrade lying with half a dozen silk gowns, or some
such thing, wrapped about him.   Others wished to attack the
different stores, and as there is something marvellously
attractive in the very name of a brandy one, it is not to be
wondered at that many of our heroes turned not only their
thoughts, but their steps also, in the direction in which these
houses lay; and from the unsparing hand with which they
supplied themselves, it might be imagined they intended to
change their habits of life and turn spirit-venders, and that
too in the wholesale line!

It was astonishing to see with what rapidity and accuracy
these fellows traversed the different parts of the town, and
found out the shops and storehouses. A stranger would
have supposed they were natives of the place, and it was not
until the following morning that I discovered the cause of
what was to me before incomprehensible.

In all military movements in a country which an army
is not thoroughly acquainted with, (and why not in a large
town?) there are no more useful appendages than good
guides. Lord Wellington was most particular on this point,
and had attached to his army a corps of this description.
I suppose it was this knowledge of tactics which suggested
to the soldiers the necessity of so wise a precaution; accordingly, every group of individuals was preceded by a Spaniard,
who, upon learning the species of plunder wished for by his

employers, instantly conducted them to the most favourable ground for their operations.   By this means the houses were unfurnished with less confusion than can be supposed ; and had it not been for the state of intoxication that some of the young soldiers—mere tyros in the art of sacking a town —had indulged themselves in, it is inconceivable with what facility the city of Ciudad Rodrigo would have been eased of its superfluities.   And the *conducteur* himself was not always an idle spectator.   Many of these fellows realised something considerable from their more wealthy neighbours, and being also right well paid by the soldiers, who were liberal enough, they found themselves in the morning in far better circumstances than they had been the preceding night, so that all things considered, there were about as many cheerful faces as sad ones.   But although the inhabitants were, by this sort of transfer, put more on an equality with each other, the town itself was greatly impoverished.   Many things of value were destroyed, but in the hurry so natural to the occasion, many also escaped ; besides, our men were as yet young hands in the arcana of plundering a town in that *au fait* manner with which a French army would have done a business of the sort : but they most unquestionably made up for their want of tact by the great inclination they showed to profit by any occasion that offered itself for their improvement.

By some mistake, a large spirit store situated in the Plaza Mayor took fire, and the flames spreading with incredible fury, despite of the exertions of the troops, the building was totally destroyed ; but in this instance, like many others which we are obliged to struggle against through life, there was a something that neutralised the disappointment which the loss of so much brandy occasioned the soldiers : the light which shone forth from the building was of material service to them, inasmuch as it tended to facilitate their movements in their excursions for plunder; the heat also was far from disagreeable, for the night was piercingly cold, yet, nevertheless, the soldiers exerted themselves to the utmost to put a stop to this calamity. General Picton was to be seen in the midst of them, encouraging them by his example and presence to make still greater efforts; but all would not do, and floor after floor fell in, until at last it was nothing but a burning heap of ruins.

Some houses were altogether saved from plunder by the interference of the officers, for in several instances the women ran out into the streets, and seizing hold of three or four of us, would force us away to their houses, and by this stroke of political hospitality saved their property. A good supper was then provided, and while all outside was noise and pillage, affairs within went on agreeably enough. These instances were, however, but few.

In the house where I and four other officers remained, we fared remarkably well, and were passing the night greatly to our satisfaction, when we were aroused by a noise like a crash of something heavy falling in the apartment above us. As may be supposed, we did not remain long without seeking to ascertain the cause of this disturbance; the whole party sprang up at once—the family of the house secreting themselves behind the different pieces of furniture, while we, *sabre à la main*, and some with lights, advanced towards the apartment from whence the noise proceeded; but all was silent within. Captain Seton of my corps proposed that the door should be forced, but he had scarcely pronounced the words, when a voice from within called out, not in Spanish or French, but in plain English, with a rich Irish

M

brogue, " Oh, Jasus, is it you, Captain?" On entering we
found a man of the Connaught Rangers, belonging to Seton's
company, standing before us, so disfigured by soot and filth
that it was impossible to recognise his uniform, much less
his face—his voice was the only thing recognisable about
him, and that only to his Captain; and had it not been for
that, he might have passed for one just arrived from the
infernal regions, and it may be questioned whether or not
the place he had quitted might not be so denominated. It
appeared, from the account he gave of himself, that he had
been upon a plundering excursion in one of the adjoining
houses, the roof of which, like most of those in Rodrigo,
was flat; and wishing to have a distinct view of all that was
passing in the streets, he took up his position upon the top
of the house he had entered, and not paying due attention
to where he put his foot, he contrived to get it into the
chimney of the house we occupied, and, ere he could resume
his centre of gravity, he tumbled headlong down the chimney
and caused us all the uneasiness I have been describing. His
tout ensemble was as extraordinary as his adventure. He had
eighteen or twenty pairs of shoes round his waist, and
amongst other things a case of trepanning instruments,
which he immediately offered as a present to his Captain!
Had the grate of this fireplace been what is called in
England the " Rumford grate," this poor fellow must have
been irretrievably lost to the service, because it is manifest,
encumbered as he was, he would have stuck fast, and must
inevitably have been suffocated before assistance could be
afforded him; but, fortunately for him, the chimney was of
sufficient dimensions to admit an elephant to pass down it,
and, in truth, one not so constructed would have been
altogether too confined for him.

Morning at length began to dawn, and with it the horrors
of the previous night's assault were visible. The troops not
on guard were directed to quit the town, but this was not a
command they obeyed with the same cheerfulness or expedition which they evinced when ordered to enter it; in their
eyes it had many attractions still, and, besides, the soldiers
had become so unwieldy from the immense burdens they
carried, it was scarcely possible for many of them to stir,
much less march. However, by degrees the evacuation of
the fortress took place, and towards noon it was effected
altogether.

The breaches presented a horrid spectacle. The one
forced by the Light Division was narrower than the other,
and the dead, lying in a smaller compass, looked more
numerous than they really were. I walked along the
ramparts towards the grand breach, and was examining
the effects our fire had produced on the different defences
and the buildings in their immediate vicinity, but I had not
proceeded far when I was shocked at beholding about a
hundred and thirty or forty wounded Frenchmen, lying
under one of the bastions and some short distance up a
narrow street adjoining it. I descended, and learned that
these men had been performing some particular duty in the
magazine which blew up and killed General Mackinnon and
so many of the 3rd Division. These miserable beings were
so burnt that I fear, notwithstanding the considerate attention which was paid to them by our medical officers, none of
their lives were preserved. Their uniforms were barely
distinguishable, and their swollen heads and limbs gave
them a gigantic appearance that was truly terrific; added
to this, the gunpowder had so blackened their faces that
they looked more like a number of huge negroes than

soldiers of an European army. Many of our men hastened to the spot, and with that compassion which truly brave men always feel, rendered them every assistance in their power; some were carried on doors, others in blankets, to the hospitals, and these poor creatures showed by their gestures, for they could not articulate, how truly they appreciated our tender care of them.

At length I reached the grand breach—it was covered with many officers and soldiers; of the former, amongst others, was my old friend Hardyman of the 45th, and Lieutenant William Pearse of the same regiment; there were also two of the 5th whose names I forget, and others whose faces were familiar to me. Hardyman, the once cheerful, gay Bob Hardyman, lay on his back; half of his head was carried away by one of those discharges of grape from the flank guns at the breach which were so destructive to us in our advance; his face was perfect, and even in death presented its wonted cheerfulness. Poor fellow! he died without pain, and regretted by all who knew him; his gaiety of spirit never for an instant forsook him. Up to the moment of the assault he was the same pleasant Bob Hardy-man who delighted every one by his anecdotes, and none more than my old corps, although many of his jokes were at our expense. When we were within a short distance of the breach, as we met, he stopped for an instant to shake hands. " What's that you have hanging over your shoulder?" said he, as he espied a canteen of rum which I carried. " A little rum, Bob," said I. " Well," he replied, " I'll change my breath; and take my word for it, that in less than five minutes some of the 'subs' will be scratching a Captain's ——, for there will be wigs on the green." He took a mouthful of rum, and taking me by the hand squeezed it affectionately, and in ten minutes afterwards he was a corpse!

The appearance of Pearse was quite different from his companion; ten or a dozen grape-shot pierced his breast, and he lay, or rather sat, beside his friend like one asleep, and his appearance was that of a man upwards of sixty, though his years did not number twenty-five. Hardyman was stripped to his trousers, but Pearse had his uniform on; his epaulettes alone had been plundered. I did not see the body of General Mackinnon, but the place where he fell was easily distinguishable; the vast chasm which the spot presented resembled an excavation in the midst of a quarry. The limbs of those who lost their lives by that fatal explosion, thrown here and there, presented a melancholy picture of the remnants of those brave men whose hearts but a few short hours before beat high in the hope of conquest. It was that kind of scene which arrested the attention of the soldier, and riveted him to the spot; and there were few who, even in the moment of exultation, did not feel deeply as they surveyed the mangled remains of their comrades.

I next turned to the captured gun, so chivalrously taken by the three men of the 88th. The five cannoniers lying across the carriage, or between the spokes of the wheels, showed how bravely they had defended it; yet they lay like men whose death had not been caused by violence; they were naked and bloodless, and the puncture of the bayonet left so small a mark over their hearts, it was discernible only to those who examined the bodies closely.

I turned away from the breach, and scrambled over its rugged face, and the dead which covered it. On reaching the bivouac we had occupied the preceding evening, I learned, with surprise, that our women had been engaged in a contest, if not as dangerous as ours, at least one of no trivial sort. The men left as a guard over the baggage, on hearing the first shot at the trenches, could not withstand the inclination they felt to join their companions; and although this act was creditable to the bravery of the individuals that composed the baggage-guard, it was nigh being fatal to those who survived, or, at least, to such as had anything to lose except their lives, for the wretches that infested our camp attempted to plunder it of all that it possessed, but the women, with a bravery that would not have disgraced those of ancient Rome, defended the post with such valour that those miscreants were obliged to desist, and our baggage was saved in consequence.

We were about to resume our arms when General Picton approached us. Some of the soldiers, who were more than usually elevated in spirits, on his passing them, called out, "Well, General, we gave you a cheer last night; it's your turn now!" The General, smiling, took off his hat, and said, "Here, then, you drunken set of brave rascals, hurrah! we'll soon be at Badajoz!" A shout of confidence followed; we slung our firelocks, the bands played, and we commenced our march for the village of Atalaya in the highest spirits, and in a short time lost sight of a place the capture of which appeared to us like a dream.

CHAPTER XV

Results of the siege of Ciudad Rodrigo—The town revisited—Capture
of deserters—Sale of the plunder—Army rests in cantonments—
An execution of deserters—A pardon that came too late.

THE fortress of Ciudad Rodrigo fell on the eleventh day
after its investment ; and taking into account the season of
the year, the difficulty of the means to carry on the
operations, and the masterly manner in which Lord
Wellington baffled the vigilance of the Duke of Ragusa,
the capture of Rodrigo must ever rank as one of the most
finished military exploits upon record, and a *chef d'œuvre* of
the art of war. Our loss was equal to that of the enemy ; it
amounted to about one thousand *hors de combat*, together
with three generals ; of the garrison but seventeen hundred
were made prisoners, the rest being put to the sword.

So soon as my regiment reached the village, I obtained
leave to return to Rodrigo, for I was anxious to see in what
situation the family were with whom I, in common with
my companions, had passed the preceding night. Upon
entering the town, I found all in confusion. The troops
ordered to occupy it were not any of those which had
composed the storming divisions ; and although the task of
digging graves, and clearing away the rubbish about the
breaches, was not an agreeable one, they nevertheless per-

167

formed it with much cheerfulness; yet, in some instances, the soldiers levied contributions upon the unfortunate inhabitants,—light ones it is true, and for the reason that little remained with them to give, or, more properly speaking, withhold.   But the Provost-Marshal was so active in his vocation that this calamity was soon put a stop to, and the miserable people, who were in many instances in a state of nudity, could without risk venture to send to their more fortunate neighbours for a supply of those articles of dress which decency required.   Upon reaching the house I had rested in the evening before, I was rejoiced to find it uninjured, and the poor people, upon once more seeing me, almost suffocated me with their caresses, and their expressions of gratitude knew no bounds for our having preserved their house from pillage.

Having satisfied myself that my *padrona* and her daughters had escaped molestation, I took my leave of them, and once more visited the large breach.   On my way thither I saw the French garrison preparing to march, under an escort of Portuguese troops, to the fortress of Almeida; they were a fine-looking body of men, and seemed right well pleased to get off so quietly; they counted about eighteen hundred, and were all that escaped unhurt of the garrison.   At the breach there were still several wounded men, who had not been removed to the hospitals; amongst them was a fellow of my own corps, of the name of Doogan; he was badly wounded in the thigh, the bone of which was so shattered as to protrude through the skin.   Near him lay a French soldier, shot through the body, quite frantic from pain, and in the agonies of death.   The moment Doogan observed me, he called out most lustily, "Och! for the love of Jasus, Mr. Grattan, don't lave me here near this villain that's afther

cursing me to no end." I observed to Doogan that the poor
fellow was in a much worse state than even himself, and that
I doubted whether he would be alive in five minutes. At
this moment the eyes of the Frenchman met mine, "*Oh!*
monsieur," exclaimed he, "*je meurs pour une goutte d'eau!*
Oh, mon Dieu! mon Dieu!"—"Now," ejaculated Doogan,
addressing me, "will you believe me (that never tould a lie
in my life!) another time? Did you hear him, then, how he
got on with his *mon dew?*" I caused Doogan to be carried
to an hospital, but the French soldier died as we endeavoured
to place him in a blanket.

I quitted the breach, and took a parting glance at the
town; the smell from the still burning houses, the groups of
dead and wounded, and the broken fragments of different
weapons, marked strongly the character of the preceding
night's dispute; and even at this late hour, there were many
drunken marauders endeavouring to regain, by some fresh act
of atrocity, an equivalent for the plunder their brutal state
of intoxication had caused them to lose by the hands of their
own companions, who robbed indiscriminately man, woman, or
child, friend or foe, the dead or the dying! Then, again,
were to be seen groups of deserters from our army, who,
having taken shelter in Rodrigo during the winter, were now
either dragged from their hiding-places by their merciless
comrades, or given up by the Spaniards, in whose houses they
had sought shelter, to the first officer or soldier who would
be troubled, at the moment, with the responsibility of taking
charge of them.

In the midst of a group of a dozen men deserters from
different regiments, stood two of the Connaught Rangers.
No matter what their other faults might be, desertion was
not a species of delinquency they were addicted to; and as

the fate of one of these men—indeed both of them, for that matter—was a little tragical, I purpose giving it a nook in my adventures. The two culprits to whom I have made allusion were as different in their characters as persons; one of them (Mangin) was a quiet well-disposed man, short in stature, a native of England, and, as a matter of course, a heavy feeder, one that could but ill put up with "short allowance," and in consequence left the army when food became as scarce as it did in the winter of 1811. The other, a fellow of the name of Curtis, an Irishman, tall and lank, was, like the rest of the "boys" from that part of the world, mighty aisy about what he ate, provided he got a reasonable supply of drink; but as neither the one nor the other were "convenient" during the period in question, they both left an advanced post one fine night, and resolved to try the difference between the French commissariat and ours. This was their justification of themselves to me, and I believe, for I was not present at it, the *summum bonum* upon which the basis of their defence at their trial rested. There were also six Germans of the 60th Rifles in the group, but they seemed so unnerved by their unexpected capture that they were unable to say anything for themselves.

Towards evening I reached the village which my regiment occupied. An altered scene presented itself. The soldiers busied in arranging their different articles of plunder; many of them clad in the robes of some priest, while others wore gowns of the most costly silk or velvet; others, again, nearly naked; some without pantaloons, having been plundered, while drunk, of so essential a part of their dress; but all, or almost all, were occupied in laying out for sale their different articles of plunder, in that order which was essential to their being disposed of to the crowds of

Spaniards which had already assembled to be the purchasers ;
and if one could judge by their looks, they most unquestionably committed a breach in their creed by " coveting their
neighbours' goods." And had the scene which now presented
itself to our sight been one caused by an event the most
joyous, much less by the calamity that had befallen the
unfortunate inhabitants of Rodrigo, to say nothing of the
human blood that had been spilt ere that event had taken
place, the scene could not have been more gay. Brawny-
shouldered Castilians, carrying pig-skins of wine on their
backs, which they sold to our soldiers for a trifling sum ;
bolero-dancers, rattling their castanets like the clappers of
so many mills ; our fellows drinking like fishes, while their
less fortunate companions at Rodrigo—either hastily flung
into an ill-formed grave, writhing under the knife of the
surgeon, or in the agonies of death—were unthought of, or
unfelt for. *Sic transit gloria mundi!* The soldiers were
allowed three days *congé* for the disposal of their booty ; but
long before the time had expired, they had scarcely a rag to
dispose of, or a *real* of the produce in their pockets.

A few days sufficed for the reorganisation of the soldiers
after they had disposed of their hard-earned plunder, and
we were once more ready and willing for any fresh enterprise, no matter how difficult or dangerous. Badajoz was
talked of, but nothing certain was known, and the quiet
which reigned throughout all our cantonments was such as
not to warrant the least suspicion that any immediate attack
against that fortress was contemplated by the Commander-
in-Chief.

On the sixth day after our arrival at Atalaya, we were
again in motion ; the village of Albergaria was allotted for
our quarters, and a court-martial was ordered to assemble for

the trial of the deserters from our army found in Rodrigo.
The men of the 60th, and the two men of the 88th (Mangin
and Curtis) were amongst the number. The court held its
sitting—the prisoners were arraigned, found guilty, and
sentenced to be shot! All were bad characters, save one,
and that one was Mangin. He received testimonials from
the Captain of his company (Captain Seton—ever the soldier's
friend) highly creditable to him, and Lord Wellington, with
his accustomed love of justice, resolved that his pardon
should be promulgated at the time of the reading the proceedings and sentence of the court-martial. Three days
after the trial it was made known to the prisoners, and the
army generally, that they were to die the following morning.

At eight o'clock the division was under arms, and formed
in a hollow square of small dimensions; in the centre of it
was the Provost-Marshal, accompanied by his followers, with
pick-axes, spades, shovels, and all the necessary etceteras for
marking out and forming the graves into which the unfortunate delinquents were to be deposited as soon as they
received the last and most imposing of military honours—
that of being shot to death! In a few moments afterwards
the rolling of muffled drums—the usual accompaniment of
the death-march—was heard, and the soldiers who guarded
the prisoners were soon in sight. The division observed a
death-like silence as the prisoners defiled round the inside of
the square; every eye was turned towards them; but Mangin,
from his well-known good character, was an object of general
solicitude. The solitary sound of the muffled drums at last
died away into silence; the guard drew up in the centre of
the square, and the prisoners had, for the last time, a view
of their companions from whom they had deserted, and of
their colours which they had forsaken; but if their counte-

nances were a just index of their minds, they seemed to repent greatly the act they had committed! The three men of the 60th were in their shirts, as was also Mangin of the 88th, but Curtis wore the " old red rag," most likely from necessity, having, in all human probability, *no shirt to die in*—a circumstance by no means rare with the soldiers of the Peninsular army.

The necessary preliminaries, such as reading the crime and finding the sentence, had finished, when the Adjutant-General announced the pardon granted to Mangin, who was immediately conducted away, and placed at a short distance in rear of the division; the rest staggered onward to the spot where their graves had been dug, and having been placed on their knees, their legs hanging over the edge of the grave, a bandage was tied over their eyes. The Provost-Marshal then, with a party of twenty musketeers, their fire-locks cocked, and at the recover, silently moved in front of the prisoners until he reached to within five paces of them, and then giving two motions of his hand—the one to present, the other to fire—the four men fell into the pit prepared to receive them. The three Germans were dead—indeed they were nearly so before they were fired at! and if the state of their nerves was a criterion to go by, a moderate-sized popgun would have been sufficiently destructive to have finished their earthly career; but Curtis sprang up, and, with one of his jaws shattered and hanging down upon his breast, presented a horrid spectacle. Every one seemed to be electrified, the Provost-Marshal excepted; he, I suppose, was well accustomed to such sights, for, without any ceremony, he walked up to Curtis, and with the most perfect composure levelled a huge instrument (in size between a horse-pistol and blunderbuss) at his head, which blew it nearly off his shoulders, and he fell upon the bodies of the Germans without moving a muscle.

This ceremony over, the division defiled round the grave, and as each company passed it the word "eyes right" was given by the officer in command, by which means every man had a clear view of the corpses as they lay in a heap. This is a good and wholesome practice, for nothing so much awakes in the mind of the soldier, endowed with proper feeling, the dishonour of committing an action which is almost certain to bring him to a disgraceful end, while it deters the bad man from doing that which will cost him all that he has to lose—for such persons have no character—his life. It was ten o'clock before the parade broke up, and we returned to our quarters, leaving to the Provost-Marshal and his guard the task of filling up the grave. Several Portuguese peasants crowded near the fatal spot, and so soon as all danger was passed, they flocked to wi ness he interment, making, all the time, divers appeals to the Virgi i Mary; but whether these were intended for the preser ation of the souls departed, or their own bodies corporate, I either knew nor inquired.

Mangin, the man who had received his pardon, was still in a state of stupor. After the lapse of an hour or so his Captain went to see him; but the shock he had received was too severe; he had not nerve to bear up against it; he replied in an incoherent manner, soon fell asleep, and awoke an idiot! Every effort that could be made by the medical men, and every assurance of favour from his Captain, proved vain—he became a palpable, irreclaimable idiot, and shortly afterwards died of convulsions.

CHAPTER XVI

Preparations against Badajoz—Description of this fortress—Its investment—Line of circumvallation formed in the night—Sortie of the
garrison repulsed—Destructive fire of the besieged—Dreadful explosion from a shell—Indifference—Deaths of Captain Mulcaster,
Majors Thompson and North.

RODRIGO having fallen, it was soon rumoured that we were
to move off to the south, to assault Badajoz. The soldiers
were full of ardour; they anxiously counted the hours as
they passed; and when at length, on the 8th of March, the
order arrived for the advance of the army to the Alemtejo,
their joy was indescribable. Badajoz had ever been looked
upon by them as unfriendly to our troops, and they contemplated with delight the prospect of having it in their power
to retaliate upon the inhabitants their treatment of our men.
On the 9th, the army was in movement; the Light Division
opened the march, followed by the 3rd and 4th; they
crossed the Tagus by a bridge of boats, thrown over that
river at Villa Velha, and pressed rapidly forward towards
Elvas. One division of infantry and a brigade of cavalry
remained on the Agueda. On the 14th, the Light and 3rd
Divisions were concentrated in the neighbourhood of Elvas;
they were joined by the 4th Division on the following day,
while the remainder of the army, under Hill and Graham,
were pushed forward to Llerena, Merida, and Almendralejo,

175

to observe the motions of Soult, who by this time was
informed of the preparations, though not to their full extent,
that had been formed against Badajoz.

On the 16th of March, everything being in readiness, a
pontoon bridge was thrown across the Guadiana; fifteen
thousand men broke up from their bivouac at Elvas, and
advanced towards the river; the enemy disputed the ground,
and here—even here, with only a handful of cavalry opposed
to us—the French horsemen had actually the best of it, and
kept us at bay during a march of three hours. At length
we gained the river's edge, passed the bridge, drove back
the enemy's outposts, and completed the investment. The
following day, the 17th, Lord Wellington, accompanied by
his engineers, carefully reconnoitred the place. The point of
attack which his lordship decided upon, notwithstanding the
advantages which were on the side of the enemy, was quite
at variance with that of the preceding year, so it must be
naturally presumed that the former was found to be faulty.
Then the outworks were by no means so formidable as now
on the side about to be assailed, while on the San Christoval
side, the scene of the former attack, little progress had been
made towards its amelioration.

The evening of the 17th of March had scarcely closed
when three thousand men broke ground before the fort of La
Picurina, at the distance of one hundred and fifty yards.
The night was unusually dark, the wind was high, and the
rain fell in torrents—all of which favoured the enterprise.
The soldiers, accustomed to fatigues, and knowing by experience, if for nothing but their own safety, the necessity of
getting on rapidly with their work, exerted themselves to
their utmost, and when the grey dawn of morning made its
appearance, the enemy beheld with surprise, through the

mist that surrounded them, the first parallel of our works completed, without their having anticipated it, or having thrown one shot in the direction of our workmen; but as the fog cleared away, it was too palpable to be misunderstood that, despite of the sagacity of General Count Phillipon and his devoted garrison, a line of circumvallation had been cut close to one of the best of their outworks, without their having the remotest idea of the attempt. The different alarm-bells in the town rang a loud peal, and in less than half an hour a tremendous cannonade was opened upon us from the guns of the fort as well as the town itself. Some men were killed and several wounded, but excepting this, no loss was sustained; the works were uninjured, their progress unimpeded, and this, our first attempt, for the third time, was crowned with that unlooked-for success which was a good omen for the future.

The entire of the 18th the rain continued to fall, and the trenches were already nearly knee-deep with water, but by the great exertions of the engineers, and the persevering resolution of the soldiers, the works were pushed on with extraordinary vigour, the earth not being as yet sufficiently saturated to lose its consistency. On the night of the 18th it rained still more heavily; nevertheless some guns were dragged through the slough by the soldiers, into the batteries marked out to act against La Picurina, and the following morning the works were in that forward state as to cause the French Governor much alarm for the fate of this outwork. Towards mid-day on the 19th, a dense vapour, issuing from the Guadiana and Rivillas, caused by the heavy rains that had fallen, made Phillipon consider the moment a favourable one to make a rush into our works; he accordingly placed two thousand chosen troops at the different

N

gates and sally-ports with fixed bayonets, ready to storm the batteries at a given signal. At this time our soldiers were working in the trenches, nearly up to their hips in water; the covering party were too distant to afford immediate relief if required to do so, because they were kept out of the wet ground as far as was consistent with the safety of our lines; and the soldiers that composed the working party were in a helpless and defenceless state, their arms and appointments being thrown aside.

I happened to be in the works on this day, and having a little more experience than the officer who commanded the party, I observed with distrust the bustle which was apparent, not only in the fort of Picurina, but also along the ramparts of the town. Without waiting the formality of telling the commanding officer what I thought, I, on the instant, ordered the men to throw by their spades and shovels, put on their appointments, and load their firelocks. This did not occupy more than three minutes, and in a few seconds afterwards the entire trenches to our right were filled with Frenchmen, the workmen massacred, and the works materially damaged; while at the same moment several hundred men attempted to throw themselves into the battery we occupied. But the workmen were armed and ready to receive them; they had just been placed—I must say it, for it is the truth —by me in a posture not only to save their own lives, but the battery also. The Frenchmen advanced with that impetuous burst so well known to those who have witnessed it, and so difficult to stand before by any. They had a double motive to urge them on on this occasion: honour had a forcible auxiliary in the shape of a dollar, which they were to receive for every pick-axe or shovel they carried out of our trenches; and, well as I know the French character, it is difficult for me

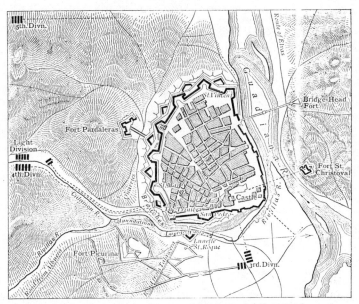

PLAN OF SIEGE OF BADAJOZ. March 16–April 6, 1812.

to say which of the two, honour or avarice, most predominated upon the present occasion; I shall only say that it is my firm conviction—and I judge from the spirit of the attack—that both had their share in stimulating those heroic and veteran plunderers to seek for a footing within our trenches, for I never saw a set of fellows that sought with greater avidity than they did the spades and shovels that were thrown aside by our men. Lieutenant D'Arcy of the 88th and Lieutenant White of the 45th pursued them almost to the glacis of the town; and had the movement been foreseen, there can be little hazard in saying that, with a sufficient supply of ladders at the moment, the fort of Picurina could have been carried by the workmen alone, so great was their enthusiasm, with a less loss of lives than it cost us (after six days' labour) on the 25th!

The sortie had been well repulsed at this point, but higher up, on the right, we were not so fortunate; the workmen were surprised, and, in addition to the injury inflicted upon the works, a great loss of men and officers was sustained before the covering party reached the spot. General Picton soon after arrived in the battery where I was stationed, and seemed to be much alarmed for its safety, not knowing in the confusion of the moment, which was great, that the enemy had attacked it, and had been driven back; but when he learned from me that the workmen alone had achieved this act, he was lavish in his praise of them, and spoke to myself in flattering terms—for him; but there was an austerity of demeanour which, even while he gave praise—a thing he seldom did to the Connaught Rangers at least!—kept a fast hold of him, and the caustic sententiousness with which he spoke rather chilled than animated. He was on foot, but his aide-de-camp, Captain

Cuthbert of the Fusiliers, was mounted, and while in the
act of giving directions to some of the troops (for by this
time the whole of the besieging force, attracted by the
cannonade, was in motion towards the works) he was struck
in the hip by a round shot, which killed his horse on the
spot, leaving him dreadfully mangled and bleeding to death.
This officer was a serious loss to Picton, and was much
regretted by the division; he possessed all the requisites for
a staff-officer, without that silly arrogance—the sure sign of
an empty mind, as well as head—which we sometimes meet
with amongst the gentlemen who compose the *état major* of
our army.

We lost in this affair about two hundred men, many of
whom were cut down in the works, and several in the depots
far in the rear, by a body of the enemy's light cavalry that
galloped out of the town at the moment the sortie commenced.   Absurd as this may read, it is nevertheless true:
the garrison of Badajoz, cooped up within its walls, without
a foot of ground that they could call their own beyond the
glacis, and, in a manner, begirt by an army of fifteen
thousand men, were—by their admirable arrangement of their
forces, or by the superlative neglect of our people, enabled
to ride through our lines—unopposed by a single dragoon!—
from right to left!   Brilliant, however, as was this exploit,
it was of no such service to the garrison; their loss exceeded
four hundred men, and the capture of a few dozen spades
and shovels but ill repaid them for so great a sacrifice of
lives, at any time valuable, but in their present position
doubly so.

The sortie being at length repulsed, and order once more
restored, the works in the trenches were continued under a
torrent of rain and fire of artillery.   Lieutenant White of

the 45th, who had been much distinguished in the batteries, was struck by a shell (without a fuse) on the head, which killed him on the spot; he was reading a book at the moment, and Lieutenant Cotton of the 88th, who was sitting beside him, was so covered with his blood, that it was thought at first he had been frightfully wounded.

Up to this time the fall of rain had been so violent as to threaten the total failure of the operation; it had never ceased since the 17th, and the trenches were a perfect river. The soldiers were working up to their knees in water, and the fatigue and hardships they endured were great indeed, but there was no complaint—not even a murmur to be heard! The next day, the 22nd, the pontoon bridge over the Guadiana was carried away by the floods which the late rains had caused in the river, and the stream became so rapid that the flying bridges could not be made use of, and, in short, all supplies from the other side were cut off. In the trenches matters were in as bad a state, for the earth no longer retained its consistency, and it was impossible to get it into any shape. On the 24th, however, the weather happily settled fine, and much progress was made towards forwarding the works; but this and the following day were perhaps two of the most dreadful recorded in the annals of sieges. The soldiers laboured with a degree of hardihood bordering on desperation, while the engineers braved every danger with as much composure as if they either set no value upon their lives, or thought their bodies impregnable to shot or shell. In proportion as our works advanced, the enemy redoubled his fire, and the attempt made by us to drag the heavy guns through the mud, or to form magazines for the gunpowder, was almost certain death; but not content with the destruction which his fire carried throughout our ranks,

Phillipon brought to his aid a battery from San Christoval, which he placed close to the edge of the river; the fire of this battery completely enfiladed our works, and rendered it difficult and hazardous for the workmen to keep their ground.

Half a battalion was ordered down to the water's edge, and the effect of their fire against these guns was soon appreciated by the soldiers in the batteries; the cannonade of the enemy lost its effect, their fire became irregular, their shot passed over our heads, and finally they were compelled to limber up their park of artillery, and retrace their steps, at a gallop, up the Christoval height. Nevertheless, this battery did an incalculable hurt to us; many men were struck down by its fire, but, above all, our engineers suffered the most. This was a loss that could be but ill spared, for we were so scantily supplied with this description of force, that it was found necessary to substitute officers of the infantry to act as such during the siege. These officers were very zealous in the performance of the dangerous duties they had to fulfil: some had a tolerable knowledge of the theory, but none, if I except Major Thomson of the 74th, and one or two that had served at Rodrigo, knew anything of the practical part; they strove, however, by great intrepidity, to make up for their other defects; they exposed themselves to every danger, with a bravery bordering on foolhardihood, and consequently, under such a fire as we were exposed to, scarcely one escaped death. Lieutenant Fairclough of the 5th, and Rammage of the 74th, both acting engineers, were cut asunder by a round shot from the San Christoval battery; others, whose names I forget, shared the same fate, and several were wounded.

Towards three o'clock in the afternoon our works had

been materially advanced, several small magazines were in progress, the batteries destined to act against La Picurina were armed, and the losses which we sustained amongst our engineers repaired by the arrival of others to replace their fallen companions.   It was at this time, while I was seriously occupied with thirty men, in covering with boards and sandbags a magazine which had been, with great labour, formed during the forenoon, that a shell of huge dimensions exploded at the entrance of it.   There were, at the moment, above a dozen or so of the Staff Corps and Engineers, with some of the line, placing a quantity of gunpowder in the vault which had been prepared to receive it.   The roof of the magazine was, in defiance of the dreadful fire which was incessant upon this point, crowned by a few soldiers of the party under my command; some kegs of gunpowder, which were at the entrance of the cave, unfortunately blew up, destroying all at that side of the magazine, and hurling the planks which were but in part secured upon its top, together with the men that were upon them, into the air: it caused us great loss of lives and labour, but fortunately the great store of powder which was inside escaped.   The planks were shivered to pieces, and the brave fellows who occupied them either blown into atoms, or so dreadfully wounded as to cause their immediate death; some had their uniforms burned to a cinder, while others were coiled up in a heap, without the vestige of anything left to denote that they were human beings.

An 88th soldier, of the name of Cooney, barber to the company he belonged to, escaped the effects of the explosion unhurt, except a slight scratch in the face, caused by a splinter from a rock that had been rent in pieces by the blowing up of the magazine; he was an old and ugly man, but yet so vain of his personal appearance as to be nearly in despair at the idea, as he said, "of his good looks being spoiled." While he was in the midst of his lamentation, a round shot struck his head and carried it off. In his coat pocket was found his soap and razor, which were instantly drawn lots for, but to whose "lot" they fell I know not.

The French cannoniers were loud in cheering when they discovered the effects of their fire upon Cooney's sconce; our men cheered in turn, and continued to crown the top of the already half-dismantled magazine, but as fast as they mounted it, they were swept off its face by the overwhelming fire from the town; yet notwithstanding the great loss of lives that had already taken place, and the almost certain death which awaited all who attempted to remain on the magazine, it was never for five minutes unoccupied, and by four o'clock in the afternoon it might be said to be perfectly finished. Baffled in his endeavours to stop our progress, Phillipon was determined to make it cost us as dear as he could. Twelve additional guns were brought from the unemployed batteries and placed along the curtain *en barbette*. These, at half-range distance, without the means on our side to reply to them, were fired with a fearful precision; it was next to impossible to stand under it, but the soldiers, on this day, surpassed all their former efforts. The fire of threescore pieces of artillery was employed in vain against them; the works were repaired so soon as injured, and everything warranted the opinion that, should the night prove fine, our batteries would open the following day.

Captain Mulcaster, of the Engineers, by his heroic conduct, stimulated the soldiers wonderfully; no danger could unnerve him, or prevent his exposing himself to the hottest of the French fire, and for a time he escaped unhurt, but at length,

while standing on a rising ground, in front of the battery
No. 1, a twenty-four pound shot struck him in the neck, and
carried away his head and part of his back and shoulders.
The headless trunk was knocked several yards from the spot,
but was speedily carried to the engineer camp by some of
the brave men who, but a few short moments before, looked
upon what was now an inanimate lump of clay, with that
admiration naturally inspired by one of the finest as well as
the most intrepid young men in the army; for he had
endeared himself to the soldiers as much by his kind manner
to them as by his total disregard of danger to himself. It
is well known that infantry soldiers had a great dislike to
being placed under the control of the engineer officers, who
exacted, or at least they thought so, too much from them;
but Captain Mulcaster had a manner, peculiar to himself,
that gained him the goodwill of all.

Major Thompson of the 88th soon after fell. He was
observing a party of the enemy who were rowing a *bateau*
across the inundation of the Rivillas with a reinforcement
of men intended to succour the troops that occupied the
ravelin of San Roque. This operation, although embracing
but a small portion of the garrison, was one of a very delicate
nature, inasmuch as the distance between our works and the
inundation was so short as to enable us to command with
musketry its entire span; but the Governor, ever ready in
strategy, provided against even this chance of his plans for
defence being marred. He caused to be constructed a large
bateau, or, perhaps, more properly speaking, a raft. The
side of it which faced our lines was raised by light poles to
the height of four feet, through which were intertwined
wattles of osier; by this means, a support sufficiently strong,
without being too cumbrous to impede the movement of the

raft, was completed, and the inside was carefully padded with hay, or such light matter; it made a sufficient defence against musketry without any danger of the machine's losing its centre of gravity. To stop as much as possible this operation, several hundred riflemen were placed in advance, and so soon as the machine was discovered in motion on the water, a heavy fire was opened; a corresponding demonstration was made by the enemy, sustained by several batteries, and those mutual efforts were always productive of a heavy loss of lives on both sides, but particularly on ours, because the enemy's line of musketry commanded us at a distance of three hundred and fifty yards, and up to this time we had not one gun to answer their powerful salvos.

Major Thompson, who was in command of the riflemen, was in conversation with an aide-de-camp belonging to the staff of Marshal Beresford at the moment he fell; a musket ball struck him in the right temple, and passing through the brain, killed him on the spot. He had been but just *gazetted* to his majority, by purchase, and had served with the army from the campaign in Holland in 1794 to the moment of his death, without ever having been absent from his regiment in any of the battles in which it had been engaged, a few of which have been recorded by me. Captain Seton, an officer of precisely the same standing and services, succeeded him in the command of the 88th, and led his regiment up the ladders on the night of the storming of Badajoz, but he gained no promotion, except in his regular turn! and he was the *only* commanding officer of a battalion in the 3rd Division that did not get a brevet step.

Towards evening the fire against La Picurina was so effective that Lord Wellington resolved to storm it after dark.

CHAPTER XVII

State of the enemy's fort La Picurina from our fire—Attempt to storm it—Desperate defence of the garrison—It is carried by assault— Preparations for the grand attack—Frightful difficulties of the enterprise—The attack and defence—Slaughter of the besiegers— Badajoz taken.

At about three o'clock in the afternoon of the 25th of March, almost all the batteries on the front of La Picurina were disorganised, its palisades beaten down, and the fort itself, having more the semblance of a wreck than a fortification of any pretensions, presented to the eye nothing but a heap of ruins. But never was there a more fallacious appearance : the work, although dismantled of its cannon, its parapets crumbling to pieces at each successive discharge from our guns, and its garrison diminished, without a chance of being succoured, was still much more formidable than appeared to the eye of a superficial observer. It had yet many means of resistance at its disposal. The gorge, protected by three rows of palisades, was still unhurt; and although several feet of the scarp had been thrown down by the fire from our battering-park, it was, notwithstanding, of a height sufficient to inspire its garrison with a well-grounded confidence as to the result of any effort of ours against it; it was defended by three hundred of the *élite* of Phillipon's force, under the command of a colonel of Soult's staff, named Gaspard Thiery, who volunteered his services on the occasion. On this day a deserter came over to us from the fort, and gave an exact account of how it was circumstanced.

Colonel Fletcher, the chief engineer, having carefully examined the damage created by our fire, disregarding the perfect state of many of the defences, and being well aware that expedition was of paramount import to our final success, advised that the fort should be attacked after nightfall.

At half-past seven o'clock the storming party, consisting of fifteen officers and five hundred privates, stood to their arms. General Kempt, who commanded in the trenches, explained to them the duty they had to perform; he did so in his usual clear manner, and every one knew the part he was to fulfil. All now waited with anxiety for the expected signal, which was to be the fire of one gun from No. 4 battery. The evening was settled and calm; no rain had fallen since the 23rd; the rustling of a leaf might be heard; and the silence of the moment was uninterrupted, except by the French sentinels, as they challenged while pacing the battlements of the outwork; the answers of their comrades, although in a lower tone of voice, were distinguishable— "*Tout va bien dans le fort de la Picurina*" was heard by the very men who only awaited the signal from a gun to prove that the *réponse*, although true to the letter, might soon be falsified.

The great cathedral bell of the city at length tolled the hour of eight, and its last sounds had scarcely died away when the signal from the battery summoned the men to their perilous task; the three detachments sprang out of the works at the same moment, and ran forwards to the glacis, but the great noise which the evolution unavoidably created gave warning to the enemy, already on the alert,

and a violent fire of musketry opened upon the assailing
columns. One hundred men fell before they reached the
outwork ; but the rest, undismayed by the loss, and unshaken
in their purpose, threw themselves into the ditch, or against
the palisades at the gorge. The sappers, armed with axes
and crow-bars, attempted to cut away or force down this
defence ; but the palisades were of such thickness, and so
firmly placed in the ground, that before any impression could
be made against even the front row, nearly all the men who
had crowded to this point were struck dead. Meanwhile,
those in charge of the ladders flung them into the ditch, and
those below soon placed them upright against the wall; but
in some instances they were not of a sufficient length to reach
the top of the parapet. The time was passing rapidly, and
had been awfully occupied by the enemy; while as yet our
troops had not made any progress that could warrant a hope
of success. More than two-thirds of the officers and privates
were killed or wounded ; two out of the three that commanded detachments had fallen ; and Major Shawe, of the
74th, was the only one unhurt. All his ladders were too
short; his men, either in the ditch or on the glacis, unable
to advance, unwilling to retire, and not knowing what to do,
became bewildered. The French cheered vehemently, and
each discharge swept away many officers and privates.

Shawe's situation, which had always been one of peril,
now became desperate ; he called out to his next senior
officer (Captain Oates of the 88th) and said, "Oates, what
are we to do ? " but at the instant he was struck in the neck
by a bullet, and fell bathed in blood. It immediately occurred
to Oates, who now took the command, that although the
ladders were too short to mount the wall, they were long
enough to go across the ditch ! He at once formed the

desperate resolution of throwing three of them over the
fosse, by which a sort of bridge was constructed; he led the
way, followed by the few of his brave soldiers who were
unhurt, and, forcing their passage through an embrasure
that had been but bolstered up in the hurry of the moment,
carried—after a brief, desperate, but decisive conflict—the
point allotted to him. Sixty grenadiers of the Italian
guard[1] were the first encountered by Oates and his party;
they supplicated for mercy, but, either by accident or design,
one of them discharged his firelock, and the ball struck Oates
in the thigh; he fell, and his men, who had before been
greatly excited, now became furious when they beheld their
commanding officer weltering in his blood. Every man of
the Italian guard was put to death on the spot.

Meanwhile Captain Powis's detachment had made great
progress, and finally entered the fort by the salient angle.
It has been said, and, for aught I know to the contrary,
with truth, that it was the first which established itself in
the outwork; but this is of little import in the detail, or to
the reader. All the troops engaged acted with the same
spirit and devotion, and each vied with his comrade to keep
up the character of the "fighting division." Almost the
entire of the privates and non-commissioned officers were
killed or wounded; and of fifteen officers, which constituted
the number of those engaged, not one escaped unhurt! Of
the garrison, but few escaped; the Commandant, and about
eighty, were made prisoners; the rest, in endeavouring to
escape under the guns of the fortress, or to shelter themselves
in San Roque, were either bayoneted or drowned in the

---

[1] There were no troops of the Italian guard in this part of Spain,
though there were some of the "*Velites*" in Catalonia. Italians there
were, but only men incorporated in ordinary French line regiments.

Rivillas; but this was not owing to any mismanagement on the part of Count Phillipon. He, with that thorough knowledge of his duty which marked his conduct throughout the siege, had, early in the business, ordered a body of chosen troops to *débouche* from San Roque, and to hold themselves in readiness to sustain the fort; but the movement was foreseen. A strong column, which had been placed in reserve, under the command of Captain Lindsey of the 88th, met this reinforcement at the moment they were about to sustain their defeated companions at La Picurina. Not expecting to be thus attacked, these troops became panic-struck, soon fled in disorder, and, running without heed in every direction, choked up the only passage of escape that was open for the fugitives from the outwork, and, by a well-meant but ill-executed evolution, did more harm than good.

So soon as the result of this last effort to succour the fort was apparent to Phillipon, he caused a violent cannonade to be opened against it, but it was not of long duration; and our engineers, profiting by the quiet which reigned throughout the enemy's batteries, pushed forward the second parallel with great success. A corps of sappers, under my command, were charged with the work of dismantling the fort, and before day we had nearly completed its destruction.

Thus terminated the siege and storming of La Picurina, after a lapse of eight nights and nine days of unprecedented labour and peril. It might be said that its capture opened to us the gates of Badajoz, or at all events put the key of that fortress into our hands; it nevertheless cost us some trouble before we could make use of the key so gained. Never, from the commencement of the war until its termination, was there a more gallant exploit than the storming of this outwork.

On the 30th of March two breaching-batteries, armed with twenty-six guns of heavy calibre, and of the very best description, opened their fire to batter down the face of the two bastions of Santa Maria and the Trinidad ; and, notwithstanding every effort which the powerful resources of the enemy enabled him to command, it was abundantly manifest that a few days would suffice to finish the labours of the army before Badajoz.

The breaching-batteries, which opened their fire on the 30th, were effective beyond our expectations against the works, and the sappers had made considerable progress towards completing a good covered way for the troops to *débouche* from in their attack of the breaches.   On the 25th thirty-two sappers were placed under my command, but on the night of the 4th of April their numbers were reduced to seven.   I lost some of the bravest men I ever commanded ; but, considering the perils they encountered, it is only surprising how any escaped.   We were frequently obliged to run the flying-sap so close to the battlements of the town that the noise of the pick-axes was heard on the ramparts, and, upon such occasions, the party were almost invariably cut off to a man.   But it was then that the courage of the brave fellows under my orders showed itself superior to any reverse, and what was wanted in force was made up by the most heroic bravery of individuals.   There were three men of my own regiment, Williamson, Bray, and Macgowan, and I feel happy in being able to mention the names of those heroes. When a fire, so destructive as to sweep away all our gabions, took place, those men would run forward with a fresh supply, and, under a fire in which it was almost impossible to live, place them in order for the rest of the party to shelter themselves, while they threw up a sufficiency of earth to render

them proof against musketry. This dangerous duty was
carried on for eleven successive nights, that is to say, from
the 25th of March to the 5th of April.

On this day the batteries of the enemy were nearly crippled,
and their replies to our fire scarcely audible; the spirits of
the soldiers, which no fatigue could damp, rose to a frightful
height—I say frightful, because it was not of that sort which
alone denoted exultation at the prospect of their achieving
an exploit which was about to hold them up to the admiration of the world; there was a certain *something* in their
bearing that told plainly that they had suffered fatigues, which
they did not complain of, and had seen their comrades
and officers slain while fighting beside them without repining,
but that they smarted under the one, and felt acutely for
the other; they smothered both, so long as their minds and
bodies were employed; now, however, that they had a
momentary license to *think*, every fine feeling vanished, and
plunder and revenge took their place. Their labours, up to
this period, although unremitting, and carried on with a
cheerfulness that was astonishing, hardly promised the success
which they looked for; and the change which the last twenty-
four hours had wrought in their favour, caused a material
alteration in their demeanour; they hailed the present
prospect as the mariner does the disappearance of a heavy
cloud after a storm, which discovers to his view the clear
horizon. In a word, the capture of Badajoz had long been
their idol. Many causes led to this wish on their part; the
two previous unsuccessful sieges, and the failure of the attack
against San Christoval in the latter; but, above all, the
well-known hostility of its inhabitants to the British army,
and perhaps might be added a desire for plunder, which the
sacking of Rodrigo had given them a taste for. Badajoz

O

was, therefore, denounced as a place to be made an example of; and, most unquestionably, no city, Jerusalem excepted, was ever more strictly visited to the letter than was this ill-fated town.

The demeanour of the soldiers on this evening faithfully exemplified what I have just written: a quiet but desperate calm had taken the place of that gayness and buoyancy of spirits which they possessed so short a time before, and nothing now was observable in their manner but a tiger-like expression of anxiety to seize upon their prey, which they considered as already within their grasp.

Towards five o'clock in the afternoon all doubts were at an end, in consequence of some officers arriving in the camp from the trenches: they reported that Lord Wellington had decided upon breaching the curtain that connected the bastions of La Trinidad and Santa Maria, and as this operation would necessarily occupy several hours' fire, it was impossible that the assault could take place before the following day, the 6th, and the inactivity that reigned in the engineer camp, which contained the scaling-ladders, was corroborative of the intelligence. For once I saw the men dejected; yet it was not the dejection of fear, but of disappointment. Some of the most impetuous broke out into violent and unbecoming language; others abused the engineers; and many threw the blame of the delay upon the generals who commanded in the trenches; but all, even the most turbulent, admitted that the delay must be necessary to our success, or Lord Wellington would not allow it.

The night at length passed over, and the dawn of morning ushered in a day pregnant with events that will be recorded in our history as amongst the most brilliant that grace its annals. The batteries against the curtain soon reduced it

to a heap of ruins; and the certainty that the trial would
be made the same evening re-established good-humour
amongst the soldiers.   It was known, early in the day, that
the breaches were allotted to the Light and 4th Divisions;
to the 5th, the task of escalading the town on the side of
the St. Vincent bastion; and to Picton, with his invincible
3rd, to carry the castle by escalading its stupendous walls,
upwards of thirty feet high.   The Portuguese brigade, under
General Power, were to divert the enemy's attention on the
side of San Christoval; while three hundred men, taken
from the guard in the trenches, were to carry the outwork
of San Roque.

To ensure the success of an enterprise upon which so
much was at stake, twenty thousand men were to be brought
into action as I have described; by five o'clock all the ladders
were portioned out to those destined to mount them.   The
time fixed for the assemblage of the troops was eight; that
for the attack ten.   The day passed over heavily, and hour
after hour was counted, each succeeding one seeming to
double the length of the one that preceded it; but, true as
the needle to the pole, the long-expected moment arrived,
and the clear but deep note of the town clock was now heard
throughout our lines, as it tolled the hour of eight, and ere
its last vibration had ceased the vast mass of assailants were
in battle array.   A thick and dusky vapour, issuing from the
Guadiana and Rivillas, hung above the heads of the hostile
forces, and hid alike, by its heavy veil, each from the view
of its opponent; the batteries on both sides were silent, as
if they reserved their efforts for the approaching struggle;
and, except the gentle noise which the rippling of the
Guadiana created, or the croaking of the countless frogs that
filled the marshes on each side of its banks, everything was

as still as if the night was to be one of quiet repose; and a passing stranger, unacquainted with the previous events, might easily have supposed that our army were no otherwise occupied than in the ordinary routine of an evening parade; but Phillipon, profiting by this cessation, retrenched and barricaded the breaches in a manner hereafter to be described.

So soon as each division had formed on its ground in open column of companies, the arms were piled, and the officers and soldiers either walked about in groups of five or six together, or sat down under an olive-tree to observe, at their ease, the arrangements of the different brigades which were to take a part in the contest. Then, again, might be seen some writing to their friends—a hasty scroll, no doubt, and, in my opinion, an ill-timed one. It is a bad time, at the moment of entering a breach, to write to a man's father or mother, much less his wife, to tell them so; and, besides, it has an unseasonable appearance in the eyes of the soldiers, who are decidedly the most competent judges of what their officers should be, or, at least, what *they* would *wish* them to be, which is tantamount, at such a crisis.

There is a solemnity of feeling which accompanies the expectation of every great event in our lives, and the man who can be altogether dead to such feeling is little, if anything, better than a brute. The present moment was one that was well calculated to fill every bosom throughout the army; for, mixed with expectation, hope, and suspense, it was rendered still more touching to the heart by the music of some of the regiments, which played at the head of each battalion as the soldiers sauntered about to beguile the last hour many of them were destined to live. The band of my corps, the 88th, all Irish, played several airs which exclusively belong to their country, and it is impos-

sible to describe the effect it had upon us all; such an air
as "Savourneen Deelish" is sufficient, at any time, to inspire
a feeling of melancholy, but on an occasion like the present
it acted powerfully on the feelings of the men : they thought
of their distant homes, of their friends, and of bygone days.
It was Easter Sunday, and the contrast which their present
position presented to what it would have been were they in
their native land afforded ample food for the occupation of
their minds; but they were not allowed time for much
longer reflection. The approach of General Kempt, accompanied by his staff, was the signal for the formation of the
column of attack; and almost immediately the men were
ordered to stand to their arms. Little, if any, directions
were given; indeed, they were unnecessary, because the men,
from long service, were so conversant with the duty they
had to perform, that it would have been but a waste of
words and time to say what was required of them.

All was now in readiness. It was twenty-five minutes
past nine; the soldiers, unencumbered with their knapsacks
—their stocks off—their shirt-collars unbuttoned—their
trousers tucked up to the knee—their tattered jackets, so
worn out as to render the regiment they belonged to barely
recognisable—their huge whiskers and bronzed faces, which
several hard-fought campaigns had changed from their
natural hue—but, above all, their self-confidence, devoid of
boast or bravado, gave them the appearance of what they
in reality were—an invincible host.

The division now moved forward in one solid mass—the
45th leading, followed closely by the 88th and 74th; the
brigade of Portuguese, consisting of the 9th and 21st Regiments of the line, under Colonel de Champlemond, were
next; while the 5th, 77th, 83rd, and 94th, under Colonel

Campbell, brought up the rear. Their advance was un-disturbed until they reached the Rivillas; but at this spot some fire-balls, which the enemy threw out, caused a great light, and the 3rd Division, four thousand strong, was to be seen from the ramparts of the castle. The soldiers, find-ing they were discovered, raised a shout of defiance, which was responded to by the garrison, and in a moment after-wards every gun that could be brought to bear against them was in action; but, no way daunted by the havoc made in his ranks, Picton, who just then joined his soldiers, forded the Rivillas, knee-deep, and soon gained the foot of the castle wall, and here he saw the work that was cut out for him, for he no longer fought in darkness. The vast quantity of combustible matter which out-topped this stupendous defence was in a blaze, and the flames which issued forth on every side lighted not only the ramparts and the ditch, but the plain that intervened between them and the Rivillas. A host of veterans crowned the wall, all armed in a manner as imposing as novel; each man had beside him eight loaded firelocks; while at intervals, and proportionably distri-buted, were pikes of an enormous length, with crooks attached to them, for the purpose of grappling with the ladders. The top of the wall was covered with rocks of ponderous size, only requiring a slight push to hurl them upon the heads of our soldiers, and there was a sufficiency of hand-grenades and small shells at the disposal of the men that defended this point to have destroyed the entire of the besieging army; while on the flanks of each curtain, batteries, charged to the muzzle with grape and case shot, either swept away entire sections or disorganised the ladders as they were about to be placed, and an incessant storm of musketry, at the distance of fifteen yards, completed the resources the enemy brought into play, which, as may be seen, were of vast formidableness.

To oppose this mass of warriors and heterogeneous congregation of missiles Picton had nothing to depend upon for success but his tried and invincible old soldiers—he relied firmly upon their devoted courage, and he was not disappointed. The terrible aspect of the rugged wall, thirty feet in height, in no way intimidated them; and, under a frightful fire of small arms and artillery, the ponderous ladders were dragged into the ditch and, with a degree of hardihood that augured well for the issue, were planted against the lofty battlements that domineered above his soldiers' heads : but this was only the commencement of one of the most terrific struggles recorded during this hard-fought night. Each ladder, so soon as placed upright, was speedily mounted and crowded from the top round to the bottom one; but those who escaped the pike-thrusts were shattered to atoms by the heavy cross-fire from the bastions, and the soldiers who occupied them, impaled upon the bayonets of their comrades in the ditch, died at the foot of those ladders which they had carried such a distance and with so much labour.

An hour had now passed over. No impression had been made upon the castle, and the affair began to have a very doubtful appearance, for already well nigh half of the 3rd Division had been cut off. General Kempt, commanding the right brigade, fell wounded, early in the night; and the 88th Regiment alone, the strongest in the division, lost more than half their officers and men, while the other regiments were scarcely in a better condition. Picton, seeing the frightful situation in which he was placed, became uneasy; but the goodwill with which his brave companions exposed and laid down their lives reassured him; he called out to his men—told them they had never been defeated, and that now was the moment to conquer or die. Picton, although not loved by his soldiers, was respected by them; and his appeal, as well as his unshaken front, did wonders in changing the desperate state of the division. Major Ridge of the 5th, by his personal exertions, caused two ladders to be placed upright, and he himself led the way to the top of one, while Canch, a Grenadier officer of the 5th, mounted the other. A few men at last got footing on the top of the wall; at the same time Lieutenant William Mackie of the 88th—he who led the forlorn hope at Rodrigo (unnoticed! —still a lieutenant!!)—and Mr. Richard Martin (son of the member for Galway, who acted as a volunteer with the 88th during the siege) succeeding in mounting another. Mackie —ever foremost in the fight—soon established his men on the battlements, himself unhurt; but Martin fell desperately wounded. A general rush to the ladders now took place, and the dead and wounded that lay in the ditch were indiscriminately trampled upon, for humanity was nowhere to be found. A frightful butchery followed this success; and the shouts of our soldiery, mingled with the cries of the Frenchmen, supplicating for mercy or in the agonies of death, were heard at a great distance. But few prisoners were made; and the division occupied, with much regularity, the different points allotted to each regiment. Meanwhile the ravelin of San Roque was carried by the gorge, by a detachment drawn from the trenches, under the command of Major Wilson of the 48th; and the engineers were directed to blow up the dam and sluice that caused the inundation of the Rivillas, by which means the passage of that river between La Picurina and the breaches could be more easily effected.

One entire regiment of Germans, called the regiment of
Hesse Darmstadt, that defended the ravelin were put to
death.

While all this was taking place at the castle and San
Roque, a fearful scene was acting at the breaches. The Light
and 4th Divisions, ten thousand strong, advanced to the
glacis undiscovered—a general silence pervading the whole,
as the spirits of the men settled into that deep sobriety
which denotes much determination of purpose; but at this
spot their footsteps were heard, and, "perhaps since the
invention of gunpowder,"[1] its effects were never more powerfully brought into action. In a moment the different
materials which the enemy had arranged in the neighbourhood of the breaches were lighted up—darkness was converted into light—torches blazed along the battlements—
and a spectator, at a short distance from the walls, could
distinguish the features of the contending parties. A battery
of mortars, doubly loaded with grenades, and a blaze of
musketry, unlike anything hitherto witnessed by the oldest
soldier, opened a murderous fire against the two divisions;
but, unshaken by its effects, they pressed onward and jumped
into the ditch. The 4th Division, destined to carry the
breach to the right, met with a frightful catastrophe at the
onset. The leading platoons, consisting of the fusilier
brigade,[2] sprang into that part of the ditch that had been
filled by the inundation of the Rivillas, and were seen no
more; but the bubbles that rose on the surface of the water
were a terrible assurance of the struggles which those devoted
soldiers—the men of Albuera—ineffectually made to extricate themselves from the deadly grasp of each other, and
from so unworthy an end.

[1] Colonel Jones's Sieges, i. p. 236.   [2] 7th, 23rd, and 1st 48th.

Warned by the fate of their companions, the remainder turned to the left, and following the footsteps of the Light Division, pressed onwards in one mingled mass to the breaches of the curtain and La Trinidad. Arrived here, they encountered a series of obstacles that it was impossible to surmount, and which I find great difficulty in describing. Planks, of a sufficient length and breadth to embrace the entire face of the breaches, studded with spikes a foot long, were to be surmounted ere they reached the top of the breach; yet some there were—the brave Colonel Macleod, of the 43rd, amongst the number—who succeeded so far, but on gaining the top, *chevaux de frise,* formed of long sword-blades firmly fixed in the trunks of trees of a great size, and chained, boom-like, across the breach, were still to be passed; while at each side, and behind the *chevaux de frise,* trenches were cut, sufficiently extensive for the accommodation of three thousand men, who stood in an amphitheatrical manner —each tier above the other—and armed with eight muskets each, like their companions at the castle, awaited the attack so soon as the planks on the face, and the *chevaux de frise* on the top of the breach were surmounted; but they might have waited until doomsday for that event, because it was morally impossible.

The vast glare of light caused by the different explosions, and the fire of cannon and musketry, gave to the breaches the appearance of a volcano vomiting forth fire in the midst of the army: the ground shook—meteors shone forth in every direction—and when for a moment the roar of battle ceased, it was succeeded by cries of agony, or the furious exultation of the imperial soldiers. To stand before such a storm of fire, much less endeavour to overcome a barrier so impregnable, required men whose minds, as well as frames, were cast in a mould not human; but, nevertheless, so it was. The gallant Light and 4th Divisions boldly braved every danger, and with a good will, rarely to be found, prolonged a struggle, the very failure of which, taking into account the nature of the obstacles opposed to them, and their immense losses, was sufficient to immortalise them. At length, after a dreadful sacrifice of lives—all the generals, and most of the colonels, being either killed or wounded—they were driven from the breaches, while the Frenchmen, securely entrenched behind them, might be seen waving their caps in token of defiance. This was too galling for men who had never known defeat—and they ran back headlong to the attack, and destruction. But for what end? To judge from the past, when their numbers were more numerous, they had failed; they were now reduced to less than half, while the resources of the enemy were unimpaired, and the prospect before them was hideous. Again did they attempt to pass this terrible gulf of steel and flame—and again were they driven back—cut down—annihilated. Hundreds of brave soldiers lay in piles upon each other, weltering in blood, and trodden down by their own companions. The 43rd left twenty-two officers and three hundred men on the breach; four companies of the 52nd were blown to atoms by an explosion; and the 95th, as indeed every other regiment engaged, suffered in proportion. Our batteries, from whence a clear view of all that was passing could be distinguished, maddened by the havoc at the breaches, poured in a torrent of shot; and, in the excitement of the moment, killed friends as well as foes. Finally, the remnant of the two divisions retired; and, with a valour bordering upon desperation, prepared for a third trial; but the success of Picton's attack was by this time whispered amongst them, and the evacuation of the breaches soon after confirmed the rumour.

While the attack of the castle and breaches was in progress, the 5th Division, under General Leith, maintained a fierce and dangerous struggle on the other side of the city beyond the Pardeleras fort; but the resistance at those points was feeble, as compared with the other two. In some instances the French troops deserted the walls before they were carried; and it is worthy of remark, that while the 38th Regiment were mounting the ladders, the imperial soldiers were scrambling down them at the reverse side—in many instances treading upon the fingers of our own men! The few men of Leith's division, thus established on the ramparts, boldly pressed on in the hope of causing a change in favour of the men at the breaches; but the multitude that had fled before this handful of troops became reassured when they beheld the scantiness of their numbers, and, returning to the fight, forced them up a street leading to the ramparts. Leith's men became panic-struck by this unexpected burst, and retraced their steps in confusion; many were killed ere they reached the wall; and some, infected by the contagion of the moment, jumped over the battlements, and were dashed to pieces in their fall. One, an officer, bearing the flag of his regiment, fearing it might be captured, flung himself from the wall, and falling into a part of the ditch that was filled with the slime of the river, escaped unhurt. At this critical moment General Walker reached the spot with a fresh body of troops, and driving back the French with ruinous disorder, established his men at this point; and from that moment the fate of Badajoz was sealed. The enemy fled in every direction towards the bridge leading to San Christoval; and the remnant of the ill-fated Light and 4th

Divisions with difficulty entered the town by the breaches, although unopposed.

It was now half-past two o'clock in the morning, and the fighting had continued, without cessation, from ten the preceding night.   More than three hundred and fifty officers and four thousand men had fallen on our side ; yet the enemy's loss was but small in proportion ; because, with the exception of the castle, where the 3rd Division got fairly amongst them, the French, with that tact for which they are so remarkable, got away the moment they found themselves out-matched.

Shortly after the last attack at the breaches had failed, and long after the castle had been carried (although it was not generally known at the time), I was occupied, with Major Thomson of the 74th (acting engineer), in placing some casks of gunpowder under the dam of the Rivillas, in front of San Roque ; when, while leaning on his shoulder, I was struck by a musket-bullet in the left breast ; I staggered back, but did not fall, and Thomson, bandaging my breast and shoulder with his handkerchief, caused me to be removed inside the ravelin ; but the firing continued with such violence upon this point, that it was long before I could venture out of it.   At length, nearly exhausted from loss of blood, and fearing that I might be unable to reach the camp if I delayed much longer, I quitted it, accompanied by two sappers of my own corps (Bray and Macgowan), who supported me as I walked towards the trenches.   Bray was wounded in the leg while he tried to cover me from the enemy's fire ; but this brave fellow soon recovered, and afterwards greatly distinguished himself in the battle of the Pyrenees, by killing a French colonel at the head of his battalion.

By this time the attack of Badajoz was, in effect, finished. Some irregular firing was still to be heard as the fugitives

hurried from street to street towards the Roman bridge
leading to San Christoval, but all resistance might be said to
have ceased.   An attempt to retake the castle was made in
vain ; but the brave Colonel Ridge of the 5th, who had so
distinguished himself, lost his life by almost one of the last
shots that was fired in this fruitless effort to recover a place
which had cost the army the hearts' blood of the 3rd Division;
and the dawn of the morning of the 7th of April showed to
the rest of the army, like a speck in the horizon, the shattered
remnant of Picton's invincible soldiers, as they stood in a lone
group upon the ramparts of a spot that, by its isolated
situation, towering height, and vast strength, seemed not to
appertain to the rest of the fortifications, and which the
enemy, with their entire disposable force, were unable to
take from the few brave men who now stood triumphant
upon its lofty battlements.   Nevertheless, triumphant and
stern as was their attitude, it was not without its alloy, for
more than five-sixths [1] of their officers and comrades either
lay dead at their feet, or badly wounded in the ditch below
them.   All their generals, Picton amongst the number, and
almost all their colonels, were either killed or wounded ; and
as they stood to receive the praises of their commander, and
the cheers of their equally brave but unfortunate companions
in arms, their diminished front and haggard appearance told,
with terrible truth, the nature of the conflict in which they
had been engaged.

Early on the morning of the 7th of April, Phillipon and
his garrison, which had taken refuge in San Christoval,
hoisted the white flag in token of submission, and from that
moment the beautiful and rich town of Badajoz became a
scene of plunder and devastation.

[1] An exaggeration: the 3rd Division lost about 1100 men out of 4300.

CHAPTER XVIII

The sacking of Badajoz—Neglect of the wounded—Spaniards and their plunderers—Disgraceful occurrences—Calamities of war—The author's wound and uncomfortable couch—Extent of plunder—An auction in the field—Neglect of the 88th by General Picton.

BADAJOZ, one of the richest and most beautiful towns in the south of Spain, whose inhabitants had witnessed its siege in silent terror for one-and-twenty days, and who had been shocked by the frightful massacre that had just taken place at its walls, was now about to be plunged into all the horrors that are, unfortunately, unavoidable upon an enterprise such as a town taken by storm. Scarcely had Count Phillipon and his garrison commenced their march towards Elvas, when the work of pillage commenced. Some—many indeed —of the good soldiers turned to the ditch of the castle and to the breaches to assist and carry off their wounded companions; but hundreds were neglected in the general and absorbing thirst for plunder.

The appearance of the castle was that of a vast wreck; the various ladders lying shattered at the base of its walls, the broken piles of arms, and the brave men that lay as they had fallen—many holding their firelocks in their grasp— marked strongly the terrible contest in which they had been engaged, and presented to the eye of a spectator ample food for reflection. It was not possible to look at those brave men, all of them dead or frightfully maimed, without recollecting what they had been but a few short hours before; yet those feelings, fortunately perhaps, do not predominate with soldiers, and those sights, far from exciting reflections of a grave nature, more usually call forth some jocular remark, such as "that he will have no further occasion to draw rations"; or "that he has stuck his spoon in the wall and left off messing"—such is the force of habit.

At the breaches, the Light and 4th Division soldiers lay in heaps upon each other—a still warm group; and many of those veterans, from whom the vital spark had not yet fled, expired in the arms of the few of their companions who sought to remove them to a place better suited to their miserable condition. But war, whatever its numerous attractions to a young mind may be, is but ill calculated to inspire it with those softer feelings so essential to soothe us in the moment of our distress; it must not, therefore, be wondered at that a wish for plunder and enjoyment took the place of humanity, and that hundreds of gallant men were left to perish from neglect.

Before six o'clock in the morning of the 7th of April, all organisation amongst the assaulting columns had ceased, and a scene of plunder and cruelty, that it would be difficult to find a parallel for, took its place. The army, so fine and effective on the preceding day, was now transformed into a vast band of brigands, and the rich and beautiful city of Badajoz presented the turbulent aspect that must result from the concourse of numerous and warlike multitudes nearly strangers to each other, or known only by the name of the nation to which they belonged. The horde of vagabonds— Spaniards as well as Portuguese, women as well as men—

that now eagerly sought for admission to plunder, nearly augmented the number of brigands to what the assailing army had reckoned the night before; and it may be fairly said that twenty thousand people—armed with full powers to act as they thought fit, and all, or almost all, armed with weapons which could be turned, at the pleasure or caprice of the bearer, for the purpose of enforcing any wish he sought to gratify—were let loose upon the ill-fated inhabitants of this devoted city. These people were under no restraint, had no person to control them, and in a short time got into such an awful state of intoxication that they lost all control over their own actions.

In the first burst, all the wine and spirit stores were forced open and ransacked from top to bottom; and it required but a short time for the men to get into that fearful state that was alike dangerous to all—officers or soldiers, or the inhabitants of the city. Casks of the choicest wines and brandy were dragged into the streets, and when the men had drunk as much as they fancied, the heads of the vessels were stove in, or the casks otherwise so broken that the liquor ran about in streams.

In the town were a number of animals that belonged to the garrison, several hundred sheep, numerous oxen, as likewise many horses; these were amongst the first taken possession of; and the wealthy occupier of many a house was glad to be allowed the employment of conducting them to our camp, as, by doing so, he got away from a place where his life was not worth a minute's purchase. But terrible as was this scene, it was not possible to avoid occasionally laughing, for the *conducteur* was generally not only obliged to drive a herd of cattle, but also to carry the bales of plunder taken by his employers—perhaps from his own house

P

—and the stately gravity with which the Spaniard went through his work, dressed in short breeches, frilled shirt, and a hat and plumes that might vie with our eighth Henry, followed, as he was, by our ragamuffin soldiers with fixed bayonets, presented a scene that would puzzle even Mr. Cruikshank himself to justly delineate. The plunder so captured was deposited in our camp, and placed under a guard chiefly composed of the soldiers' wives.

The shops were rifled, first by one group, who despoiled them of their most costly articles, then by another, who thought themselves rich in capturing what had been rejected by their predecessors; then another, and another still, until every vestige of property was swept away. A few hours was sufficient for this; night was fast drawing near, and then a scene took place that has seldom fallen to the lot of any writer to describe. Every insult, every infamy that human invention could torture into practice was committed. The following day, the 8th of April, was also a fearful one for the inhabitants; the soldiers became reckless, and drank to such an excess that no person's life, no matter of what rank, or station, or sex, was safe. If they entered a house that had not been emptied of all its furniture or wine, they proceeded to destroy it; or, if it happened to be empty, which was generally the case, they commenced firing at the doors and windows, and not unfrequently at the inmates, or at each other! They would then sally forth into the streets, and fire at the different church-bells in the steeples, or the pigeons that inhabited the old Moorish turrets of the castle —even the owls were frighted from this place of refuge, and, by their discordant screams, announced to their hearers the great revolution that had taken place near their once peaceful abodes. The soldiers then fired upon their own comrades, and many men were killed, in endeavouring to carry away some species of plunder, by the hands of those who, but a few hours before, would have risked their own lives to protect those they now so wantonly sported with : then would they turn upon the already too deeply injured females, and tear from them the trinkets that adorned their necks, fingers, or ears ! and, finally, they would strip them of their wearing apparel.   Some 'tis said there were—ruffians of the lowest grade, no doubt—who cut the ear-rings out of the ears of the females who bore them.

Hundreds of those fellows took possession of the best warehouses, and for a time fulfilled the functions of merchants; those, in their turn, were ejected by a stronger party, who, after a fearful strife and loss of lives, displaced them, and occupied their position, and those again were conquered by others, and others more powerful! and thus was Badajoz circumstanced on the morning of the 8th of April 1812.   It presented a fearful picture of the horrors that are inevitable upon a city carried by assault; and although it is painful to relate these disgraceful facts, it is essential nevertheless.   I feel as much pride as any man can feel in having taken a part in actions that must ever shed lustre upon my country; but no false feeling of delicacy shall ever prevent me from speaking the truth— no matter whether it touches the conduct of one man or ten thousand !

To put a stop to such a frightful scene, it was necessary to use some forbearance, as likewise a portion of severity. In the first instance, parties from those regiments that had least participated in the combat were ordered into the town to collect the hordes of stragglers that filled its streets with crimes too horrible to detail ; but the evil had spread to such

an extent that this measure was inadequate to the end proposed, and in many instances the parties so sent became
infected by the contagion, and in place of remedying the
disorder, increased it, by joining once more in revels they had
for a time quitted. At length a brigade of troops was
marched into the city, and were directed to stand by their
arms while any of the marauders remained; the Provost
Marshals attached to each division were directed to use that
authority with which they are of necessity invested.   Gibbets
and triangles were in consequence erected, and many men
were flogged, but, although the contrary has been said, none
were hanged—yet hundreds deserved it.

A few hours more were sufficient to purge the town of the
infamous gang of robbers that still lurked about its streets,
and those ruffians—chiefly Spaniards or Portuguese, not in
any way attached to the army—were infinitely more dangerous than our fellows, bad as they were. Murder—except
indeed in a paroxysm of drunkenness, and in many cases, I
regret to say, it did occur in this way—never entered their
thoughts, but the miscreants here referred to would commit
the foulest deed for less than a dollar.

Towards evening tranquillity began to return, and, protected as they now were by a body of troops untainted by
the disease which had spread like a contagion, the unfortunate
inhabitants took advantage of the quiet that reigned; yet it
was a fearful quiet, and might be likened to a ship at sea,
which, after having been plundered and dismasted by pirates,
is left floating on the ocean without a morsel of food to
supply the wants of its crew, or a stitch of canvas to cover
its naked masts; by degrees, however, some clothing, such
as decency required, was procured for the females, by the
return of their friends to the town; and many a father and

mother rejoiced to find their children alive, although too often seriously and grossly injured. But there were also many who were denied even this sad consolation, for numbers of the townspeople had fallen in the confusion that prevailed; some of our officers also were killed in this way, and it has been said, I believe truly, that one, a colonel commanding a regiment, lost his life by the hands of his own men.

The plunder with which our camp was now filled was so considerable, and of so varied a description, that numerous as were the purchasers, and different their wants, they all had, nevertheless, an opportunity of suiting themselves to their taste; still the auction had not commenced in form, although, like other markets, "some private sales were effected." From the door of my tent I had a partial view of what was taking place; but for the present I shall leave the *marché*, and describe how I myself was circumstanced from the period I reached my tent, wounded, on the morning of the 7th.

The two faithful soldiers, Bray and Macgowan, that conducted me there, on entering, found my truss of straw, or bed, if the reader will so allow me to designate it, occupied by Mrs. Nelly Carsons, the wife of my batman, who, I suppose, by the way of banishing care, had taken to drinking divers potations of rum to such an excess that she lay down in my bed, thinking, perhaps, that I was not likely again to be its occupant; or, more probably, not giving it a thought at all. Macgowan attempted to wake her, but in vain—a battery of a dozen guns might have been fired close to her ear without danger of disturbing her repose! "Why then, sir," said he, "sure the bed's big enough for yees both, and she'll keep you nate and warm, for, be the powers, you're

kilt with the cold and the loss ov blood." I was in no mood
to stand on ceremony, or, indeed, to stand at all. I allowed
myself to be placed beside my partner, without any further
persuasion; and the two soldiers left us to ourselves and
returned to the town. Weakness from loss of blood soon
caused me to fall asleep, but it was a sleep of short duration.
I awoke, unable to move, and, in fact, lay like an infant.
The fire of small arms, the screams of the soldiers' wives, and
the universal buzz throughout the camp, acted powerfully
upon my nervous and worn-out frame; but Somnus conquered
Mars, for I soon fell into another doze, in which I might have
remained very comfortable had not my companion awoke
sooner than I wished; discharging a huge grunt, and putting
her hand upon my leg, she exclaimed, "Arrah! Dan, jewel,
what makes you so stiff this morning?"

It required but few words from me to undeceive her. Tea
and chocolate were soon in readiness, and having tasted some
of the former, I sat up in my bed waiting the arrival of the
first surgeon to dress my wound. My batman, Dan Carsons,
shortly afterwards made his appearance; he led up to the
door of my tent three sheep, and had, moreover, a pig-skin
of enormous size filled with right good wine which the
Spaniards call *la tinta de la Mancha:* "And sure," said he,
"I heard of your being kilt, and I brought you this (pointing
to the pig-skin of wine), thinking what a nate bolster it i'd
be for you while you slept at your aise," and, without waiting
for my reply, he thrust the pig-skin under my head. "And
look," said he, shewing me a spigot at the mouth of my
bolster, "when you're thirsty at-all-at-all, you see nothing is
more pleasant or aisy than to clap this into your mouth, and
sure won't it be mate and dhrink for you too?"

"Oh, Jasus!" responded Nelly, "he's kilt out and

out; see, Dan, how the blood is in strames about the blankets."

A little learning is a dangerous thing,

so—under certain circumstances—is a little laughing! and Dan Carsons and his wife made me laugh so immoderately, that a violent discharge of blood from my wound nearly put an end to my career in this world. Had it not been for the arrival of Dr. Grant, the staff-surgeon of the division, who just now made his appearance, I doubt much if any of my readers would ever have had the pleasure of reading these my reminiscences. But I must have done with myself, Dan Carsons, and his wife Nelly, and resume my narrative of the sale of the plunder with which our camp was, to use a mercantile phrase, glutted.

Early on the morning of the 9th of April a great concourse of Spaniards had already thronged our lines; the neighbouring villages poured in their quota of persons seeking to be the purchasers of the booty captured by our men, and each succeeding hour increased the supply for their wants, numerous and varied as they were, and our camp presented the appearance of a vast market. The scene after the taking of Rodrigo was nothing in comparison to the present, because the resources of Badajoz might be said to be in the ratio of five to one as compared with her sister fortress, and, besides, our fellows were, in an equal proportion, more dexterous than they had been in their maiden effort to relieve Rodrigo of its valuables. It may, therefore, be well supposed, and the reader may safely take my word for it, that the transfer of property was, on the present occasion, considerable. Some men realised upwards of one thousand dollars (about £250), others less, but all, or almost all, gained handsomely by an enterprise in which they had displayed such unheard-of acts of devotion and bravery; and it is only to be lamented that they tarnished laurels so nobly won by traits of barbarity for which it would be difficult to find a parallel in the annals of any army. The sale of the different commodities went on rapidly, notwithstanding we had no auctioneers; there was no "king's duty," but, most undeniably, if the Spaniards paid no "king's duty," they paid the piper! While the divers articles were carried away by the purchasers, the wounded were removed to the hospitals and camp, and the lamentations of the women for their dead or wounded husbands made a striking contrast to the scene of gaiety which almost everywhere prevailed.

Towards the evening of the 9th our camp was nearly emptied of all its saleable commodities, and the following morning was occupied in getting rid of the many Spaniards who still hovered about us, endeavouring to get a bargain of some of the unsold articles. By noon all traffic had ceased, and the men began to arrange themselves for a fresh combat with Marshal Soult, who was advancing towards Badajoz. The appearance and demeanour of the soldiery in no way warranted the idea that they had been occupied as they were for the last three weeks, but more especially for the last three days. They were the same orderly set of men they had been before the attack on the town, and were just as eager to fight Soult as they were to storm Badajoz: the only change visible was their *thinned ranks*. In my regiment alone, out of seven hundred and fifty privates, four hundred and thirty-four had fallen; and of the officers, who at the commencement of the siege counted twenty-four, but five remained unhurt! Our total loss exceeded five thousand men; and although no officer of a higher rank than colonel was killed, it is a singular circumstance that every general actively engaged was wounded on the night of the assault. Picton, Colville, Kempt, Walker, and Bowes, who headed the assaulting divisions and brigades, were every one of them hurt on that fatal 8th of April.[1]

[1] Picton headed the 3rd Division ; Kempt its 1st Brigade. Colville commanded the 4th Division ; Bowes its 2nd Brigade. Walker the 2nd Brigade of the 5th Division. The total loss of the British during the siege was 72 officers and 963 men killed, and 306 officers and 3483 men wounded. There were also 100 missing, mostly, it is believed, men whose bodies fell into the Guadiana or the Rivillas and were not found. This gives a total of 4924, so that Grattan's figure of "over 5000 " is hardly exaggerated.

CHAPTER XIX

Departure from Badajoz—The wounded left to the protection of
Spanish soldiers—Subsequently removed to Elvas—The author
leaves Elvas to join the army—Spaniards and Portuguese—Rodrigo
revisited—A Spanish ball—Movements of Marshal Marmont—Fall
of the forts of Salamanca—Amicable enemies.

ON the 15th of April, 1812, the heroes of Badajoz took a
last farewell of the scene of their glory and the graves of
their fallen companions, and marched towards the banks of
the Coa and Agueda, where, but a few months before, they
had given proofs of their invincible valour.   Indeed it might
be said, without any great stretch of historical truth, that
every inch of ground upon which they trod was a silent
evidence of their right to be its occupant—so far, at least, as
right of conquest goes.

Ill as I was, in common with many others, who, like
myself, lay wounded, and were unable to accompany our
friends, I arose from my truss of straw to take a parting look
at the remnant of my regiment as it mustered on the parade;
but in place of upwards of seven hundred gallant soldiers,
and four-and-twenty officers, of the former there were not
three hundred, and of the latter but five!   At any time,
when in the full enjoyment of health and vigour, this sad
diminution would have affected me; but in my then frame of
mind it acted powerfully upon my nerves.   I asked myself,

where are the rest ?   I suppose I spoke louder than I
intended ; for my man, Dan Carsons, ran out of his tent to
inquire " who I was looking after ? "—" Dan," I replied, " I am
looking for the men that are absent from parade ; where are
they ? "—" Kilt, sir," replied Dan, " and the greater part of
them buried at the fut of the ould castle forenent ye."
" Their *bodies* are there, Dan, but where are they themselves?"
" Och, Jasus ! " cried Dan to his wife, " he's out of his sinces !
Nelly ! run and fetch the pig-skin of wine ; you know how it
sarved him last night when he was raving."   Nelly brought
the remnant of the Tinta de la Mancha, and a few mouthfuls
of it raised my spirits considerably, but the fever with which
I was attacked was increasing rapidly.

The drums of the division beat a ruffle ; the officers took
their stations ; the bands played ; the soldiers cheered, and,
in less than half an hour, the spot which, since the 17th of
the preceding month, had been a scene of the greatest excitement, was now a lone and deserted waste, having no
other occupants than disabled or dying officers and soldiers,
or the corpses of those who had fallen in the strife.   The
contrast was indeed great, and of that cast that made the
most unreflecting think, and the reflecting feel.   The sound
of the drums died away ; the division was no longer visible,
except by the glittering of their firelocks ; at length we lost
sight of even this, and we were left alone, like so many
outcasts, to make the best of our way to the hospitals in
Badajoz.

It is a task of more difficulty than may appear to the
reader to describe the feelings that a separation, such as I
have told of, caused in our breasts.   More than half of our
old companions—dear to us from the intimate terms upon
which we had lived together, fought together, and, I might

say, died together, for three years—were parted from us, most
of them for ever!—the others gone to a distant part of the
theatre of war, while we, enervated and worn down, either
by loss of limb, or by loss of strength and vigour, were left
to seek shelter under the roofs of those very people who had
been so barbarously maltreated by our own soldiers.   Nevertheless every one betook himself to the method he thought
best suited to the occasion.   Some caused themselves to be
conveyed in waggons; others rode on horseback; and many,
from a disinclination to bear the jolting of the carts, or the
uneasy posture of sitting astride a horse, hobbled on towards
the dismantled walls of the fortress.   As we continued our
walk, we met, at almost every step, heaps of newly turned-up
earth, beneath which lay the bodies of some of our companions; and a little farther in advance was the olive-tree, at
the foot of which so many officers of the 3rd Division had
been buried.   At length we reached the ravelin of San Roque.

The Talavera gate was opened for our admission; it was
guarded by a few ill-looking, ill-fed, and ill-appointed
Spanish soldiers.   As we entered, each man we passed saluted
us with respect; but the contrast between these men, who
were now our protectors, and the soldiers we had but a short
time before commanded, was great indeed; and the circumstance, trifling as it may appear, affected us proportionably.
We walked on towards our wretched billets, and as we
passed through the streets that led to them, we saw nothing
but the terrible traces of what had taken place.   Piles of
dismantled furniture lay scattered here and there; houses,
disfigured by our batteries, in a ruined state; the streets
unoccupied except by vagabonds of the lowest grade, who
prowled about in search of plunder; while at the windows
of some houses were to be seen a few females in disordered

dresses; but their appearance was of that caste that served rather to increase the gloom which overhung the city. Nevertheless, as the wounded men and officers passed, they waved their handkerchiefs and saluted us with a *viva*; but it was pitiable to witness the wretched state to which the unfortunate inhabitants had been reduced.

Upon reaching the house allotted to me, I was met at the door by an old woman who showed me my apartment. It was scantily garnished with furniture, most of which was broken; the bed was on the tiles, but that was rather an advantage than the contrary, because the heat was excessive. I stood in no need of any refreshment; my man, Dan, having been so active during the *bouleversement* that he supplied my cellar as well as larder; and it was fortunate that he did so, for the inhabitants of the house, as I after-wards learned, were without a morsel of food or a stitch of clothing, having been plundered of everything.

I lay down upon my mattress, soon fell asleep, and in less than an hour awoke in a high fever. Dan wished that I should attack the pig-skin of the Tinta de la Mancha, but I positively refused to do so: "Why then, sir," said he, "hasn't it been the making ov yee?"—"You mean the killing of me, Dan. Go and seek for a surgeon." He went, and soon returned with a young man in the uniform of the staff surgeons of our army; but from his youthful appear-ance, and the unworkmanlike manner he went about dressing my wound, I opine he was but an hospital mate. My man Dan was decidedly of my opinion; for after the doctor had examined my breast, and applied some dressing to it, he was about to retire, when Dan said with an air of authority, "You're not going to be afthur going without looking at his hinder part?" meaning my back. The doctor took the

hint, and, turning me on my face, found a large piece of the
cloth of my coat, which had been carried in by the ball,
protruding through the wound. The doctor looked confounded; Dan looked ferocious, and though he spoke with
respect to the medical man, I plainly saw the storm which
was gathering. I feared that he was about to make use of
the *fortiter in re*, in preference to the *suaviter in modo;* so I
dismissed the doctor, upon an assurance that he would visit
me the following morning.

After a lapse of three days, all the wounded capable of
being removed were ordered to Elvas. Spring waggons,
carts drawn by oxen, mules harnessed with pack-saddles, and
in default of them, asses prepared in like manner, were put
in requisition for the purpose of freeing Badajoz of as many
of the disabled men, who crowded the hospitals, as possible.
I was among the number, but so ill was I as to have no
recollection of how I was transported, except that a waggon
stopped at my door, and, after some hours, I found myself in
the streets of Elvas. From the waggon I was placed in a
car, and it was night before my man Dan, with all his tact,
was enabled to procure me a billet. During a space of
fifteen days I lay in a state of great pain, accompanied by
fever, but after that I soon recovered my strength, and
being allowed the option of either joining the second
battalion of my regiment, to which I then belonged,
quartered at home, or going back to the army, I preferred
the latter.

My friends, Darcy and Adair, were my companions on my
route to the army; and, punctual at the appointed hour, we
left Elvas at six o'clock on the morning of the 3rd of June,
without any encumbrance, such as a detachment to look
after. We had no escort except our three servants, and

Dan's wife Nelly; and it is needless to say that they were perfectly competent to take care of themselves, without causing us one moment's uneasiness, either on their account or our own; and never did any three officers in the service of His Britannic Majesty, or in the service of any other sovereign, set out on a route to join their companions with a more fervent intention of making the time pass as agreeably as possible. Our route towards Salamanca, near which city the army was stationed, lay through the old line of march, and we were obliged, unfortunately, once more to encounter that place of dirt and wretchedness, Niza. No matter what change had taken place either amongst ourselves or the different towns through which we passed, Niza was still the same; positively dirt—comparatively dirt— superlatively dirt!—dirt! dirt! dirt! The ditches were filled with reptiles, the houses with bugs and fleas, and Adair, who was already blind of one eye, had the other nearly darkened by the bite of a huge centipede. We poulticed his eye with rye bread and cold water, and in the morning carried him, with a *wry* face, to his saddle.

Once clear of Niza, we traversed the country towards the Spanish frontier; at length we got clear of Portugal, and once more reached the village of Fuentes d'Oñoro; every house, I might almost say every face, was familiar to me. The heaps of embanked earth, which denoted the places where many of our old companions had been interred, were covered with grass, which grew luxuriantly over the graves of the men who had once stood there victorious, but who were now lifeless clay. We traversed the churchyard where so many of the Imperial Guard and our Highlanders had fallen; and we marked well the street where three hundred of the former had been put to death by the 88th Regiment.

Many of the doors still retained the marks of the contest; and the chimneys, up which the Guard had sought shelter, bore the traces of what had taken place. The torn apertures in the large twigged chimneys, broken down by the Guard in attempting to get up them, were in the same state we had left them—untouched, unmended. Even the children could trace with accuracy the footsteps of those fallen heroes.

We walked on to the chapel wall, where the 79th had suffered so severely, and through which the French had forced their passage, under a torrent of shot, against the bayonets of the brave Highlanders. The chapel door was riddled through and through with bullets, and the walls bore the marks of the round shot fired from the French batteries. Several mounds of earth, covered as they were with herbage, still pointed out the grave of some one who had fallen; yet, to a passing stranger, the inequality of the ground would scarcely have been noticed, so little attention had been paid to the arrangement of the graves, which were dug in the hurry of the moment; but with us it was different. We could point out every spot, and lay our finger on the place where a grave ought to be found.

It so happened that the house I was quartered in for the night was one of those in which some of the Imperial Guard had sought shelter. I asked my patron why he had not mended the broken chimney? His reply was, that he preferred the inconvenience of the smoke which the aperture caused, for the pleasure he derived from viewing the grave, as he termed it, of the base French who had so scandalously ravaged his country. I cannot say that I much admired his feeling.

From Fuentes d'Oñoro we reached Rodrigo, which we had

left only five months before. The breaches were repaired, the trenches levelled, and were it not for the different spots that had been assigned to many of our fallen companions, which we found untouched, there was no trace of those works which had caused us so much time and labour to construct. But those places, well known to us, brought back to our recollection the ground upon which we had stood a short time before, under circumstances so different; and the change that had taken place during the short interval—the thousands that had fallen in the two sieges,—and the difference of our attitude as compared to what it was when we before trod the spot we were then standing upon, afforded ample food for reflection. From the period of our investment of Rodrigo to the capture of Badajoz, that is to say, eighty-eight days, we lost in my regiment alone twenty-five officers and five hundred and fifty-six men; and it cannot be wondered at that we, who were alive and in health, should have a feeling of regret for our less fortunate companions, as also a feeling of thankfulness for our own escape.

There may be some who will think that such ideas are out of place, but, in my opinion, they are not so. No truly brave man ever looked upon the graves of his fallen companions without a feeling of regret. A man falling in the heat of battle is quite a different thing, because *there* all are alike, and subject to the same chance; and it is, moreover, wrong to mourn over the death of a comrade while the strife is going on; but the strife once ended, then will the feelings be brought into play, and the man who is incapable of a pang of regret for his fallen companion is unworthy of the name of a British soldier.

My man, Dan, had scarcely arranged my billet, ere I bent my steps to the house where I had slept on the night of the storming of the town. I had scarcely made my appearance at the portal, when the old lady to whom the house belonged recognised my voice. She ran forward to meet and welcome me; her daughters accompanied her, and it was in vain that I said I had a billet in a distant part of the town. The excuse would not be taken, and I was forced, absolutely forced, to have my baggage conveyed to the house where I had so short a time before entered under far different circumstances. The old lady asked how long I was to remain at Rodrigo. I replied, for that night only. *"J'en suis fâché,"* she replied in French, which language she spoke tolerably well,—*"mais j'essayerai de faire votre séjour ici plus agréable qu'elle ne l'était la dernière fois"*—and she immediately sent an invitation to her friends to assemble at her house the same evening.

Profiting by the confusion which of necessity took place in arrangements for the *soirée*, I left the house and took a survey of the town and breaches. The houses which were destroyed in the Great Square, by the fire which had taken place on the night of the assault, as also those near the breaches, remained in the same ruined state we had left them; but excepting this, and a few gabions which outtopped the large breach, whose reconstruction had not been quite completed, we could find nothing to denote the toil and labour we had sustained during our operations. An hour sufficed for me to make my "reminiscence" of past events. It was eight o'clock before Darcy and Adair joined me, and when we reached my billet, we found the saloon filled by a large and varied company.

Upon entering the room, all eyes were turned towards us, for the good hostess had said a thousand kind things in my praise, and the height and imposing look of Darcy were in

themselves sufficient to cause a *stare*; but the elegance of
Adair's manners, who had passed the greater part of his life
on the Continent—his perfect knowledge of the Portuguese,
Spanish, Italian, and French languages—captivated all. And
although he was some fifteen or twenty years our senior, he
decidedly bore away the palm; and in less than an hour after
our *entré*, he made, to my own knowledge, five conquests;
while Darcy and myself could boast of but two each! I never
felt so humiliated—and from that moment I resolved that
if ever I had a son I would make him a linguist.

The ball was opened by Avandano de Alcantara, a young
Portuguese captain, belonging to the garrison of Almeida,
and Señora Dolores de Inza, a Spanish lady, a relative of the
Governor. The dance was the bolero, of which I had heard
so much, but had never seen danced before. All eyes were
turned towards the spot which the youthful couple occupied.
I was an attentive spectator. Avandano danced well, and
kept his elbows—a material point by the way—in that
position which no bolero dancer should depart from (I
obtained this information at Madrid), not to raise them
higher than his ear; but he danced mechanically, like one
that had been taught, and had his lesson by rule more than
by heart. Although he moved his arms with much grace,
and kept the proper measure with his feet, there was nothing
inspiring in his mode of dance, or in the manner he used his
castanettes. His partner, on the contrary, had all the fire
of the true Andalusian breed. Her movements, though not
perhaps as correct as his, were spirited, and drew down
thunders of applause from the spectators; and each plaudit,
as was natural, caused her to increase her exertions. She
danced beautifully, and every one expressed by their appro-
bation the gratification they felt by her display; but the

dance had scarcely ended when she fainted away, in consequence, no doubt, of the exertions she had made. She soon recovered, and would have once more joined the dance, had not her friends dissuaded her from so foolish an act, and she was reluctantly obliged to be a spectator for the remainder of the night. Waltzing was continued to a late hour; but there was no lady hardy enough to attempt the bolero after the success of Señora Dolores in this most difficult and graceful dance. The company at length retired to their different homes; I bade an affectionate good-night to my hostess and her daughters; and long before they were awake in the morning, I was several miles on the road leading to Salamanca.

On the 17th, Darcy, Adair, and I rejoined the 88th and the 3rd Division on the heights of San Christoval. We found that we were engaged in "covering" the siege of the forts of Salamanca, which Marshal Marmont was most anxious to disturb. On the 23rd of June he came up against us, tried our lines at several points, did not like the look of them, and after some futile manœuvring on both sides of the Tormes, fell back upon Huerta, where he remained until the 27th, and then retreated towards the Douro.

Meanwhile our bombardment of the Salamanca forts continued, and on the 27th its effect was so powerful that one of the magazines in the principal fort blew up, and the fire communicating with a quantity of wood which had been incautiously placed near the magazine, the whole fort was soon one vast fire, and a general attack by our troops taking place at the moment, completed the disorder which naturally prevailed. The three forts were thus taken; our loss, which was estimated by the enemy at thirteen hundred, did not much exceed one-third of that number; and Salamanca was freed from the enemy.

As soon as the garrison of the forts were made prisoners, they were marched through the streets leading from the out-works to that part of the town that had been allotted for their reception ; but it was painful to witness the degradation which these men were obliged to endure at the hands of the excited population.   Women of the lowest grade insulted them, and some there were base enough to spit in their faces ; yet the French soldiers bore all these insults with com-posed—I might say, with truth,—gentlemanly demeanour ; but it is not possible for me to express the disgust I felt at seeing brave men so treated by a base rabble who, but a few hours before, were on the most friendly terms with these very men.   At one time, when I saw such an indignity as mud thrown at them, and a likelihood of something more serious taking place, I expressed myself in strong terms against the ruffians who so acted ; and whether it was that I spoke Spanish well enough to be understood, or that I suited the action to the word by knocking down two fellows who were the ringleaders, I know not ; but from that moment the prisoners were allowed to move on quietly.

Thus fell the forts of Salamanca.   The news soon reached Marmont, and on the 28th he retrograded towards the Douro, and on the following day rested at Alaejos.   Lord Wel-lington followed the enemy's movement, who, on the 2nd of July, passed the Douro at Tordesillas, which post was sufficiently formidable to embarrass a general who might be desirous of forcing it.   The line of the Douro is unexcep-tionable ; it possesses all the requisites which a retreating army could wish for—uneven banks, narrow fords, and abundance of woods, sufficient to mask the operations of a large body of troops ; and Marmont did all that a general could do to render any effort to force it more than hazardous.

230 WITH THE CONNAUGHT RANGERS

On the evening of the 3rd, Picton's division was abreast of the ford of Pollos; some cavalry tried the depth of the river, which was deemed fordable; but the attitude of the enemy on the opposite bank was so imposing that the idea of forcing the passage was given up. From the 3rd until the 12th of July the two armies remained in presence of each other, encamped on each side of a river which at times is a formidable sheet of water, but which was then little more than an insignificant stream. Nevertheless, although both armies kept their guards on their respective sides of the water, and the movements of each were cautiously watched, not one life was lost, nor one shot fired by either army.

Indeed so different from hostility was the conduct of both nations, that the French and British lived upon the most amicable terms. If we wanted wood for the construction of huts, our men were allowed to pass without molestation to the French side of the river to cut it. Each day the soldiers of both armies used to bathe together in the same stream, and an exchange of rations, such as biscuit and rum, between the French and our men was by no means uncommon. A stop was, however, soon to be put to this friendly intercourse; and it having been known in both armies that something was about to be attempted by Marmont, on the evening of the 12th of July, we shook hands with our *vis-à-vis* neighbours and parted the best friends.

It is a remarkable fact that the part of the river of which I am speaking was occupied, on our side, by our 3rd Division, on the French side by the 7th Division. The French officers said to us on parting, "We have met, and have been for some time friends. We are about to separate, and may meet as enemies. As 'friends' we received each other warmly—as 'enemies' we shall do the same." In ten days afterwards the British 3rd and the French 7th Divisions were opposed to each other at the battle of Salamanca— and the 7th French were destroyed by the British 3rd. But I am now about describing one of the most memorable battles ever fought by the British army—the battle of Salamanca.

CHAPTER XX

THE situation and position of the hostile armies have been
described in the last chapter; it left them on the banks of
the Douro; and the probability, nay the certainty, that a
collision was about to take place between them was manifest
to the lowest soldier of both.

The passage of the line of the Douro in presence of an
army in a condition for battle is difficult, and it requires
much circumspection on the part of the General to hazard
it in the face of an enemy. Yet Marmont managed to cross.
He employed the days of the 13th, 14th, 15th, and 16th of
July in a series of evolutions we had hitherto been unaccustomed to witness; and, in fine, on the morning of the
17th, after having made a night-march of thirteen Spanish
leagues, his army was over the river, in battle array on the
plain to the right of Nava del Rey, while the bulk of our
army was in full movement upon Toro, distant several leagues
from the 4th and Light Divisions and the two brigades of

heavy horse. The village of Torrecilla de la Orden was in their front.

Marmont, finding how well the passage of the Douro had been masked by his night-march, and seeing the small number of troops that were at hand to oppose his movement, ordered his masses forward in the hope of crushing them. The 4th and Light Divisions, covered by Bock's dragoons,[1] retired upon the rising ground behind the villages. At this point various charges were made by the cavalry of both armies; and it was not until after a retreat of three hours, under a burning sun and a torrent of shot, that the two divisions reached the heights of the Guarena. The soldiers, famishing with thirst, their tongues cleaving to their mouths, and fainting with fatigue, rushed headlong towards the river; and before they had drank sufficiently to satisfy their burning thirst, the heights above them were crowned with forty pieces of cannon at half-range. Great was the confusion caused by the cannonade; and it was not without suffering some loss that they effected their retreat to the opposite bank. In less than an hour they joined the 1st and 3rd Divisions, and the entire continued the retrograde movement.

The French then advanced in two columns of twenty-five thousand men each; the intervening space between them might be reckoned at two miles. The right wing was commanded by Clausel, the left by Marmont in person. Clausel had scarcely arrived before the point occupied by the 4th Division, when, seeing the smallness of their force, he conceived the idea of making a sudden rush, in the hope of cutting them off. His troops had scarcely formed when he pushed onward at the head of two divisions of infantry and the brigade of dragoons

[1] The 1st and 2nd Heavy Dragoons of the King's German Legion, lately arrived from England.

commanded by General Carrié; but Cole, placing himself at
the head of the 27th and 40th Regiments, received him with
steadiness, and drove the French infantry back in disorder.
Meanwhile Carrié, seeing some open spaces in Cole's line,
caused by their movement against Clausel's infantry, thought
to profit by this disorder, and galloping forward at the head
of his troopers, sabred many men; but at this moment the
cavalry sent to sustain Cole met them, and after a severe but
short conflict totally overthrew the brigade of Carrié, who
was himself numbered amongst the prisoners.

The defeat of Clausel and Carrié checked in a great
degree the ardour of the French Marshal. The following
day he rested, and on the 19th threw back his right wing,
and moving forward with the left of his army, menaced the
right of the British; but Lord Wellington, anticipating the
movement, was prepared for him, and offered battle on the
plain of Velosa. This was refused on the part of the French
General; and from this until the 20th, the two armies
manœuvred within half cannon-shot of each other, the
British retiring as it had advanced—moving, not directly
rearward, but rather in a line parallel with the march of the
French. The columns were in movement in an open country,
fairly in the view of each other, and their respective attitudes
were of that novel sort that it would be difficult to find the
like recorded in the history of any two armies. At times
the French and British were within musket-shot of each
other, the soldiers of both in momentary expectation of
being engaged, yet not one shot was fired by either.

On the 20th, the British army reached the strong position
of San Christoval, on the right bank of the Tormes, distant
a league from Salamanca, the French General likewise resting
for the night upon the heights of Aldea Rubea, holding the

ford of Alba on the Tormes. Towards mid-day on the 21st
the French passed the river in two compact bodies, and,
screened by the woody nature of the country, established
themselves upon a new line of operations, threatening, in a
manner, the communication of the British with Rodrigo.
This manœuvre—a bold one it may well be called—under
the cannon of an army that had proffered battle but a few
days before on a plain of vast extent, was enough to puzzle
a man less capable of command than he who was at the head
of the allied army; but, unruffled in his temper by such
vacillating conduct, and keeping a steady eye upon his
opponent, the British General diligently followed his track.
He passed his army, the 3rd Division under Pakenham
excepted, across the Tormes, and taking hold of one of two
isolated hills called Arapilles, he resolved to rest the right
of his army upon this point while his left leaned upon the
Tormes river at Santa Martha, and, in the event of a battle
taking place, to stand the issue on the ground I have described. The 3rd Division still held the position of San
Christoval on the right bank, but was in readiness to pass
over the river by the bridge of Salamanca, in the event of a
battle taking place. The British General thus threw down
the gauntlet for the second time; and whether it was the
impetuous spirit of the French soldiers, or the temper of
their leader, or both combined, that wrought a change in
either, it is not easy to say; but one thing is certain, that
from this moment Marmont made up his mind to try the
issue of a battle.

In front of the Arapilles hill, which was the *point d'appui*
for our right, stood another, of the same name and greater
altitude, distant five hundred yards from the one we possessed.
This mound commanded the one occupied by us, and, after

some severe contention, was finally held by the French; and
it was evident from the earnest manner in which they sought
to gain the possession of it, that it was destined to be the
support of the left of their army, as the other was clearly
marked out, by the previous events, to be intended for our
right.

All doubts as to a battle not taking place were now
hushed, and the soldiers of both armies were aware that the
result was to decide to whom Madrid belonged. The die
was cast; neither were inclined to back out of it, or to gain-
say what they had in a manner pledged themselves to fulfil;
and the evening of the 21st July 1812 closed upon the
heads of many a soldier who was destined never to
behold the setting of another sun.   Nevertheless, the 3rd
Division under Pakenham had not been recalled; on the
contrary, we were busy in throwing up breastworks, and by
other means adding to the strength of the position we occupied.   Our division, though encamped on a height of considerable altitude, had received strict orders to entrench
themselves; the earth was thrown up, the works were
palisaded, and in fine they were so well secured that we
had no fear of an attack or surprise.   It is this precaution
that marks the great general.   Lord Wellington had no
idea of being taken aback by any change in Marmont's
plans during the night: on the contrary, he was convinced
that he was serious in his desire to give battle; but to guard
against any and every chance was but right.   Marmont
might have again, on the night of the 21st, passed the river,
and brought his army in battle array before a handful of
men, and cut them off piecemeal before his movement could
have been arrested by the British General.   The thing was
not probable—barely possible; but where possibilities, much

less probabilities, exist, it is essential that the mind of the
commander should be awake, and instead of brooding over
what is likely to take place the following day, look to what
may take place in the night. It was a remark of that
eminent general, Kleber, that to be surprised was much
more disgraceful than to be defeated: he said, "the bravest
man may be beaten; but whoever suffers himself to be surprised is unworthy of being an officer."

The evening of the 21st of July was calm, and appeared
settled, but persons well versed in the symptoms of the
horizon, which were unobserved by those intensely occupied
with the anticipations of the events which the morrow was
to produce, pronounced that a hurricane was not far distant.
Pakenham's division was occupied, as I have before said, in
entrenching itself, when about ten at night a torrent of rain
fell in the trenches, and so completely filled them with water
that the soldiers were obliged to desist from their labour.
Later in the night a storm arose, and the wind howled in
long and bitter gusts. This was succeeded by peals of
thunder and flashes of lightning, so loud and vivid that the
horses of the cavalry, which were ready saddled, took alarm,
and forcing the pickets which held them, ran away affrighted
in every direction. The thunder rolled in rattling peals, the
lightning darted through the black and almost suffocating
atmosphere, and presented to the view of the soldiers of the
two armies the horses as they ran about from regiment to
regiment, or allowed themselves to be led back to their
bivouac by the troopers to whom they belonged. The vivid
flashes of lightning, which seemed to rest upon the grass, for
a few moments wholly illuminated the plain, and the succeeding flashes occurred with such rapidity that a constant blaze
filled the space occupied by both armies. It was long before

the horses could be secured, and some in the confusion ran away amongst the enemy's line and were lost. By midnight the storm began to abate, and towards morning it was evidently going farther: the lightning flashed at a distance through the horizon; the rain fell in torrents, and the soldiers of both armies were drenched to the skin before the hurricane had abated. Towards five o'clock the storm was partially over, and by six the dusky vapour which had before veiled the sun disappeared, and showed the two armies standing in the array they had been placed the evening before. All doubts were now set at rest as to which side of the river the battle would be fought. The entire army of Marmont remained on the left bank, and Pakenham was ordered to move across the Tormes with the 3rd Division, by the bridge of Salamanca, with as much speed as possible; but it was one o'clock before he reached the station allotted to him— the extreme right of the British.

At half-past one o'clock the two armies were within gunshot of each other. The British, placed as follows, awaited with calmness the orders of their General. We of the 3rd Division, under Pakenham, were on the right of the line, but hid by the heights in our front, and unseen by Marmont; two squadrons of the 14th Light Dragoons and a brigade of Portuguese horse, commanded by General D'Urban, supported us. Next to the 3rd Division stood the 5th, led on by Leith; next to the 5th, and at the head of the village of Arapilles, were placed the 4th and 7th Divisions; beyond them, and a little in the rear, was the 6th Division, under General Clinton; and to the left of all was the Light Division, commanded by Colonel Barnard. The 1st Division, composed of the Guards and Germans, was in reserve; and the cavalry, under Sir Stapleton Cotton, was behind the

3rd and 5th Divisions, ready to act as circumstances might require. The guns attached to each brigade were up with the infantry; the park in reserve was behind the cavalry of Cotton, while in the rear of all, and nearly *hors de combat*, might be seen the Spanish army, commanded by Don Carlos D'España. Thus stood affairs, on the side of the British, at half-past one o'clock.

The French army, composed of eight divisions of infantry, amounting to forty-two thousand bayonets, four thousand cavalry, and seventy pieces of artillery, occupied a fine line of battle behind a ridge whose right, supported by the Arapilles height held by them, overlooked the one upon which the left of our army rested. Their 5th Division occupied this point; the 122nd Regiment, belonging to Bonnet's division, with a brigade of guns, crowned the Arapilles; the 7th Division supported the 122nd Regiment; the 2nd Division was in reserve behind the 7th; the 6th were at the head of the wood, protected by twenty pieces of artillery; and Boyer's dragoons occupied the open space in front of the wood to the left of all.

There was some irregularity in the arrangement of these troops, and the Duke of Ragusa essayed in person to remedy the evil. He marched with the 3rd and 4th Divisions to the head of the wood occupied by Boyer, and it was then he conceived the idea of extending his left, which afterwards proved so fatal to him. On our side all was arranged for defence; the bustle which was evident in the ranks of the enemy caused no change in our dispositions. Lord Wellington, having surveyed what was passing, and judging that something was meant by it, gave his glass to one of his aide-de-camps, while he himself sat down to eat a few mouthfuls of cold beef. He had scarcely commenced when his aide-de-

camp said, "The enemy are in motion, my lord!"—"Very
well; observe what they are doing," was the reply. A
minute or so elapsed, when the aide-de-camp said, "I think
they are extending to their left."—"The devil they are!"
said his lordship, springing upon his feet,—"give me the
glass quickly." He took it, and for a short space continued
observing the motions of the enemy with earnest attention.
"Come!" he exclaimed, "I think this will do at last; ride
off instantly, and tell Clinton and Leith to return as rapidly
as possible to their former ground."

In a moment afterwards Lord Wellington was on horseback, and all his staff in motion. The soldiers stood to their
arms—the colours were uncased—bayonets fixed—the order
to prime and load passed, and in five minutes after the false
movement of Marmont was discovered, our army, which so
short a time before stood on the defensive, was arrayed for
the attack! It was twenty minutes past four when these
dispositions were completed; and here it may not be amiss
to tell the reader the nature of the movement made by the
French General, which so materially altered his position, as
likewise that of his antagonist—and in doing so I shall be
as brief as I can.

It has been already seen that both armies were so circumstanced as to almost preclude the possibility of a battle not
taking place. Marmont coveted it—Wellington did not
seek to decline it—both had the confidence of their soldiers
—and both, as to numbers, might be said to be on an
equality. When I speak of "numbers" I include the
Portuguese troops. Military men know what was the *real*
value of these soldiers! At two o'c'ock in the afternoon
Marmont was the aggressor; he held the higher hand; yet
at four, in two short hours afterwards, the relative situation

of both was altogether changed. The natural question will be—How was this? It occurred just as I am about to describe.

The two armies took their ground under the impression that the French would attack, the British defend. All this was plain; but Marmont had no sooner mounted his horse and taken a survey of the field of battle than he conceived the idea—like Melas at Marengo—of extending his line; by marching his 7th Division to his left he might cause an alarm in the breast of the British General for the safety of his communication with the Rodrigo road, and in a manner circumvent his position. Lord Wellington, at a glance, saw all that was passing in the mind of his antagonist—he saw the error he had committed; and calculating that his 3rd Division (distant but three-quarters of a league from the French 4th) would reach them before the 7th French Division could retrace their steps and be in a position fitted for fighting, he decided upon attacking the left, before this division, commanded by Thomières, could regain its ground, or at all events be in an efficient state to resist the attack of his invincible Old Third. The result proved the soundness of the calculation, because, although Thomières got into his place in the fight, he did so before his men had foreseen or expected it, and their total overthrow was in itself sufficient to cause the loss of this great battle.

The 3rd Division had but just resumed their arms when Lord Wellington, at the head of his staff, appeared amongst them. The officers had not taken their places in the column, but were in a group together in front of it. As Lord Wellington rode up to Pakenham every eye was turned towards him. He looked paler than usual, but notwithstanding the sudden change he had just made in the dis-

R

position of his army, he was quite unruffled in his manner, and as calm as if the battle about to be fought was nothing more than an ordinary assemblage of the troops for a field-day. His words were few and his orders brief. Tapping Pakenham on the shoulder, he said, "Edward, move on with the 3rd Division—take the heights in your front—and drive everything before you."—"I will, my lord," was the laconic reply of the gallant Sir Edward.[1] Lord Wellington galloped on to the next division, gave, I suppose, orders to the same effect, and in less than half an hour the battle commenced.

The British divisions were scarcely in line when fifty pieces of artillery crowned the ridge occupied by the French. A heavy fire was soon opened from this park at half range, and as the 4th and 5th Divisions advanced they were assailed by a very formidable fire; but as yet the French infantry, posted behind the ridge, were not visible. Cole's troops advanced to the left of the Arapilles height, while Pack, with his brigade of Portuguese, two thousand strong, pressed onward to attain it. The 5th Division, under Leith, advanced by the right of Cole's troops; and at this moment the French 7th Division were seen hurrying back to occupy the ground they had so short a time before quitted, while the 3rd and 4th French Divisions were arranging themselves to receive the attack of Cole and Leith.

When all was in readiness Pakenham departed at the head of ten battalions[2] and two brigades of guns, to force the left of the enemy. Three battalions, the 45th, 74th,

---

[1] Grattan evidently discredits Londonderry's story that when starting Pakenham cried to his brother-in-law, "Give me one grasp of that conquering hand before I go"—a tale not much in consonance with the character of either of the two men.

[2] It should rather be *twelve* battalions, as each Portuguese regiment was composed of two weak battalions.

and 88th, under Colonel Alexander Wallace of the 88th, composed the first line; the 9th and 21st Portuguese of the line, under the Portuguese colonel, De Champlemond, formed the second line; while two battalions of the 5th, the 77th, 83rd, and 94th British, under the command of Colonel Campbell, were in reserve. Such was the disposition of the 3rd Division. In addition, General D'Urban, with six Portuguese squadrons, had orders to make head against Boyer's dragoons; and that the 3rd Division might not be molested in its operation, Le Marchant's three regiments of heavy cavalry were placed in reserve in the rear of it. It now only remains to relate what actually happened.

No sooner was Pakenham in motion towards the heights than the ridge he was about to assail was crowned with twenty pieces of cannon, while in the rear of this battery was seen Thomières' division endeavouring to regain its place in the combat. A flat space, one thousand yards in breadth, was to be crossed before Pakenham could reach the heights. The French batteries opened a heavy fire, while our two brigades of artillery, commanded by Captain Douglas, posted on a rising ground behind the 3rd Division, replied to them with much warmth. Pakenham's men might thus be said to be within two fires—that of their own guns firing over their heads, while the French balls passed through their ranks, ploughing up the ground in every direction; but the veteran troops which composed the 3rd Division were not to be shaken even by this.

Wallace's three regiments advanced in open column until within two hundred and fifty yards of the ridge held by the French infantry. Thomières' column, five thousand strong, had by this time reached their ground, while in their front the face of the hill had been hastily garnished with *tirailleurs*.

All were impatient to engage, and the calm but stern advance of Wallace's brigade was received with beating of drums and loud cheers from the French, whose light troops, hoping to take advantage of the time which the deploying from column into line would take, ran down the face of the hill in a state of great excitement; but Pakenham, who was naturally of a boiling spirit and hasty temper, was on this day perfectly cool. He told Wallace to form line from open column without halting, and thus the different companies, by throwing forward their right shoulders, were in line without the slow manœuvre of a deployment. Astonished at the rapidity of the movement, the French riflemen commenced an irregular and hurried fire, and even at this early stage of the battle a looker-on could, from the difference in the demeanour of the troops of the two nations, form a tolerably correct opinion of what would be the result.

Regardless of the fire of the *tirailleurs*, and the showers of grape and canister, Pakenham, at the head of Wallace's brigade, continued to press onward; his centre suffered, but still advanced; his left and right being less oppressed by the weight of the fire, continued to advance at a more rapid pace, and as his wings inclined forward and outstripped the centre, the brigade assumed the form of a crescent. The manœuvre was a bold, as well as a novel one, and the appearance of the brigade imposing and unique, because it so happened that all the British officers were in front of their men—a rare occurrence. The French officers were also in front; but their relative duties were widely different: the latter, encouraging their men into the heat of the battle; the former keeping their devoted soldiers back!—what a splendid national contrast! Amongst the mounted officers were Sir Edward Pakenham and his staff, Wallace of the

88th, commanding the brigade, and his gallant aide-de-camp, Mackie (at last a Captain—in his regular turn!), Majors Murphy and Seton of the 88th, Colonels Forbes and Greenwell of the 45th, Colonel Trench of the 74th, and several others whose names I cannot now remember.

In spite of the fire of Thomières' *tirailleurs*, they continued at the head of the right brigade, while the soldiers, with their firelocks on the rest, followed close upon the heels of their officers, like troops accustomed to conquer.   They speedily got footing upon the brow of the hill, but before they had time to take breath, the entire French division, with drums beating and uttering loud shouts, ran forward to meet them, and belching forth a torrent of bullets from five thousand muskets, brought down almost the entire of Wallace's first rank, and more than half of his officers.   The brigade staggered back from the force of the shock, but before the smoke had altogether cleared away, Wallace, looking full in the faces of his soldiers, pointed to the French column, and leading the shattered brigade up the hill, without a moment's hesitation, brought them face to face before the French had time to witness the terrible effect of their murderous fire.

Astounded by the unshaken determination of Wallace's soldiers, Thomières' division wavered ;   nevertheless they opened a heavy discharge of musketry, but it was unlike the former,—it was irregular and ill-directed, the men acted without concert or method, and many fired in the air.   At length their fire ceased altogether, and the three regiments, for the first time, cheered!   The effect was electric; Thomières' troops were seized with a panic, and as Wallace closed upon them, his men could distinctly remark their bearing.   Their mustachioed faces, one and all, presented the same ghastly hue, a horrid family likeness throughout; and as they stood to receive the shock they were about to be assailed with, they reeled to and fro like men intoxicated.

The French officers did all that was possible, by voice, gesture, and example, to rouse their men to a proper sense of their situation, but in vain. One, the colonel of the leading regiment (the 22nd), seizing a firelock, and beckoning to his men to follow, ran forward a few paces and shot Major Murphy dead in front of the 88th. However, his career soon closed: a bullet, the first that had been fired from our ranks, pierced his head; he flung up his arms, fell forward, and expired.

The brigade, which till this time cheerfully bore up against the heavy fire they had been exposed to without returning a shot, were now impatient, and the 88th greatly excited; for Murphy, dead and bleeding, with one foot hanging in the stirrup-iron, was dragged by his affrighted horse along the front of his regiment. The soldiers became exasperated, and asked to be let forward. Pakenham, seeing that the proper moment had arrived, called out to Wallace "to let them loose." The three regiments ran onward, and the mighty phalanx, which but a moment before was so formidable, loosened and fell in pieces before fifteen hundred invincible British soldiers fighting in a line of only two deep.

Wallace, seeing the terrible confusion that prevailed in the enemy's column, pressed on with his brigade, calling to his soldiers "to push on to the muzzle." A vast number were killed in this charge of bayonets, but the men, wearied by their exertions, the intolerable heat of the weather, and famishing from thirst, were nearly run to a standstill.

Immediately on our left, the 5th Division were discharging

volleys against the French 4th; and Park's brigade could be
seen mounting the Arapilles height. But disregarding everything except the complete destruction of the column before
him, Pakenham followed it with the brigade of Wallace,
supported by the reserves of his division. The battle at
this point would have been decided on the moment, had the
heavy horse, under Le Marchant, been near enough to
sustain him. The confusion of the enemy was so great, that
they were mixed pell-mell together without any regard to
order or regularity; and it was manifest that nothing short
of a miracle could save Thomières from total destruction.
Sir Edward continued to press on at the head of Wallace's
brigade, but the French outran him. Had Le Marchant
been aware of this state of the combat, or been near enough
to profit by it, Pakenham would have settled the business
by six o'clock instead of seven. An hour at any time,
during a battle, is a serious lapse of time; but in this action
every minute was of vital import. Day was rapidly drawing
to a close; the Tormes was close behind the army of
Marmont; ruin stared him in the face; in a word, his left
wing was doubled up—lost; and Pakenham could have
turned to the support of the 4th and 5th Divisions had our
cavalry been on the spot ready to back Wallace at the
moment he broke Thomières' column. This, beyond doubt,
was the moment by which to profit, that the enemy might
not have time to recollect himself; but while Le Marchant
was preparing to take a part in the combat, Thomières, with
admirable presence of mind, remedied the terrible confusion
of his division, and calling up a fresh brigade to his support,
once more led his men into the fight, assumed the offensive,[1]

---

[1] It was Maucune's division; Thomières had been killed by now,
and his regiments entirely scattered.

and Pakenham was now about to be assailed in turn. This was the most critical moment of the battle at this point. Boyer's horsemen stood before us, inclining towards our right, which was flanked by two squadrons of the 14th Dragoons and two regiments of Portuguese cavalry; but we had little dependence on the Portuguese, and it behoved us to look to ourselves.

Led on by the ardour of conquest, we had followed the column until we at length found ourselves in an open plain, intersected with cork-trees, opposed by a multitude who, reinforced, again rallied and turned upon us with fury. Pakenham and Wallace rode along the line from wing to wing, almost from rank to rank, and fulfilled the functions of adjutants, in assisting the officers to reorganise the tellings-off of their men for square. Meanwhile the first battalion of the 5th drove back some squadrons of Boyer's dragoons; the other six regiments were fast approaching the point held by Wallace, but the attitude of the French cavalry in our front and upon our right flank caused some uneasiness.

The peals of musketry along the centre still continued without intermission; the smoke was so thick that nothing to our left was distinguishable; some men of the 5th Division got intermingled with ours; the dry grass was set on fire by the numerous cartridge-papers that strewed the field of battle; the air was scorching; and the smoke, rolling onward in huge volumes, nearly suffocated us. A loud cheering was heard in our rear; the brigade half turned round, supposing themselves about to be attacked by the French cavalry. Wallace called out to his men to mind the tellings-off for square. A few seconds passed, the trampling of horses was heard, the smoke cleared away, and the heavy

brigade of Le Marchant [1] was seen coming forward in line at
a canter. "Open right and left" was an order quickly
obeyed; the line opened, the cavalry passed through the
intervals, and, forming rapidly in our front, prepared for
their work.

The French column, which a moment before held so
imposing an attitude, became startled at this unexpected
sight. A victorious and highly-excited infantry pressing
close upon them, a splendid brigade of three regiments of
cavalry ready to burst through their ill-arranged and beaten
column, while no appearance of succour was at hand to
protect them, was enough to appal the boldest intrepidity.
The plain was filled with the vast multitude; retreat was
impossible; and the troopers came still pouring in to join
their comrades, already prepared for the attack. Hastily,
yet with much regularity, all things considered, they
attempted to get into square; but Le Marchant's brigade
galloped forward before the evolution was half completed.
The column hesitated, wavered, tottered, and then stood
still! The motion of the countless bayonets as they clashed
together might be likened to a forest about to be assailed by
a tempest, whose first warnings announce the ravage it is
about to inflict. Thomières' division [2] vomited forth a
dreadful volley of fire as the horsemen thundered across the
flat! Le Marchant was killed, and fell downright in the
midst of the French bayonets; but his brigade pierced
through the vast mass, killing or trampling down all before
them. The conflict was severe, and the troopers fell thick
and fast; but their long heavy swords cut through bone as
well as flesh. The groans of the dying, the cries of the

[1] 5th Dragoon Guards and 3rd and 4th Dragoons.
[2] It should rather be Maucune's.

wounded, the roar of the cannon, and the piteous moans of the mangled horses, as they ran away affrighted from the terrible scene, or lay with shattered limbs, unable to move, in the midst of the burning grass, was enough to unman men not placed as we were; but upon us it had a different effect, and our cheers were heard far from the spot where this fearful scene was acting.

Such as got away from the sabres of the horsemen sought safety amongst the ranks of our infantry, and scrambling under the horses, ran to us for protection—like men who, having escaped the first shock of a wreck, will cling to any broken spar, no matter how little to be depended upon. Hundreds of beings, frightfully disfigured, in whom the human face and form were almost obliterated—black with dust, worn down with fatigue, and covered with sabre-cuts and blood—threw themselves amongst us for safety. Not a man was bayoneted—not one even molested or plundered; and the invincible old 3rd Division on this day surpassed themselves, for they not only defeated their terrible enemies in a fair stand-up fight, but actually covered their retreat, and protected them at a moment when, without such aid, their total annihilation was certain. Under similar circumstances would the French have acted so? I fear not. The men who murdered Ponsonby at Waterloo, when he was alone and unprotected, would have shown but little courtesy to the 3rd Division, placed in a similar way.

Nine pieces of artillery, two eagles, and five thousand prisoners were captured at this point; still the battle raged with unabated fury on our left, immediately in front of the 5th Division. Leith fell wounded as he led on his men, but his division carried the point in dispute, and drove the enemy before them up the hill.

While those events were taking place on the right, the 4th Division, which formed the centre of the army, met with a serious opposition. The more distant Arapilles, occupied by the French 122nd, whose numbers did not count more than four hundred,[1] supported by a few pieces of cannon, was left to the Portuguese brigade of General Pack, amounting to two thousand bayonets. With fatal, though well-founded reliance—their former conduct taken into the scale—Cole's division advanced into the plain, confident that all was right with Pack's troops, and a terrible struggle between them and Bonnet's corps took place. It was, however, but of short duration. Bonnet's soldiers were driven back in confusion, and up to this moment all had gone on well. The three British divisions engaged overthrew every obstacle, and the battle might be said to be won, had Pack's formidable brigade —formidable in numbers at least—fulfilled their part; but these men totally failed in their effort to take the height occupied only by a few hundred Frenchmen, and thus gave the park of artillery that was posted with them full liberty to turn its efforts against the rear and flank of Cole's soldiers. Nothing could be worse than the state in which the 4th Division was now placed; and the battle, which ought to have been, and had been in a manner, won, was still in doubt.

Bonnet, seeing the turn which Pack's failure had wrought in his favour, re-formed his men, and advanced against Cole, while the fire from the battery and small arms on the Arapilles height completed the confusion. Cole fell wounded; half of his division were cut off, the remainder in full retreat; and Bonnet's troops, pressing on in a compact body, made it manifest that a material change had taken

---

[1] This is unfair to the Portuguese; the 122nd had 1000 bayonets.

place in the battle, and that ere it was gained some ugly up-hill work was yet to be done.

Marshal Beresford, who arrived at the moment, galloped up at the head of a brigade of the 5th Division, which he took out of the second line, and for a moment covered the retreat of Cole's troops; but this force—composed of Portuguese—was insufficient to arrest the progress of the enemy, who advanced in the full confidence of an assured victory; and at this critical moment Beresford was carried off the field wounded. Bonnet's troops advanced, loudly cheering, while the entire of Cole's division and Spry's brigade of Portuguese were routed. Our centre was thus endangered. Boyer's dragoons, after the overthrow of the French left, countermarched and moved rapidly to the support of Bonnet; they were close in the track of his infantry; and the fate of the battle was still uncertain. The fugitives of the 7th and 4th French Divisions ran to the succour of Bonnet, and by the time they had joined him his force had indeed assumed a formidable aspect; and thus reinforced, it stood in an attitude far different from what it would have done had Pack's brigade succeeded in its attack.

Lord Wellington, who saw what had taken place by the failure of Pack's troops, ordered up the 6th Division to the support of the 4th; and the battle, although it was half-past eight o'clock at night, recommenced with the same fury as at the onset.

Clinton's division, consisting of six thousand bayonets, rapidly advanced to assert its place in the combat, and to relieve the 4th from the awkward predicament in which it was placed; they essayed to gain what was lost by the failure of Pack's troops in their feeble effort to wrest the Arapilles height from a few brave Frenchmen; but they were received

by Bonnet's troops at the point of the bayonet, and the fire
opened against them seemed to be threefold more heavy than
that sustained by the 3rd and 5th Divisions.   It was nearly
dark ; and the great glare of light caused by the thunder of
the artillery, the continued blaze of the musketry, and the
burning grass, gave to the face of the hill a novel and terrific
appearance : it was one vast sheet of flame, and Clinton's
men looked as if they were attacking a burning mountain,
the crater of which was defended by a barrier of shining
steel.   But nothing could stop the intrepid valour of the 6th
Division, as they advanced with a desperate resolution to
carry the hill.   The troops posted on the face of it to arrest
their advance were trampled down and destroyed at the first
charge, and each reserve sent forward to extricate them met
with the same fate.   Still Bonnet's reserves, having attained
their place in the fight, and the fugitives from Thomières'
division joining them at the moment, prolonged the battle
until dark.   Those men, besmeared with blood, dust, and
clay, half naked, and some carrying only broken weapons,
fought with a fury not to be surpassed; but their impetuosity
was at length calmed by the bayonets of Clinton's troops,
and they no longer fought for victory but for safety.   After
a frightful struggle, they were driven from their last hold in
confusion ; and a general and overwhelming charge, which
the nature of the ground enabled Clinton to make, carried
this ill-formed mass of desperate soldiers before him, as a
shattered wreck borne along by the force of some mighty
current.

The mingled mass of fugitives fled to the woods and to
the river for safety, and under cover of the night succeeded
in gaining the pass of Alba over the Tormes.   It was now
ten o'clock at night : the battle was ended.   At this point

it had been confined to a small space, and the ground, trampled and stained deep, gave ample evidence of the havoc that had taken place. Lord Wellington, overcome as he was with fatigue, placed himself at the head of the 1st and Light Divisions and a brigade of cavalry, and following closely the retreating footsteps of the enemy, with those troops who had not fired a shot during the conflict, left the remnant of his victorious army to sleep upon the field of battle they had so hardly won.[1]

[1] The reader will note a considerable number of echoes from Napier in this interesting and well-written chapter. But the narrative differs in many points from that of Napier, especially as to the sequence of events in that part of the field where the 88th served—notably as to the moment at which Le Marchant's dragoons charged. Grattan, being an eye-witness, is probably nearer the truth than Napier, who was on the other wing in the ranks of the Light Division. On the other hand, he makes some slips, especially in stating that Pakenham's *second* assault was made upon Thomières' division instead of Maucune's.

CHAPTER XXI

Importance of the battle of Salamanca—Anecdotes of the 88th—
Gallantry of Captain Robert Nickle—Pursuit of the defeated army
of Marshal Marmont—French infantry in square broken and
destroyed by cavalry—March on Madrid—Frolics at St.
Ildefonso —Sudden attack of the French Lancers—Disgraceful conduct of
the Portuguese Dragoons.

No battle since that of Marengo, in 1800, which opened the
gates of Vienna to the first Consul of France, had been fought
whose consequences ought to be more duly appreciated than
the battle of Salamanca.

Had that battle been lost, the disasters of the French
army before Moscow would have been of little account in
the scale of the south, and the imperial eagles would have
soared with the same splendour, from Madrid to Cadiz, or
perhaps to Lisbon, as if no event of importance had occurred
beyond the Vistula. Portugal would have been then open
to invasion—the siege of Cadiz continued—the lines of Lisbon
once more invested—and what then?—why, the probable
withdrawal of the British army from the Peninsula. Portugal
would be thus conquered—Spain laid prostrate—England in
utter dismay—and one hundred and fifty thousand veteran
French troops marched across the Pyrenees to take a part in
the combats of Lutzen and Leipsic. These would have been
the results of a defeat at Salamanca ; and who is the man bold

enough to say what the results in the north of Europe would have been, had such an augmentation of force—which would have been certain—joined Napoleon in the end of 1812, or even in the spring of 1813 ? As it was, he gained the battle of Lutzen with a " green army." Had he been backed by one hundred and fifty thousand veteran troops from Spain, it requires no conjuror to tell what the upshot would have been. These are the consequences which would have followed a defeat at Salamanca. The gaining that battle placed matters on a different footing. Portugal had nothing to dread— Soult was forced to raise the siege of Cadiz—Madrid was evacuated, and Castille and Andalusia were freed from the presence of a French force; but, above all, no reinforcement of any account durst leave Spain to succour the French army in the north of Europe; and the European struggle was brought to a favourable result, and England saved from invasion—perhaps ultimate conquest! But those services of the Peninsular army are forgotten, and unrewarded.

At ten o'clock at night, Lord Wellington at the head of twelve thousand infantry, and two thousand horsemen, was in pursuit of the routed and discomfited army of Marmont, while the bulk of his own soldiers lay on the field of battle. The results of that battle were—prisoners, one hundred and thirty officers, seven thousand five hundred men, two eagles, and fourteen guns. The field of battle was heaped with the slain, and the total loss of the enemy may be estimated at seventeen thousand : it has been reckoned by some writers as exceeding twenty thousand ; but I apprehend I am nearer the mark, and that seventeen thousand was the outside. The dead and wounded on the side of the British and Portuguese (for the Spanish army, commanded by Don Carlos de España, lost *four men!*) were nearly five thousand ; but the greater number of the Portuguese either fell in their feéble attempt against the Arapilles height, or by the shot that passed over the first line, composed of British, which fell at random amongst the Portuguese placed in the rear.

The troops that had gained the victory lay buried in sleep until two o'clock of the morning following, when the arrival of the mules carrying rum aroused them from their slumber, but the parties sent out in search of water had not yet reached the field. The soldiers, with parching lips, their tongues cleaving to their mouths from thirst, their limbs benumbed with cold, and their bodies enfeebled by a long abstinence from food, and the exertion of the former day, ran to the casks, and each man drank a fearful quantity. This for a short time satisfied them, but a burning thirst followed this rash proceeding, and before any water arrived, we were more in need of it than at the close of the battle.

The inhabitants of Salamanca, who had a clear view of what was passing, hastened to the spot, to afford all the relief in their power. Several cars, most of them loaded with provisions, reached the field of battle before morning; and it is but due to those people to state, that their attentions were unremitting, and of the most disinterested kind, for they sought no emolument.

They brought fruit, and even quantities of water, well knowing how distant the river was from us, and how scantily the countryside around was provided with so necessary a relief to men who had not tasted a drop for so many hours, under a burning sun, and oppressed with the fatigue they had endured during the fight.

During the battle there were many circumstances which, if related in their places, at the period they occurred, would

S

have broken in upon the narrative, but may be told with more propriety now.

When the 3rd Division under Pakenham had crossed the flat, and were moving against the crest of the hill occupied by Thomières' *tirailleurs*, a number of *Caçadores* commanded by Major Haddock were in advance of us. The moment the French fire opened, these troops, which had been placed to cover our advance, lay down on their faces, not for the purpose of taking aim with more accuracy, but in order to save their own sconces from the French fire. Haddock dismounted from his horse and began belabouring with the flat side of his sabre the dastardly troops he had the misfortune to command, but in vain ; all sense of shame had fled after the first discharge of grape and musketry, and poor Haddock might as well have attempted to move the great cathedral of Salamanca as the soldiers of his Majesty the King of Portugal.

At the time the Colonel of the 22nd French Regiment stepped out of the ranks and shot Major Murphy dead at the head of his regiment, the 88th, a number of officers were beside Murphy. It is not easy at such a moment to be certain who is the person singled out. The two officers who carried the colours of the regiment, and who were immediately in the rear of the mounted officers, thought that the shot was intended for either of them. Lieutenant Moriarty, carrying the regimental flag, called out, "That fellow is aiming at me!"—"I hope so," replied Lieutenant D'Arcy, who carried the other colour, with great coolness—"I hope so, for I thought he had *me* covered." He was not much mistaken : the ball that killed Murphy, after passing through him, struck the staff of the flag carried by D'Arcy, and also carried away the button and part of the strap of his epaulette! This fact is not told as an extraordinary occurrence, that the ball which killed one man should strike the coat of him who happened to stand in his rear, for such casualties were by no means uncommon with us; but I mention it as a strong proof of the great coolness of the British line in their advance against the enemy's column.

When the cavalry of Le Marchant passed through Wallace's brigade, in their advance against Thomières' column, Captain William Mackie of the 88th, the discountenanced leader of the forlorn hope at Rodrigo, who acted as aide-de-camp to Colonel Alexander Wallace, was missing. In the confusion that prevailed it was thought he had fallen. No one could give any account of him; but in a short lapse of time, after the cavalry had charged, he returned covered with dust and blood, his horse tottering from fatigue, and nothing left of his sabre—but the hilt! He joined the cavalry so soon as the fighting amongst the infantry had ceased, and those who knew the temperament of the man were not surprised at it: wherever glory and danger were to be met, there was Mackie to be found, and nothing—not even the chilling slights he had experienced—could damp his daring spirit.

At the first dawn of the morning of the 23rd of July Lord Wellington continued the pursuit of the defeated army of Marmont. He placed himself at the head of the Light Division, which opened the march, followed by the heavy German cavalry under General Bock, and Anson's brigade of light horse. Those two superb brigades of dragoons had only joined the army the night before. The 1st Division of infantry, composed of the Guards and German Legion, followed the cavalry, and Lord Wellington, at the head of thirteen thousand men that had not pulled a trigger,

or unsheathed a sabre in the battle, followed the enemy's
track; but the retreat was so quick that Marmont's headquarters were thirty miles from Salamanca the day after the
battle.   Nevertheless, the corps that covered the retreat,
consisting of three battalions of infantry and five regiments
of cavalry, were overtaken near the village of La Serna.   The
infantry formed themselves into three squares, the cavalry
were posted on the flanks for its support, but the panic with
which all were infected by the defeat of the preceding day
had taken such a fast hold of them, that the French horse
in advance could not be prevailed upon to show a front.
This threw those that were at hand to support them into
disorder; confusion was communicated to the remainder,
and the field of battle was precipitately abandoned by the
cavalry, who, in the most unaccountable manner, left their
companions, the infantry, to their fate.

The cavalry having thus fled, Bock, with his German
horse, galloped at the squares, and breaking through, slew
or took prisoners the entire; and the contest ended in one
dreadful massacre of the French infantry.   Nevertheless,
many of the troopers fell; for one regiment in particular,
the 105th French, bravely stood their ground, but the
ponderous weight of the heavy cavalry broke down all
resistance; and arms lopped off, heads cloven to the spine,
or gashes across the breast and shoulders, showed to those
who afterwards passed the spot the fearful encounter that
had taken place; and from this moment nothing more of
the army of Portugal was to be seen.

The overthrow of the rear-guard which covered the flight
of the army of the Duke of Ragusa, and the rapid manner
in which Clausel made good his retreat from the heights of
La Serna, where that army for the last time made any show

of a stand against the British troops that had defeated it on the plains of Salamanca, finished the campaign, so far, at least, as regarded the army of Portugal.

The leading regiments followed the enemy's track as far as Flores de Avila, which town, distant ten leagues from Salamanca, had been evacuated by them two days after the battle. The cavalry and artillery of the northern army met them on their retreat near Arevalo; but nothing—not even this reinforcement—could inspire them with confidence; and the mass of fugitives hastily followed the road leading to Valladolid. The good generalship displayed by Clausel, and the steady front he showed when in the presence of a victorious army, raised him considerably, and justly so, in the estimation of his own troops; but all his skill would have been of no avail had the battle not been unavoidably prolonged until dark.

The march of the British army continued without interruption. Those divisions which followed the enemy were enthusiastically welcomed as they passed through the different towns and villages on the Valladolid road; the inhabitants met us in vast numbers with a supply of wine, fruit, bread, and vegetables, which were all bought up by the soldiers. Arrived at Valladolid, and finding himself as far as ever from being able to overtake the army of Marmont, Lord Wellington made a full stop. Giving the troops one day's rest for the purpose of allowing the stragglers to come up, he, on the 1st of August, turned off abruptly towards the grand Madrid road; while Hill, with the second corps, reached Zafra.

Marmont being thus disposed of for the present, and Lord Wellington having formed the resolution of marching to the Spanish capital, every road leading to it was occupied, and thronged by cavalry, infantry, and artillery, baggage and commissariat mules, stores of all descriptions, the reserve park guns, and the followers of the camp, such as sutlers, Portuguese servants, and women who followed the soldiers. These, when assembled together, formed one vast mass of between sixty thousand and seventy thousand souls. The sight was an imposing one; the weather was beautifully fine, and the advance of the army as it moved onward towards the capital was one scene of uninterrupted rejoicing. Never was the general feeling in Spain so much in favour of the British nation, the British army, and the Hero who commanded it, as on the present occasion. The news of the great victory gained by the British army only a few days before, under the walls of Salamanca, which was witnessed by thousands upon thousands of Spaniards, was spread afar; and the different routes which the army traversed were crowded almost to suffocation by the Spanish people, who vied with each other to gain a passing view of the men who had so distinguished themselves, and to supply them with every assistance in their power. Every face was cheerful; and at the termination of each day's march, our bivouacs, or the villages we occupied, were crowded with Spanish girls and young men, who either brought wine, lemonade, or fruit; the evening was wound up by boleros and fandangos; and, in short, our march to Madrid more resembled a triumphal procession—which, in point of fact, it really was —than the ordinary advance of an army prepared for battle.

Meanwhile King Joseph hastily endeavoured to make arrangements to stop the torrent which threatened his capital. He had advanced upon Blasco Sancho on the 25th of July; but there, hearing of the fate that had befallen his favourite general at Salamanca, he retraced his steps, and gaining the passes of the Guadarama, retired towards the palace of the Escurial.   He collected all the disposable force that could be taken from the capital; but his army, chiefly composed of *Juramentados* (Spaniards that entered into King Joseph's service), counted not quite fifteen thousand bayonets and sabres—a force as to number, without taking into account its *morale*, not of that formidableness very likely to disconcert the grand designs of Lord Wellington.   In short, the army continued its march towards the Spanish capital without molestation.   On the 6th of August the headquarters were at Cuellar; on the 7th, at the ancient town of Segovia, so celebrated in Spanish romance; and on the 8th the divisions destined to march upon Madrid were concentrated at St. Ildefonso.

St. Ildefonso is beautifully situated.   The magnificent waterworks, the elegant taste with which the gardens and pleasure-grounds are laid out, and the vast concourse of people who thronged them on the day of our arrival, gave to it the appearance, in our eyes at least, of the most enchanting spot on the face of the globe.   At each of the principal walks, bands of music played inspiring airs; and at half-past six in the evening the waterworks were in full play.   These works, situated at the base of a lofty blue mountain, cast up water to an immense height; and one in particular seemed to us to be much superior to anything we afterwards witnessed at either Versailles or St. Cloud.   To me it certainly seems so; but I, in common with many others, may be wrong; for, in truth, we were so charmed with the novelty of the scene we then witnessed, and the vast contrast it presented to the scenes we had for such a length of time not only witnessed, but taken an active part in, that all due allowance ought to be made—if we are wrong—for our prepossession in favour of this spot.

At eight o'clock Lord Wellington, surrounded by a number of generals of different nations, a splendid staff, and many grandees of Spain, entered the gardens. All the bands, at one and the same moment, played "See the Conquering Hero comes," the singers joined in chorus, and the vast multitude rent the air with acclamations. The females, disregarding all form or etiquette, broke through the crowd to get a nearer view of his Lordship, and many embraced him as he passed down the different alleys of the gardens. The groups of singers continued to sing; this was succeeded by bolero-dancing, fandango-dancing, and waltzing; and all was wound up by one of the most intoxicating and delightful nights of pleasure that we had ever witnessed, and, if I mistake not greatly, that was ever acted on the same spot. It was late before we retired to rest—and indeed we had need of repose: our minds as well as bodies required it; and when the shrill note of the bugle the following morning (for that matter it was the same morning) aroused us from our sleep, all that had passed seemed but as a dream.

The causeway leading to Madrid is broad and well arranged; as we reached each league-stone we counted with anxiety the distance we had yet to pace ere we arrived at the capital of Spain. The mountains which overhang the Guadarama passes are bold and lofty; these passes, easy of defence, and requiring but a small force, were abandoned without a musket-shot being fired for their protection; and, in fine, on the 11th, Lord Wellington was near the village of Majadahonda, distant but one march from the capital. Thirty thousand infantry were encamped half a league in its rear; the different brigades of horse and artillery attached

to the infantry were at hand—in short, all was in readiness;
but the advanced guard of cavalry, unfortunately entrusted
to the brigade of Portuguese of D'Urban, was in front of
all. Behind them, at the distance of a mile, were the two
regiments of heavy German horse, while the splendid troop
of horse artillery, commanded by Captain Macdonald, was
ready to support D'Urban.

The greatest part of the day had passed over without any
event taking place between the advanced posts; some slight
skirmishing between the enemy's lancers and D'Urban's cavalry
left matters as they were at the commencement. The army
was preparing its arrangements for the night's repose and
the march of the following day, when the thunder of Macdonald's artillery aroused us in an instant from our occupa-
tions. It was soon manifest that the enemy's advance had
attacked the Portuguese cavalry; and the vast cloud of dust
that came rolling onward towards the village, where the
German horse were placed in reserve, told but too plainly
that the Portuguese were routed, and the Germans about to
be cut off. The infantry betook themselves to their arms,
and in a few moments the entire were in readiness to march
to the scene of action—for so in fact it was. The Portuguese
dragoons fled at the first onset, without waiting to exchange
one sabre-cut with the French; and so rapid was their flight
—for they rode through the village where the reserve of
Germans were posted to support them—that not more than
half of the Germans were mounted. Many men thus fell
before they could defend themselves, and their Colonel was
cut down while in the act of shaving himself; but his brave
soldiers, forming themselves together in the best manner the
time would admit of, closed with drawn sabres upon the
French lancers, which turned the stream, broke the mad

fury of the attack, and drove back the lancers in confusion.

Up to this time the combat was one scene of desperation. An irregular and furious crowd might be seen mixed together, fighting without order or regularity, and from the confusion that prevailed it was not possible to see distinctly to which side the victory belonged; but at a distance, far from the scene of action, the burnished helmets of the Portuguese troopers were distinguishable as they fled from the post they had deserted, and from their brave companions, the Germans, whom they left to be massacred. The din of arms, the clashing of swords, and the thunder of the cannon, mingled with shouts from every side, completed the confusion. In the hurry of the moment some tents belonging to the 74th Regiment took fire, the flames soon communicated with those of the next regiment, and the camp was enveloped with smoke; but this was soon overcome; and by the time we approached near the point in dispute, the French cavalry had been driven off the field, but not before many of the Germans had fallen. Two guns of Macdonald's brigade had also been taken; and upon the whole, it was one of the most disgraceful and unlooked-for events that had taken place during the campaign. To be beaten at any time was bad enough, but to be beaten by a handful of lancers, on the eve of our entering Madrid, almost in view of the city, was worse than all. But what caused our defeat—our disgrace—under the eyes of the people of Madrid? The placing undue reliance on the Portuguese troops.

CHAPTER XXII

The British army approach Madrid—Enthusiastic welcome—Preparations to carry by assault the fortress of La China—It surrenders—Description of Madrid—The Puerto del Sol—The Prado—Unsociability of English officers—Seizure of a Spanish priest—Proved to be a spy in the service of the enemy—His execution by the garrotte.

ORDER having been at length restored, and the French pushed back again to their former ground, the German horse took the advance, and the night passed over quietly; but in the disgraceful encounter, which I have related in my last chapter, two guns of Macdonald's troop, which were upset during the clamour, fell for a time into the enemy's hands.

As we passed over the ground which had been the object of dispute the preceding evening, we beheld many of the brave Germans lying dead and naked. Every wound was in the breast, and at the skirts of the village lay the two captured guns; their carriages were broken, and they could not in consequence be removed; the French had set fire to the wheels, which were still smoking.

In less than two hours we reached the heights which command Madrid; the soldiers ran forward to catch a glimpse of the countless steeples that were distinguishable through the haze, and their joy was at its height when they beheld a city that had cost them so much toil and hard fighting to gain the possession of. Ten thousand voices, at one and the same moment, vociferated "Madrid! Madrid!" The enthusiasm of the army was still further increased by the thousands upon thousands of Spaniards that came from the town to accompany us in our entry; for miles leading to the capital the roads were crowded, almost to suffocation, by people of all ranks, who seemed to be actuated by one simultaneous burst of patriotism, and it was with difficulty that the march was conducted with that order which we were in the habit of observing. The nearer we approached the city the greater was the difficulty of getting on, for the people forced themselves into the midst of our ranks, and joined hand in hand with the soldiers. Wine was offered and accepted, though not to the extent the Spaniards wished, but the soldiers were too well-disciplined, and felt too proud of the station they held in the estimation of the people, and in the estimation of themselves, to allow anything bordering on excess to follow the latitude they thus had. There was nothing like intoxication, not the slightest irregularity, and the appearance of the officers, almost all of whom were mounted, and the respect with which they were accosted by the soldiers when occasion required it, was so strongly contrasted with the loose discipline of the French army, to say nothirg of the bands of half-naked creatures that composed the army of their own nation, that it may be fairly said no troops ever entered any capital with all the requisites necessary to ensure them a cordial as well as a respectful reception, as the British army did on the present occasion.

At length we entered that part of the town near which the palace stands, but the obstacles which impeded our march, great as they were before, now became tenfold greater. Nothing could stop the populace, which at this period nearly embraced all that Madrid contained, from mixing themselves amongst us. The officers were nearly forced from their horses in the embraces of the females, and some there were who actually lost their seats, if not their hearts. Old or young, ugly or well-looking, shared the same fate; and one in particular, an old friend of my own, and a remarkably plain-looking personage, was nearly suffocated in the embraces of half a dozen fair Castilians. When he recovered himself and was able to speak, he turned to me and said, "How infer-nally fond these Madrid women must be of kissing, when they have nearly hugged to death such an ill-looking fellow as me." I would mention his name, but as he is still alive he might not like the joke second-hand. We soon reached the Convent of St. Domingo, near the Plaza Mayor, which was destined for our quarters, and for a time took leave of these people who had so cordially welcomed us to their capital. The soldiers, thus quartered, were left to arrange their barracks; while the officers, who were billeted in those parts of the city adjoining the barrack, proceeded to occupy the houses allotted to them, and to partake of the hospitality of their patrons.

Evening had scarcely closed when every house was illumin-ated. The vast glare of light which the huge wax candles and torches, placed outside each balcony, threw out, so com-pletely lighted the town, that night seemed to be converted into day, and the whole population of Madrid might be said to fill the streets. Nothing could exceed the popular feeling in favour of the British, and although the ancient palace of the Retiro was garrisoned by two thousand five hundred French troops, with a park of artillery at its disposal, sufficient to batter down the city, the gaiety was continued as if no enemy was within several leagues of the place. The illuminations lasted for three nights, during which not the slightest irregularity or misunderstanding took place.

On the morning of the 13th of August, the General commanding the fortress of La China having refused to give it up, orders were given to carry it by storm. The 3rd, or "fighting division," as ours was called, was selected by Lord Wellington for this duty. At eight o'clock in the morning all the ladders were in readiness, and the division, commanded by Sir Edward Pakenham, defiled under the walls of the botanic gardens. The sappers had succeeded in opening several breaches in the wall, and the fire of the riflemen in the interior of the gardens announced that the attack of the outposts had commenced. One hundred thousand people of all ranks, ages, and sex crowded the streets, houses, and house-tops to witness the contest. No sooner was the first gun fired, which was the signal for attack, than an universal shout was raised by this vast multitude of spectators, and it would be very difficult indeed, if not quite impossible, to describe this animated scene. The soldiers, infected by the example thus set them, cheered in turn, and it was several minutes before any word of command could be heard from the Babel-like tumult that prevailed. Little or no orders were given—they were unnecessary. The men were directed to carry the fort at the bayonet's point, and this was all that was said or that was necessary to be said. The troops were then put in motion, and this was the signal for another burst of enthusiasm from the Spaniards, several of whom joined our ranks. The *vivas* now became so tremendous that nothing else could be heard, and the leading platoons had made some progress through the shrubberies before the order to halt was known; owing to this a few men were killed and wounded, and those old and tried soldiers lost their lives or were disabled in a mere *bagatelle*, for the French general commanding in the fort displayed the white flag in token of submission the moment he saw the 3rd Division in movement towards the Retiro.

The fall of this place was of vast importance to us. In it was found a large supply of provisions, as well as one hundred and eighty-nine pieces of cannon, including a complete battering train. There was likewise a great quantity of powder and ball, and some clothing, as likewise twenty thousand stand of arms. The garrison, consisting of three thousand veteran soldiers, were made prisoners and sent to Lisbon, and the fort was converted into a state prison for disaffected or suspected Spaniards.

Thus ended our operations for the present, and we had leisure to make our observations upon Madrid, and avail ourselves of the hospitality of such of our patrons as were disposed to show us attention.

Madrid stands in a flat uninteresting country, devoid of scenery; fields of tillage encompass the city up to the mud wall that surrounds it, and the rivulet that meanders round it is in summer so insignificant as to be barely able to supply the few baths on its banks with a sufficiency of water; nevertheless this side of the town, which is next the Grand Park, and the regal cottage called Casa del Campo, is far from uninteresting, and as the Park, which abounds with game of all sorts, was open to the British officers, we had abundance of sport when we wished to avail ourselves of it. The streets are wide, and the principal ones, generally speaking, clean, but the part of the town possessing the greatest interest is the great street called Puerto del Sol. Some centuries ago it was the eastern gate of the town, but as the city became enlarged from time to time, it is now, like the University

College of Dublin, in the heart of the metropolis, instead of at the verge of it.   Half a dozen or so of the principal streets empty, in a manner, their population into this gangway, where the Exchange is held, and all public business carried on, so that any one desirous of hearing the news of the day, the price of the funds, or any other topic discussed, has but to station himself here and his curiosity will be satisfied, as almost the entire of the population of Madrid pass and repass under his eye during the day.   Merchants, dealers, higglers, charcoal venders, fellows with lemonade on their backs, girls with pannellas of water incessantly crying out " *Quien quiere agua ?* " all congregate to this focus, where everything is to be known.

Next to the Puerto del Sol must be placed the Prado or public walk, which is decidedly the most agreeable lounge that Madrid can boast of; but as the promenade never commences before five in the evening, while, on the contrary, the bustle of the Puerto lasts during the forenoon, it must have from me the precedence though not the preference.   By five o'clock, as I before said, the walk begins to be frequented, the great heat having by this time subsided, and the siesta over.   At seven it is crowded almost to suffocation, and groups of singers with guitars slung across their shoulders enliven the scene.   At each side of the walk are tables at which sit groups of people enjoying the scene, but you rarely see men and women seated at the same table; indeed, it would seem as if the men totally shunned the company of the fairer sex, and engrossed themselves more with the news of the day than the gaiety of the Prado.   Much has been said of the jealousy of the Spaniards, and in England it is a generally received opinion that they are a jealous race, but I never found them such—quite the contrary.   In Madrid a married woman may go to any house she pleases, or where and with whom she wishes. They might have been a different people when Spanish romances and Spanish plays—old ones, I mean —were written, but if the manners and habits of the people were then truly narrated, I can with truth say that no nation in the world has undergone a more wholesome, thorough, and radical reform than Spain.

In some instances we experienced much hospitality from the people, but those occurrences were rare ; for the Spaniards are naturally a lofty and distant people, and most unquestionably our officers did not endeavour by any act on their part to do away with this reserve, and in fact after a sojourn of nearly three months in the Spanish capital they knew nearly as little of its inhabitants as they did of the citizens of Pekin. This is a fatal error, and I fear one that it will be difficult to counteract, for it is not easy to correct national habits and national prejudices ; but if the officers of the British army were to reflect upon the effect their conduct must have on the people of a different nation, and if they could be made to understand how different, how far different, their reception in foreign countries would be if they unbent themselves a little, and conformed themselves to the modes of those nations amongst whom they were sent by their sovereign, they would at once come to the resolution of changing their tone, and they would by so doing get themselves not only respected and regarded, but the British nation as much beloved as it is respected.

While we thus continued to pass our time in gaiety and idleness, other divisions of the army had moved onwards towards Burgos, which was strongly held by a chosen garrison under the command of an experienced and skilful general of the name of Dubreton. Meanwhile we continued

T

at Madrid, and either enjoying the amusement of the theatres, the luxuries of the hotel called El Fuente d'Oro, the hospitality of the good citizens, or the gay but noisy scenes at the Calle de Baimos, we passed our time as agreeably as men could do, considering the scanty amount of pay which was issued to us; for from the difficulty of getting a supply of animals sufficient to bring up specie from Lisbon, where there was an abundance, the army was at this period five months in arrear of pay, and except for the commissaries and some paymasters who cashed our bills (at seven shillings the dollar!) many of us would have been in a sad plight. Those who were enabled to raise money at this enormous percentage got on well enough, but others, who were limited in their resources, were obliged, per force, to be lookers-on at all that was passing.

An event was now about to take place that engrossed much of the conversation of all Madrid, and created amongst the army no little curiosity. It was the condemnation to death, by the *garrotte*, of a Spanish priest named Diego Lopez. This ill-fated man, it appears, had been, for some time previously to his arrest, in the pay of King Joseph; he acted as a spy, and gave circumstantial information of all that was passing in our army. Accurately acquainted with his proceedings, the police agents narrowly watched his motions. For some days he had been missing from his lodgings in the Calle de Barrio Nuevo. No inquiry was made after him by the police, they being too conversant in their calling to raise any suspicion in his breast by a step that they knew would be abortive; but his return was eagerly looked for, carefully watched, and his apprehension made more certain. At length he did return.

It was midnight when he reached the barrier at the

Toledo gate, where a police agent was stationed. He was asked but few questions and was allowed to pass, and mounted as he was on a jaded horse, fatigued by a long journey, it was not difficult for the agent to keep near enough to him to track him unobserved to his dwelling. The trampling of his horse was soon recognised by an old woman who kept watch for his return. A light was placed at the window as a beacon that all was safe within, and he was about to dismount when he was seized by three police agents who hurried him away to the bureau of the director, while another entered his house for the purpose of seizing his papers. He underwent an immediate examination, but nothing could be elicited from him to criminate himself, and no papers, excepting commonplace ones, were found at his lodgings. He was then stripped of his clothes, and another suit given him in their stead. Every part of his dress was examined, the linings carefully parted, his clothes in fact cut into shreds, when at last, after a scrutiny of an hour, was found, folded up in a button, covered with cloth, which corresponded with the rest, a note from King Joseph to some person in Madrid, briefly detailing the information he had received from Lopez, and asking his advice as to the plans to be pursued.

No more was required, or indeed necessary, to confirm his guilt, and the next day he was, by the orders of Don Carlos de España, Governor of Madrid, hurried before a military tribunal summoned together to try him. The only evidence brought forward against him was the concealed note; and nothing could induce him to betray the name of his confederate. The trial was, therefore, of but short duration, and when called upon by the president to make his defence, he calmly stood forward, and looking his judges full in the face, prepared to address them.

Every eye was fixed upon him, and it would be difficult to look upon a man of a more imposing figure. In stature he was about five feet eleven inches, and his make was in proportion to his height; his lank black hair lay flat on his forehead, and hung behind over the cape of his coat in loose but neglected masses; his face bore the marks of care, and his fine dark eye was sunk and wan—he was, in short, the outline of a once fine, but now broken-down man. Having wiped away the drops of sweat that covered his forehead, caused by the heat of the weather, the crowded state of the court, and, no doubt, the agitation of his mind, he spoke as follows:—

"It is now something more than two years since I first attached myself to the service of His Majesty King Joseph: during that period I have served him faithfully, and with the utmost diligence. I have rendered him some service, and he will be, I doubt not, sorry when he learns my fate. I have said that I served His Majesty faithfully: the expression is too weak—I but *lived* for him; and the only regret I feel in now laying down my life, while endeavouring to promote his interests, is, that I have not been able to succeed in this, my last mission, which is the only one I ever failed in. Gentlemen, I have done." He then bowed to the court, and resumed his former place.

During the delivery of this short but impressive speech the court and spectators were silent. When it was concluded, a buzz of admiration and pity burst forth from almost every person present, and there were many who would, if they dared, have expressed their sentiments more fully, but the strong guard which occupied the hall was sufficient to maintain order; and though no lives were lost, many arrests took place. When order was restored, the chief of police conducted the prisoner, under a strong escort, back to his dungeon; and the court being cleared, the president asked the opinion of the members as to the guilt of Lopez. They were unanimous—indeed there could be but one opinion, and by that his life became the forfeit. The sentence pronounced against him was, that he should suffer death by strangulation on the following day at two o'clock; and the Plaza Mayor, or Great Square, where a vast market is daily held, was the spot decided upon as most fitting for the execution.

It was thought necessary to augment some of the British Guards in the neighbourhood of the Plaza; and the barrack occupied by the 88th being close to it, I, as the next subaltern for duty, was ordered to repair there to take charge of thirty soldiers, lest any rioting should take place during the night. It was five o'clock in the afternoon when I reached the square on my way to the barrack. It was already much crowded with people of all classes; some led by curiosity to see if any, and what, preparations had been made towards erecting the platform upon which the *garrotte* was to be fixed; others bargaining for and cheapening seats either at the windows of the shopkeepers, or on the tops of the market stalls; others calling out a sort of programme of the offences, etc., for which López was to suffer; and, though last not least in the list, a host of beggars, who assailed the bystanders with entreaties for charity *in the name of the soul about to depart!*

The arrival of several carts carrying planks for the formation of the platform, the presence of a large body of police, and the appearance of the workmen entering the square, dissipated anything like apprehension of a disappointment. This circumstance, or announcement, had an instant and powerful effect on the price of seats—the same as the intelligence of a great victory would have on the funds in London. "Omnium was above par," and "much business was effected." Every person seemed pleased with the bargain he had made, and I myself was among the number. I paid, by way of deposit, half a dollar to ensure my place, the remaining half to be handed down the following morning. All being settled, so far as related to myself, I left the square to look after my guard. I found all quiet in the quarters of our barrack, and towards nightfall I again returned to the Plaza. It was quite deserted except by the workmen, who were busily employed in marking out and completing the rude platform for the scaffold, in which they had made considerable progress. Its height from the ground was about four feet; the square or area was fourteen by twenty; and from the quantity of materials, and their grossness, it might be supposed that it was meant to sustain, at one and the same moment, half the population of Madrid. But it yet wanted that terrible instrument of death—the iron clasp—to complete its structure.

It was three o'clock before I lay down to rest, but I slept little. The din of hammers and the creaking of waggons put sleep out of the question. I took up a volume of Gil Blas and attempted to read and laugh, but in vain: I could do neither the one nor the other—the *garrotte* was still in perspective, and nothing could banish it from my thoughts. At length the stillness which prevailed terribly told that all was prepared, and I went once more to the spot. I found it deserted by the workmen, who had done their part, and these preparations now wanted nothing to complete them but the presence of the man who was to die by the pressure of the clasp, which hung from a beam of wood placed in the centre of the platform.

I have before described the height and dimensions of this platform; at each side of it was a flight of four steps—one for the criminal, the other for the two executioners. In the centre was a beam, to which was attached a chair or stool; through the beam a clasp was introduced, and behind was a screw, or sort of vice, which at one turn crushes the neck. Having so far satisfied my curiosity, I once more returned to my post, and waited with impatience for the coming of the hour destined for the arrival of the priest. So early as ten o'clock the square was thronged with Spanish troops, and the platform upon which the scaffold stood surrounded by a strong guard. Vast multitudes already began to congregate towards the spot, in order to take possession of the places they had paid for, or to secure those which would give them an opportunity of witnessing the execution. All business was at a standstill, and every idea, except that connected with the coming event, seemed to be extinct. By mid-day the square, the market-sheds in its centre, and the houses which formed it, were filled nearly to suffocation; and the other streets leading from the prison to the Plaza were thronged with people of all ranks. At length the shouts raised in the streets nearest the prison announced the removal of the criminal, and the huzzas from that quarter were rapidly taken up as they passed onward towards the square: they increased by degrees, and, like a vast torrent which is formed by tributary streams, each stream contributed its quota to the current, until at length it reached the vast vortex, the Plaza Mayor. At this place the shouts were so deafening that for some minutes it was impossible to ask a question, much less hear one. At length the head of the cavalcade was in sight, and a death-like silence followed the tumult that had preceded it. The soldiers stationed in

the square, as also those that surrounded the platform, resumed their firelocks ; the words " Las armas a l'ombro " was
quickly obeyed, and the entire procession was soon within
the precincts of the Plaza.

The convict, Lopez, dressed in black, with a loose cloak
covering his shoulders, was on horseback, attended by two
priests, also mounted, one at each side of him. He wore a
hat of large dimensions turned up in the front, and his
demeanour was the same as at his trial—firm, collected, and
calm.   Arrived at the foot of the scaffold he dismounted
with ease, and throwing a rapid glance, first at the vast
crowd and then at the *garrotte* itself, he ascended the flight
of steps leading to it. The two priests followed but did
not speak to him, his wish being that they should not.   He
then, without flurry or agitation, took off his hat and cloak,
and handed them to the assistant executioner, to whom he
said something. He wished to address the people, but was
prevented by the officer commanding the Spanish troops.
He bowed obedience, and instantly took his seat upon the
stool under the clasp. His arms were then bound with
cords, and the iron collar passed through the stake and
placed upon his throat. This scene had a strong effect upon
the multitude : the quiet but determined self-possession of
the man, his extraordinary resolution, devoid of any bravado,
was enough to check any indecent ebullition of patriotism ;
but the sight of that terrible collar seemed to awaken
feelings, and to call forth that sympathy which, a few
moments before, was nowhere to be found. Women who,
to their shame be it told, waved their handkerchiefs with
joy upon his arrival at the scaffold, now might be seen
covering their eyes to hide from their view the horrid sight,
or to wipe away the tears that traced their cheeks.

All was now in readiness: the executioner stood behind, holding the screw with both hands; at each side was a confessor, and behind one was the assistant executioner, with a square piece of cloth in his hand; one of the priests read from a book, while the other held the hand of Lopez. This ceremony occupied but a few moments; and when the priest had finished reading he stooped down to kiss the cheek of the ill-fated Lopez. He then closed the book; the man behind him threw the cloth over the culprit's face; the executioner turned the screw—and Lopez was dead! The two priests hurried down the steps, and, in their confusion and fright, ran headlong under the horses of the cavalry which were posted round the scaffold. One of them, a corpulent man—as indeed most priests are—was dreadfully lacerated, but the other escaped uninjured.

During the entire of this scene the vast crowd preserved the most profound silence; but the sight they had just witnessed was succeeded by another of a more disgusting nature. The assistant executioner removed the cloth from the face of the dead man: it was perfectly black; the eyeballs were forced from their sockets; the throat was pressed quite flat, and the mouth, with the tongue hanging down on the chin, was dragged under the right ear.

The troops then defiled out of the square, the multitude dispersed, and by six o'clock in the evening not more than twenty persons were near the scaffold upon which the dead priest was still bound. The body was at length put into a cart, the platform was removed, and the spot which so short a time before was the theatre of this tragedy now bore no evidence of the horrid scene that had been acted upon it.

CHAPTER XXIII

Arrests at Madrid—Advantages of speaking French—Seizure of Don
Saturio de Padilla by the police—The author effects his liberation
—A bull day at Madrid—Private theatricals—French and English
soldiers—Blowing up the Retiro—Retreat from Madrid—A pig
hunt.

THE execution of the priest Lopez, narrated in the last
chapter, was followed by many arrests. In eight days no
fewer than one hundred and forty-nine persons were thrown
into prison ; some on good grounds, others on trivial circumstances, and many on the charge alone of having held
employment under the late government. The consequence
of this ill-judged severity was that all those who escaped
arrest in the first burst of tyranny practised by the local
authorities fled from Madrid, and scarcely a family was to
be found who had not to lament the loss of some individual
belonging to it, either by flight or imprisonment. Had the
siege of Burgos been successful, and the French troops driven
to Pampeluna, which would have been the natural result, a
tragical scene would have been enacted, not only at Madrid,
but throughout the whole of Spain. Yet all the time
nothing but forgiveness for the past and promises for the
future were to be heard of—except the daily and nightly
imprisonments that took place !

Two evenings after the execution of Lopez I met a

number of Spaniards at the house of my *padron*, Don Miguel de Inza, who had himself been an engineer in the employment of the late King Charles IV. ; different topics, as a matter of course, were discussed—the sieges of Rodrigo and Badajoz, the battle of Salamanca, and the triumphant entry of our troops into the capital of Spain. Most of the party seemed well inclined towards us, and towards the king we proclaimed, Ferdinand VII. ; but there was little confidence amongst the party themselves, and there was some who would, if they dared, have spoken in favour of the French.

One old Donna in particular was rather severe in her observations on the dress of the British officers, and remarked that not one in fifty of them could speak French. Whether it was that she was piqued at my paying much attention to a lady who sat near her, or that she wished to display her wit at my expense, I being nearer to her than any other Englishman, I can't say, but she turned round and asked if I spoke the French language. I replied that I understood it tolerably, but that I spoke it but indifferently. "I thought so," was her reply; "I knew by that young fellow's appearance he was a booby (*sot*)," said she, addressing one of her friends. This she spoke in the very worst French that ever came from the mouth of a Bastan peasant. I was determined to have my revenge. I mustered up all my resolution, made a rapid *repasser* of all I had ever learned of French grammar, and took the first opportunity that presented itself to attack her. In a word, I completely out-talked her, out-spoke her, and out-crowed her in the estimation of her friends; and she who had been so short a time before the "leader of the opposition," was mum for the remainder of the evening.

Harmony was once more restored, and we were beginning o forget the bickerings that party feeling had introduced

amongst us, when a violent knocking at the door from the
street threw the company into consternation and dismay.
Every one looked confounded; some were for barring the
door, others wished to escape; but this was easier said than
done, for in front stood the police agents (for it was them
and none other), and in the rear—if rear it could be called
—was nothing but a pile of buildings, to the full as lofty
as the house we inhabited. "What is to be done?" was a
demand much easier made than answered; though in fact
the proper and only reply to be made was, "Open the door,
and see who the gentlemen are looking after." Several
persons, who had nothing to dread, loudly called out for
this proceeding, but it was far from palatable to the majority
of the company. It was idle, however, to talk, and, in fine,
the massive door was heard to creak on its rusty hinges. At
the same moment six ill-looking fellows entered the saloon,
and having taken a hasty but scrutinising survey of the
company, seized the son-in-law of my patron and rudely
carried him away.

Saturio de Padilla was the name of this gentleman, and
his only crime was that of holding the situation of Juiz de
Fora, under the government of King Joseph. Nothing
could be more unjust or impolitic than this arrest: it was,
however, idle to reason so with the police agents; Saturio
was taken off to the Fort of La China and thrown into a
dungeon, without bed or any other comfort which a gentleman of his rank might have expected. At an early hour
the following morning I was awoke by his father-in-law, the
venerable Don Miguel de Inza; he begged of me to allow
my servant to convey some bedding to him, which I not only
consented to do, but, at the entreaties of his daughter, Donna
Maria Ignatia de Inza (whose sister was married to Padilla,

and who, by the way, was one of the most beautiful women in Madrid), went to the prison myself. All entreaties to allow us to see the prisoner were in vain, and had it not been for the kindness of Colonel Manners of the 74th, who was the Governor of the Fort, we should not have been allowed to send even a change of linen to this gentleman.

A week passed away, and no tidings were heard of Padilla; and his friends, fearing that he might be made away with, became extremely uneasy. Without mentioning my intention, I waited upon Colonel Manners, who was much interested in his behalf when I told him the circumstances; and, owing to his intercession, I had the happiness of seeing my friend, Don Saturio, at liberty the day but one following. I need scarcely say that this exploit of mine, for so my Spanish friends termed it, raised me considerably in the estimation of the ladies, and all of them, my old formidable antagonist not excepted, were lavish in their praises of my conduct. Nothing but balls, concerts, and parties to the theatre and the Prado were thought of, until the announcement in the newspapers, and the never-ceasing cries of *affiche* venders in the streets, that the bull-fights were to take place, put a stop to all thoughts on any other but this, to a Spaniard at least, momentous affair.

This national amusement is of so old a standing, and has been so often related in novels and romances, that a description of it may, in the present day, be thought ill-timed. The day's fighting which I witnessed was considered specially good, and a tremendous day's sport it was. Nine bulls were killed, seven horses shared the same fate, and one of the fighters was dreadfully injured. More than twenty people were hurt by the last bull, who leaped the barriers and got among the audience, but fortunately, and indeed miracu-

lously, no person was killed. Thus the "casualties" of the
day may be summed up as follows :—Killed, nine bulls, seven
horses : total, sixteen ; wounded, twenty-three men and
women : grand total of killed and wounded, thirty-nine.

The bull-fights once over, the execution of the Priest
Lopez forgotten, and the probability of our soon leaving
Madrid taking place, were not things to be passed over
lightly by the ladies of that city ; and no matter what may
be said or written of their being "a grave people," I saw,
during my sojourn amongst them, no symptoms of "gravity,"
except when they thought we were about to leave their
capital. It was palpably evident that something should be
done to drive away the gloom that had in a great measure
already begun to take a fast hold of our friends ; and the
officers of the Light Division, aided by some of the other
regiments in the garrison, resolved to treat the inhabitants
with a specimen of their dramatic powers. The play selected
was the *Revenge,* and "Zanga" was well personated by
Captain Kent of the Rifles ; but whether it was that the
other characters were ill cast, or that the tragedy was too
dull for the Spaniards to relish, it is a positive fact that,
long before the second act was ended, the audience were
heartily tired of the play ; and, notwithstanding the fine
acting of Kent, the play would have never been allowed to
proceed had not the performers been British officers, and the
object the relief of the poor of the capital. The *Mayor of
Garrett* followed, and this amusing farce was a set-off against
the *Revenge,* and put the audience quite at ease ; for from
the moment "Zanga" (or *El Preto,* as they styled him)
appeared, there was one universal buzz of disapprobation.
It is not possible for me to say why they were so averse to
the play ; it might have been their dislike to the Moors ;

but be this as it may, I would advise my friends in the army never to try the same play before a Madrid audience—that is, which is a hundred to one, should they ever have the same opportunity we had. This was the first and last play ever attempted by us to be got up at Madrid.

The season was on the wane, summer was almost over, and it was well known that Lord Wellington meditated an attack on the town of Burgos; nevertheless all was tranquillity and gaiety with the troops at Madrid, and many of the sick and wounded from Salamanca reached us. Amongst the number was my friend and companion, Frederick Meade of the 88th. He had been badly wounded in the action of the 22nd, and with his arm in a sling, his wounds still unhealed, and his frame worn down by fatigue and exhaustion, his commanding officer was surprised to see him again so soon with his regiment; but various rumours were afloat as to the advance of the Madrid army upon Burgos, and Meade was not the kind of person likely to be absent from his corps when anything like active service was to be performed by it. Endowed with qualities which few young men in the army could boast of, he soon made his way into the very best society that the capital of Spain could be said to possess. A finished gentleman in the fullest acceptation of the word; young, handsome, speaking the Castilian language well, the French fluently, a first-rate musician, endowed by nature with a fine voice, which had been well cultivated, it is not surprising that he soon became a general favourite. In a word, wherever he went he was the magnet of attraction, and when we quitted Madrid it would have required a train of vehicles much more numerous than would have suited our order of march to convey those ladies who were, and would like to be more closely, attached to him.

Poor fellow! he was greatly to blame, but it was not his fault; if the ladies of Madrid liked his face, or his voice, how could he help that? My man, Dan Carsons—and here I must say a word of apology to my friend Meade for coupling their names together—told me when we were on the eve of quitting Madrid, "that he (Carsons) didn't know how the devil he could get away at-all-at-all, without taking three women, besides his wife Nelly with him."

So far all went on gaily at Madrid; but Lord Wellington was deeply occupied with matters of a different nature, although he joined in the amusements that took place. The capture of Burgos was what he aimed at, and his stay at Madrid was but a cloak to cover his real intentions. On the 1st of September he quitted the capital, and took upon himself the direction of that part of the army which he had decided was to march upon Burgos. He crossed the Douro on the 6th, and arrived at Valladolid on the same day, and from thence he followed the enemy on their retreat to Burgos. On the 16th he was, with a portion of his army, before that fortress, which he soon invested and laid siege to. The result of that siege, its failure, and the circumstances which led to it, have nothing to do with my adventures; they are the property of Colonel Napier—the only writer that, I believe, can be held up as a standard to refer to on the Peninsular War.

I have to bring forward to the public eye, and the eye of posterity, too, the character of the Peninsular soldiers, whether they be shown up as men who were able to conquer the choicest legions of France, or as men who would sell the most essential part of their dress for a glass of brandy. No matter; they would have done both. Perfection is nowhere to be found; and if the British soldier equalled the Frenchman in habits of sobriety and caution, there could be no possible comparison between them; but the retreat from Madrid and Burgos, which I am about to relate, will give the reader a clearer insight into what I have just now written : and I will here say, without the least fear of contradiction, that the French soldier as far surpasses the British soldier in the essential qualities requisite for general operations, as the latter excels the Frenchman in a pitched battle. Let two armies of the two nations be placed in circumstances the same, in advance or retreat. The supply of provisions may be scanty or abundant—no matter which; both armies, for argument sake, we will say, are placed in the same position as to food. It may be asked what, then, is the great difference between the soldiers of two nations who have been opposed to each other for so many campaigns, and who ought to have profited by the better system followed by either? It is this: the British soldier is not so moderate in his appetites as his neighbour, and he wants the head, which the other possesses, to control him. Give to a British regiment ten days', nay five days' bread at a time, and, as may be necessary, five days' rations of spirits; at the end of the second day—not the fifth, to which period it ought to last—what quantity will be forthcoming? Not one half ounce of bread, or half pint of spirits—half pint did I say! not one thimbleful, nay, less than that, not one drop! Should the ration be limited to bread, and in all armies, even the most temperate, a large advance of spirits ought to be avoided, the danger would be the same in any British army, because the soldiers would barter their bread for spirits or wine, and would become quite as inefficient, as if they had been supplied with both by our commissaries. Added to this, what means had the soldiers of the Peninsular

U

army to compete with the French in celerity of cooking?
None. The latter carried their cooking utensils on their
backs, while the camp-kettles for our troops were often
leagues distant when the meat arrived. This was the state
of our army when the retreat from Burgos on the one side,
and Madrid on the other, commenced, and it will be seen
in the following pages how that retreat was conducted, and
how the subordinate officers of the army were blamed for not
performing a duty which was impossible; and for this reason
was it impossible, that the means did not rest with them.
Our system was altogether faulty, and no exertions of the
junior, or even senior, officers could remedy it. Lord
Wellington at length discovered this, and in his next campaign profited by the example which the enemy showed him,
and which ought to have been followed long before.

On the 20th of October, 1812, the siege of Burgos was
raised, and the troops before it retired towards the Douro,
while the portion of the army which occupied Madrid made
arrangements to join them when the proper time should
arrive. Accordingly, the fort of La China was mined, the
battering train found there removed, and all the necessary
arrangements for retreat were completed. On the 31st of
October the army quitted Madrid, and bivouacked in the
Royal Park near the palace.

The conflagration of La China continued all night, and
story after story fell in until it became a heap of ruins. The
following day, the 1st of November, the advance of the French
entered Madrid, and on that day our army commenced its
retreat upon Rodrigo and Portugal. On the side of Burgos
matters were in the same state. The attack against the
citadel having failed, in default of means to carry it on,
the army before it broke up on the 20th of October, and by

the admirable arrangements of Lord Wellington, who took the command in person, gained two marches on the enemy before he was aware of it.   Nevertheless a vigorous pursuit took place, and the Burgos army was closely pressed, until it reached the heights of San Christoval, where it was joined by the troops that had occupied Madrid.

Up to this time no serious disaster had occurred, although from the heavy rains that had fallen, which rendered the roads nearly impassable, and the scanty supply of rations which the troops received, it was feared that, if Soult pressed on vigorously, our army would shortly become much dis-organised; but the Marshal took six days, that is to say, from the 10th to the 16th of November, to examine the ground occupied by the British General.   On the 14th, our army was in battle array close to the spot where we had fought the battle of Salamanca the July before, but Soult, although at the head of 90,000 soldiers, and two hundred pieces of cannon, declined the offer, and confined his opera-tions to the sending a brigade or two on the line of our communication with Rodrigo.   On the 17th, Lord Wellington commenced his march for the frontiers of Portugal, and from that moment he was closely pursued by Marshal Soult.   The rain fell in torrents, almost without any intermission; the roads could no longer be so called, they were perfect quag-mires; the small streams became rivers, and the rivers were scarcely fordable at any point.   In some instances the soldiers were obliged to carry their ammunition boxes strapped on their shoulders to preserve them, while passing a ford which on our advance was barely ankle deep.   The baggage and camp-kettles had left us; the former we never saw until we reached Rodrigo, and the latter rarely reached us until two o'clock in the morning, when the men, from fatigue, could make but little use of them. The wretched cattle had to be slaughtered, as our rations seldom arrived at their destination before the camp-kettles, and when both arrived, there was not one fire in our bivouac sufficient to boil a mess.

Officers as well as soldiers had no covering except the canopy of heaven; we had not one tent, and the army never slept in a village. We thus lay in the open country; our clothes saturated with rain, half the men and officers without shoes, nothing to eat, or, at all events, no means of cooking it. What then could be much worse than the situation in which the army was placed? But this was not the worst, because, from the nature of the retreat, and the pursuit, neither the cavalry nor artillery horses could be supplied with forage. The retreat each day generally began at four in the morning, in the dead dark of night; towards eight the army had gained perhaps six miles', perhaps not five, start of the enemy. At ten they were at our heels. The rear, as a matter of necessity, for the preservation of the whole, was then obliged to face about and show a front, to enable the remainder to proceed on their retreat. The position taken up was, as a matter of course, according to the urgency of the moment, sometimes in a vast tract of ploughed land, where the troops were drawn up ankle deep in mud. In this position, those who were not fighting were obliged to remain, in their tattered uniforms, worn to rags after two years' service, scarcely a good pair of shoes or trousers on any, and the greater part without the former. The ague had also attacked the bulk of the army, and as the soldiers picked up the acorns that fell from the oak trees (these, by the way, are the property of the pigs in Spain, but the pigs, fortunately for themselves, had not yet appeared in the woods we now traversed), many were unable to eat them, so much were they enfeebled by the disorder.

Yet under all these privations, the soldiers, at least the "Connaught Rangers," never lost their gaiety. Without shoes they fancied themselves "at home," and there were few, I believe, who would not have wished themselves there in reality. Without food they were nearly at home, and without a good coat to their backs equally so! My man, Dan Carsons, came up to me, and with a broad grin said, "By gor, Sir, this same place" (at the time we were, and had been for hours before, standing in a wet ploughed field) "puts me greatly in mind *iv* Madrid."—"Of Madrid! why, Dan, no two places can be more unlike."—"By Jasus, Sir, the're as like as two *paise*, only that we want the houses, and the fires, and the mate, and the dhrink, and the women! But, excepting that, don't the jaws *iv* the boys with the ague, when they rattle so, put your honour greatly in mind *iv* the castonetts?" Dan's joke was not quite so palatable as it might have proved at a more fitting opportunity, or in a more fitting place, for at that moment I felt a queer sort of motion about my own jaws, which in less than an hour proved itself to be a confirmed attack of ague. On this night the rain never ceased ; the rations could not be cooked, having arrived too late, and the army had no food except biscuit.

What I have related took place on the 16th. The following day matters became worse, the rain continued to come down in torrents, and in the passage of one river, out of ten that we forded, a woman and three children were lost, as likewise some baggage mules, which the women of the army, in defiance of the order against it, still contrived to smuggle into the line of retreat. The rations arrived alive (I mean the meat), as usual after midnight, but no kettles reached us for an hour after the poor famished brutes had been knocked on the head. Each man obtained his portion of the quivering flesh, but before any fires could be re-lighted, the order for march arrived, and the men received their meat dripping with water, but little, if anything, warmer than when it was delivered over to them by the butcher. The soldiers drenched with wet, greatly fatigued, nearly naked, and more than half asleep, were obliged either to throw away the meat, or put it with their biscuit into their haversacks, which from constant use, without any means of cleaning them, more resembled a beggarman's wallet than any part of the appointments of a soldier. In a short time the wet meat completely destroyed the bread, which became perfect paste, and the blood which oozed from the undressed beef, little better than carrion, gave so bad a taste to the bread that many could not eat it. Those who did were in general attacked with violent pains in their bowels, and the want of salt brought on dysentery. A number of cavalry and artillery horses died on this night, and fatigue and sickness had already obliged several men and officers to remain behind, so that our ranks were now beginning to show that we had commenced, in downright earnest, a most calamitous retreat.

Lord Wellington wished for a battle, if he could fight one on advantageous terms, before his army became dis-organised; but this was not to the interest of the French army; and the Duke of Dalmatia, who could at any time make choice of his own field from his vast superiority in horsemen, was too experienced a tactician to be led into so fatal an error as that of fighting. Experience had shown him that a retreat, such as the one I am describing, would cost him little trouble to inflict as great a loss upon our army as if he gained the advantage in a battle, and that it would be a bloodless victory to him; whereas, if a general action took place, and the entire of the two armies were thrown into the fight, he could not expect to get off with a loss of less than six or eight thousand men, with the chance, perhaps the probability, of being defeated.

No Marshal in the French army knew the good and the bad qualities of the soldiers he now followed better, few so well, as Soult. He had pursued them to Corunna, and fought them at Albuera. Knowing then, as he did, their imperfection in retreat, and their superlative perfection in a pitched battle, it would have been strange had he risked by a battle, what it was as clear as the noon-day he would gain without one, namely, the loss to us of several thousand men and horses, who, if they did not fall into his hands, or die on the retreat, were sure to be lost to our ranks in consequence of its effects. The game was in his hands, and if he lost it by bad play, the fault would be his, and his only. He did not do so, but played a safe game, and when battle was offered him near Salamanca, he *reneged*. He finessed well, and though he did not drive us before him at the point of the bayonet, his flank movement on the Rodrigo line, by a side wipe, effected his purpose just as well for him.

A circumstance occurred on this day that so strongly marks the difference between the British soldiers and the soldiers of any other nation on such a retreat as we were engaged in, that I cannot avoid noticing it. I have already said that we had no means of cooking our meat, and that the soldiers and officers, for all shared the same privations alike, carried their meat raw, or nearly raw; consequently it was not an additional supply of "raw material" that we so much needed as the means of dressing what we had. Never-

theless, towards noon, while a portion of the army was
engaged in a warm skirmish with the enemy's advance, which
lay through a vast forest of oak, some hundreds of swine,
nearly in a wild state, were discovered feeding upon the
acorns which had fallen from the trees the autumn before.
No flag of truce ever sent from the advance post of one army
to the advance of another had a more decisive effect. Our
soldiers immediately opened a murderous fire upon the pigs,
who suffered severely on the occasion, being closely pursued
on the route, which they followed with that stupid—and for
them, on this occasion, fatal—pertinacity which the pig tribe
are so proverbial for, namely, going to the rear when they
ought to go straight forward. Had this herd of swine
deviated from the old beaten track of pigs in general—had
they, in short, gone forward instead of rearward—many
valuable lives, in the eyes of the owners at least, would have
been saved, because they would have soon reached the French
advance, and our fellows, once more placed *vis à vis* with the
riflemen of the *grande nation,* would have left off the pursuit
—if for nothing else *but to save their bacon!* This *rencontre,*
one of the most curious that came within my knowledge
during my Peninsular campaigns, or indeed during my
sojourn in this world, led to consequences the most comic as
well as tragic. Colonel O'Shea, who commanded the cavalry
of the French advance ordered to support the *tirailleurs,* was
astounded when he saw the direction which the British fire
took. He could not be mistaken; the fire of the advance
of his own soldiers had slackened—ceased. It immediately
occurred to him that some corps must have got in rear of
our advance, and he galloped up to the *tirailleurs* to ascertain
the real state of affairs. He was soon undeceived; but when
he learned the cause of the retrograde movement on the part

of our men, he could not avoid—and who could ?—laughing heartily.

Meanwhile the discomfited and routed pigs fled, and soon got out of the clutches of the advanced guard. The bulk of the fugitives took the road to their *right*, but here they were again *wrong*. Had those ill-fated animals known anything of the "rules of the road," they would have kept to the *left*. On the right they were encountered by a nearly famished brigade that had received no rations at all in the preceding twenty-four hours; and when they were, as has been seen, so roughly handled by men whose haversacks were amply stocked with meat, what chance had they—I ask the question fearlessly—of any mercy from a body of famished, ferocious fellows ? The question I have just put is easily answered. They had none to expect, and none did they receive. Neither age nor sex was spared; and out of this fine herd of swine, scarcely one in one hundred escaped unhurt. No victory was ever more complete; and the grunting and squeaking of the wounded pigs and hogs throughout the forest was a sad contrast with the merriment of the soldiers, who toasted, on the points of their bayonets—intended for other and more noble game—the mangled fragments of their former companions.

Day was drawing to its close, and the 3rd Division, commanded by Sir Edward Pakenham, was about to retire from the ground it had held during several hours in face of the enemy, when a warm fire of musketry on our left led us to suppose we were outflanked. The officers of the staff galloped in the direction from whence the firing proceeded. Sir Edward did the same, but it was some time before they reached the scene of action. In the meantime the different regiments were so arranged as to be ready either to advance or retreat, as circumstances might require; and the French corps in our front made demonstrations of a similar kind. In this state of suspense we remained for nearly an hour, when at last Sir Edward returned, with the news that the firing was caused by a fresh attack on the pigs that had escaped the first brunt of the attack against them. He ordered the different advance posts to be placed, which he superintended in person; the soldiers then prepared to fell timber for fires, and some ran to an uninhabited village—they were all uninhabited on the line of our march for that matter—for the purpose of getting dry wood, that is to say, the doors and roofs of the houses, to enable us to light up the green timber, which was the only fuel we could command. The soldiers and officers of all ranks were nearly exhausted from cold and wet; and had the village in question belonged to the king of England, much less to a parcel of Spanish peasants, it would have shared the same fate as the one in question.

The party from the village soon arrived, some bringing doors, others articles of different kinds of household furniture, such as chairs, tables, and bedsteads; but nothing in the shape of food was to be found. No doubt, had it been day, something might be got at, but warmth was what we stood in need of more than food. Several of us still carried the parboiled beef of the night before, and, when the fires were lighted, we made a shift to roast it either on our swords, bayonets, or bits of sticks, which we formed into respectable skewers. This operation finished, the fire around which each group sat or stood, in order of companies, their arms regularly piled behind them, was replenished with green and dry timber, according to our supply of each or both. The soldiers then placed their knapsacks round the outer part of the circle, and, having given the best place to their officers inside the circle, all lay down together, or at their own choice, with their feet towards the heat of the fire. Some arranged in this manner, others did not lie down at all; and those who had captured a door, propped it up as a defence against the rains and winds. There were others who got a blanket and fixed it with branches of trees and stones against some uneven spot, and lay down in the mud. It was, in fact, all mud and wet; and in whatever manner we accommodated ourselves, according to circumstances, whether walking, standing, or sleeping, it was of little difference. No matter what *mood* any of us might have been disposed to follow, the *imperative* had the call; and, as has been seen, we could not *decline* it. *Verbum sat sapienti.*

Thus ended the operations of this day; officers and soldiers were placed exactly, or nearly, as I have described. Many were so feeble as not to be capable of the least exertion; others, on the contrary, were hale and stout, and I myself was amongst the number of the latter. I had lain some time with my feet near the fire, but I dreaded an attack of ague, and I walked about to keep my body warm, which was but thinly clad. I had not been long on my legs, and I was at the moment standing near the small tent where Sir Edward Pakenham lay in his wet clothes, when a rush of pigs—the remnant, I suppose, of those that had escaped in the day— disorganised several piles of arms. The soldiers stood up, and every man seized his firelock. A Portuguese regiment near us, thinking the enemy were at their heels, began to fire right and left, without knowing what they fired at. Sir Edward Pakenham ran out of his tent, and while in the act of mounting his horse and giving directions to his orderly dragoon, the man was shot dead by the side of the General.

It required some time before the confusion that prevailed could be remedied; but the soldiers never for a moment lost their presence of mind, and the 3rd Division was formed with astonishing celerity in battle array. The error into which the Portuguese had fallen was with some difficulty remedied, and, except a few men who were wounded, nothing serious happened. The pigs, who were the cause of all, escaped without any loss, but whether they ever found their way back to their original owners I know not. Trifling as the affair was, with troops less accustomed and less ready to face an enemy than those that composed the 3rd Division, it might have had a different result.

The march was continued the following morning. The troops commenced the retreat some hours before day. Towards ten o'clock the enemy's advance were at the heels of the rear-guard, which, as before, disputed the ground. A rapid stream on the Rodrigo side of the village of San Munoz was to be passed before the rear could be considered safe. Many regiments had already forded the river, but one entire brigade was missing, and the haze was so great that it was difficult to distinguish any object clearly.

Pakenham's division was already on the left bank of the stream, while the brigade of nine-pounders, commanded by that admirable officer, Captain Douglas, opened its fire on the French advance. This, for a moment, arrested their progress; but O'Shea, at the head of fifteen hundred dragoons, passed between the French infantry and the river, and, disregarding the fire of our artillery, overtook the brigade before it had passed the ford. The confusion at this point was great; some men were sabred; but the fire of Douglas's guns caused the French dragoons many casualties, and they galloped back to their former ground. The safety of the brigade which was missing was thus ensured; but Sir Edward Paget, who had gone in quest of it, and who knew nothing of what had taken place at the river's edge, was taken prisoner by O'Shea. We thus lost our second in command, as also many men; and the cavalry and artillery horses had become so enfeebled for want of forage, that it was manifest our retreat, if vigorously followed by Soult, would, as a matter of necessity, have been protected by the infantry alone; but Soult either could not or would not press us, and the remainder of the day passed over languidly.

CHAPTER XXIV

Sufferings of the army on the retreat—Jokes of the Connaught
Rangers—Letter of Lord Wellington—The junior officers—
Costume of the author during the retreat—An unusual enjoy-
ment.

NOTWITHSTANDING the attitude of Pakenham's troops, and
the excellent arrangement of the park of artillery under
Douglas, the troopers of O'Shea still menaced the ford. A
brigade of French guns ascended the heights, and opened
their fire upon the 3rd Division, but they were replied to
with vigour by Douglas, who on this day surpassed himself;
and the decided superiority which his fire had over that of
the enemy was so palpable that, after a short trial, the
French left the heights. Day was drawing to its close, and
our march, as usual, commenced soon after dark. The entire
day had been one of drizzling wet, but, towards evening, the
rain came down in torrents; the army had to march two
leagues ere they reached the point marked out for them on
the line of retreat, and it would be difficult to describe the
wretched state of the troops. The cavalry half dismounted;
the artillery without the requisite number of horses to draw
the ammunition-cars, much less the guns; the infantry without shoes, or nearly so; and the roads, even in the broad
day, nearly impassable, made the march of this night one of

great loss. When a halt occurred, which was often unavoidable in consequence of the guide mistaking the way, or
because of the narrowness of a part of the road, or the difficulty of ascertaining the pass of a river, those in the rear
fell down asleep, and it was next to impossible to awaken
them, so much were they exhausted; it then became incum-
bent on every man who was awake to rouse those in his
front, who impeded the line of march, not only of the individual himself, but of the army in general. Nevertheless,
many were obliged to stay behind, and were abandoned to
their fate. None but the stout and hale could bear up
against the inclemency of the weather and the want of food;
but the worst of all was the wretched state of the horses of
the cavalry and artillery. These poor animals, when they
reached the place marked out for our resting for the night,
had not one morsel to eat, for it was absolutely impossible
to forage for them at such an hour and under such circumstances, and the consequence was that many died from cold
and famine, either in the harness of the artillery or under
the saddles of the dragoons.

It was nine o'clock this night of the retreat before we
reached the ground where we were to rest, and we had scarcely
lit our fires when the bullocks and kettles arrived. This circumstance—a rare one—put us in good spirits, and by the time we
had eaten our first meal that day we became more gay, and the
" boys " of the 88th had their joke about the slaughter of the
pigs by the 4th Division, of which I have made some slight
mention in the last chapter. That I might have said more on
the subject I am aware, for it was a subject that much might
be said upon; but, had I done so, my readers, perhaps,
would consider me a *bore*. However, the Connaught Rangers
would have, and had, their joke at the expense of the

defunct pigs. Jack Richardson, of the light infantry company, said, "The poor craturs must be blind intirely when they run into the mouth of the 4th Division."—"No," replied my man, Dan Carsons, "they wern't blind all out, but perhaps they had a *stye in their eye*!" This sally of Dan was loudly applauded; and this kind of gaiety of spirit never forsook the men of the 88th under any circumstances. It was well for themselves, and for the service also; for I believe no regiment in the Peninsula had more uphill work to contend against than the ill-fated 88th. No matter!—all that is past and gone now; and those who survive, and recollect the events that took place during their stay in the 3rd Division, are now changing positions; they had uphill work *then*—*now* they are going down the hill. It is, nevertheless, a galling reflection to those who bravely earned notice and promotion, to find themselves passed over, while others, of regiments in the same division, and under the same General, and placed in circumstances the same, and sometimes less hazardous, have been lauded and promoted, when we of the 88th were not even noticed!

But I am digressing. After Carsons' pun we soon fell asleep, and were again on our legs at four in the morning; but our appearance was greatly changed for the worse: several soldiers had died during the night from exhaustion and cold, and those who had shoes on them were soon stripped of so essential a necessary; and many a young fellow was too happy to be allowed to stand in a "dead man's shoes." Others were so crippled as to be scarcely able to stand to their arms. Ague and dysentery had, more or less, affected us all; and the men's feet were so swollen that they threw away their shoes in preference to wearing them.

Scarcely any provisions were to be found, but an abundance of wine could have been easily procured from the different wine-caves in each village. The troops, once let loose in this kind of way, could not be restrained, and all discipline would have been at an end; therefore, no one ought to be surprised that Lord Wellington forbade the occupation of a town. He did his part in the grand scale, but those who acted under him were deficient in every way. Sometimes the troops were bivouacked in a muddy swamp, when dry ground, in comparison at least, was nigh. The consequence of all this bungling was fatal: the troops became ill and inefficient; they became discontented; and, to wind up all, the junior officers of the army were blamed for those things over which they had as much control as they had over the actions of the Dey of Algiers or the Great Mogul. The officers divided the misery of the retreat with their men, and it is well known that many of them had scarcely a covering to their backs. Scarcely a subaltern in the army had a dollar in his pocket, the troops being four months in arrear of pay; but, even supposing he had money in abundance, what use could he make of it? There was nothing to be had for love or money—we had no money, and few of us were inclined to make love; but even if we were, there was no one (the worst of it) to make love to.

Such was the end of a campaign, the commencement of which augured the most fortunate results. The men who composed this fine army—which, at Rodrigo, Badajoz, and Salamanca, carried all before them—were now greatly changed for the worse. Scarcely a man had shoes; not that they were not amply supplied with them before the retreat commenced, but the state of the roads, if roads they could be called, was such, that so soon as a shoe fell off or stuck in the mud, in place of picking it up again, the man

x

who had thus lost one kicked its fellow-companion after it. Yet the infantry was efficient, and able to do any duty. No excesses were committed, for Lord Wellington having taken the precaution of keeping the army away from the different villages, no man had an opportunity of obtaining wine or spirits, and thus drunkenness and insubordination were not added to the list of our misfortunes.

But the cavalry and artillery were in a wretched state indeed. The artillery of the 3rd, 6th, and 7th Divisions, the heavy cavalry, together with the 7th and 12th Light Dragoons, were nearly a wreck; and the artillery of the 3rd Division lost seventy horses between Salamanca and Rodrigo. It was next to impossible that the artillery and cavalry could have made, if vigorously pursued, three marches beyond the latter place. What force, then, was to arrest the enemy in his pursuit?—The infantry, and the infantry alone; yet this main-prop of the army was, by mismanagement, left without the means of nourishment! Had not the infantry, by their firmness in bearing up against all the evils they had to surmount—such as bad clothing, no tents to shelter them from the heavy rains that fell, and no means of dressing their food—presented the front they did, the army must have been lost before it could have reached Gallegos; and, if equal zeal had been exhibited by the general officers in providing for the wants of their troops, as was shown by the subordinate officers in the maintenance of discipline amongst them, the well-known letter of Lord Wellington would never have been written.[1]

[1] Almost every officer of the Peninsular army who has written on the Burgos retreat, from William Napier downward, joins in the protest against Wellington's objurgatory general order against his regimental officers, published at the end of this retreat. Grattan's murmurs are but a sample of the rest.

The officers asked each other, and asked themselves, how or in what manner they were to blame for the privations the army endured on the retreat? The answer uniformly was— in no way whatever. The junior officers had nothing to do with it at all. Their business was to keep their men together, and, if possible, to keep up with their men on the march, and this was the most difficult duty they had to perform; for many, very many, of these officers were young lads, badly clothed, with scarcely a shoe or boot to their feet —some attacked with dysentery, others with ague, and more with a burning fever raging through their system, they had scarcely strength left to hobble on in company with their more hardy comrades, the soldiers. Nothing but a high sense of honour could have borne them on; and there were many who would have remained behind, and run all risks as to the manner in which they would be treated as prisoners, were it not for this feeling. The different bivouacs each morning presented a sad spectacle—worn-out veterans, or young lads unable to move, were abandoned to their fate. Some were thrown across the backs of the commissariat mules, and conveyed to the rear; but this was rare, for the drivers were obliged to make all haste to reach their destination, and the frames of the men, worn down by sickness, unhealed wounds, or old ones breaking out afresh, were unable to bear the jolting of the mules, and these men generally preferred taking their chance on the line of march to submitting to such an uneasy mode of conveyance.

Thus ended the year 1812, and thus ended our retreat upon Portugal. The details I have given of that retreat have not been the least exaggerated. It had, nevertheless, but little effect on my regiment, the 88th, for we scarcely lost a man by fatigue or sickness. The "boys of Connaught"

were not much put out of their way by the want of shoes, a
good coat to their backs, or a full allowance of rations: they
took all those wants *aisy!* In short, it was astonishing to
see the effective state of the regiment, as compared with
others, when we reached our cantonments.

Since I commenced these pages, I have endeavoured to
impress my readers with the idea—and I hope I have succeeded—that the 88th were none of those humdrum set of
fellows that ought to be classed with other regiments; they,
in fact, had a way of their own! There are many who will
agree—cordially on this point, at least—with me; but their
reading and mine of the text may be widely different,
nevertheless.

The 88th was a regiment whose spirit it was scarcely
possible to break, and the many curious incidents which
occurred during this retreat afforded them ample food for
that ready humour for which they were proverbial, and for
which they got *full credit;* but, nevertheless, they still are *in
arrear*, and they owe a debt to themselves which they must
pay off—no matter what the price may be. It was well for
them that they had food for their humour, for they had
little for their stomachs; but that did not cause them much
uneasiness. The state in which some of the officers were
placed was quite pitiable. Many were obliged to throw off
their boots, their feet having become so swollen that they
could not bear them. Those so circumstanced were necessitated to look to the soldiers for a new fit-out. But where
could that be found? The men themselves, not caring
much whether they had or had not shoes, left those they
had worn in the muddy roads, and it would not be an easy
matter to find on this same retreat a second pair with any
man. However, by hook or by crook, those who wanted

SERGEANT AND PRIVATE
IN WINTER MARCHING ORDER 1813.

London Raised Arnold 1913

shoes were supplied; yet, though the soldiers might be
termed the *shoemakers* of their officers, they never got the
upper hand of them!

To describe the state of the officers would be impossible;
for myself, I can truly say I was in rags. I wore a frock-
coat, made out of a dress belonging to a priest that was
captured by my man Dan Carsons at Badajoz. I wore it
during our sojourn at Madrid: it was lined with silk, and
might be termed a good turn-out there; but, as it turned
out on the retreat, it was the worst description of clothing
I, or rather my man Dan, could have pitched on. Every
copse I passed, and they were many, took a slice off my
Madrid frock, and by the time I had undergone three
marches, it was reduced to a spencer! My feet never quitted
the shoes in which they were placed, from the moment of the
retreat until its close. I knew too well their value, and if I
once got my feet out of them (no easy matter), I knew right
well it would take some days to get them back again, they
were so swollen; and even if I were dead, much less crippled,
there were many to be found anxious to stand in my shoes—
to boot!

There were others, and many others, as badly off as I was.
My friend Meade was obliged to leave his shoes behind him.
He tried to walk barefooted for a while, but it was impossible. The gravel so lacerated his feet that he could not
move, and he was obliged to make some shift to get a pair
in place of those he had abandoned. Captain Graham of the
21st Portuguese, a lieutenant in my regiment, was so worn
out with fatigue, barebacked and barefooted, that, on one
night of the retreat, having been fortunate enough to get a
loaf of bread, he joined me and my companion Meade; but,
so unable was he to eat of the food he brought to share with

us, that he fell down on the ground and never tasted a morsel of it.   It is, therefore, tolerably clear to any man possessing common understanding, that the junior officers of the army, from the neglect of their superiors, were not in a state to do more than they did.

The retreat still continued, but the army was unmolested, and at length, after an absence of so many days, we once more got sight of our baggage. The poor animals that carried it were in a bad state ; but they were even better than our cavalry or artillery horses. Of the former, three-fourths of the men were dismounted ; and the latter could, with difficulty, show three horses, in place of eight, to a gun.

On this night, I think it was the 26th of November (that is to say, four weeks, less by two days, since we left Madrid), I enjoyed what I never expected to see again—a hearty meal. A knot of us got together under a tent belonging to Captain Robert Nickle, whose batman was one of the first to arrive with his baggage, and he kept open house for as many as the tent could accommodate.   In the centre was placed a huge pannella of chocolate, which was garnished by a couple of large loaves of Spanish bread.   The contents of the pannella, as also the dimensions of the loaves, were soon altered in appearance, and so, indeed, were we.   Our stomachs, which before were as lank as half-starved greyhounds, now became plump and full, and, moreover, some fragments were left even after the servants were fed, and abundantly fed.

A dog belonging to Nickle, that had been absent with the baggage, and which had been on as short rations as his master, also got a bellyful, and soon after came into the tent, but his owner was so changed in appearance and dress that the dog did not at first recognise him—which proves the old adage to be correct that "a man is sometimes so changed that his own dog don't know him."

The army continued its retrograde movement unassailed, and by the 30th of November was established in its different stations; but here the real effects of the retreat began to be felt. The soldiers, while in action, or in a state of activity, had not time to get ill! So long as the mind and body are occupied, everything, in comparison, goes on well; but after a storm a calm succeeds, and that calm is sometimes as bad, and even worse, than the storm that has preceded it. So it was in the present instance. More than half the men were attacked with some complaint; but fever and dysentery, from overwork and bad treatment, were most prevalent, and the number of bayonets which we counted at the conclusion of the retreat was considerably diminished before we were settled in our winter quarters.

Many men, whose frames were as robust as their minds were ardent, began to sink under the accumulation of the miseries they had endured during the retreat. The continued and unsparing exposure of their bodies under such heavy rains as had fallen, and their being obliged to lie out, without any covering, for so many nights, during so inclement a season, now began to be felt, and made visible ravages amongst our ranks. The oldest and most hardy soldiers, as well as the youngest, sank alike under diseases, and it was heart-breaking to see our ranks thinned, not only of the hardy old stock, but of the promising young suckers also. But so it was! The men died by tens—twenties—thirties —and in the course of a short time every battalion was reduced to the half of its original strength. In less than a month the hospitals were overstocked, and many officers were taken ill. I, for once, was amongst the number on the sick-list. A bad ill-healed wound, which I received in the breast on the night of the storming of Badajoz, now began to revisit me. A high fever was the consequence, but I was at length relieved by the taking away of three pieces from one of my ribs. The reader is not to suppose from this confession that I was a married man at the time this operation was performed; but I had, nevertheless, a "rib," though not a wife; and as to the "pieces" which I lost, it would be but a useless task to look after them now.

The Sergeant-Major's wife, a fine, fat, well-looking woman, amongst many others, was taken ill, and visited with a bad fever. She was the sister of my man, Dan Carsons, and had kept close with the regiment from the time of its first landing in the Peninsula to the time I am now speaking of. She acted in many a useful capacity towards the officers. She supplied us with wine and bread, and every other comfort she could afford us, and was, in fact, a necessary appendage to the officers, for she was one of the best foragers I ever saw in the 88th regiment; and the army knows—the Peninsular army, I mean—that we had some good ones. But this poor woman lost two fine mules during our retrograde movement, as also the cargoes with which they were laden, amounting to a good round sum, which, at the lowest estimate, I must value to be worth three hundred dollars. This loss affected her. She had left no stone unturned to realise it, and this untoward event brought on a violent fit of illness. The fatigue she had undergone, no doubt, aided the cause of her disorder; but, be this as it may, she became quite delirious. While in her bed she could not be made to understand that the army was not in full retreat. "Where," she would exclaim, "are my mules?" My man, Dan, was in constant attendance upon his sister, and was, as a matter of course, continually intoxicated! If she got better, he would say that he took a little dhrop "more than usual " for joy; if she relapsed, he did the same "to dhrown grief." So that, between Dan's "joy" and Dan's "grief," to say nothing of my own helpless state, I was anything but well off.

At length the poor woman became quite insane, but she still looked up to Dan as her sheet-anchor; nevertheless, Dan always paid her that respect which he conceived due to the wife of the Sergeant-Major, and always called her Misthress O'Neil; she, on the contrary, forgetting the station she held, always called her brother "Dan." "Och, then," said she, "Dan, what do the Frinch mane at all—where do they mane to dhrive us to?—an't my mules gone, and our baggage gone, and still we're on the rethrate? Haven't they taken all from us, even our necessaries?—where do they mane to send us to?"—"By gob! Misthress O'Neil," replied Dan, with a broad grin, "I think they mane to *send us all to pot!*"

CHAPTER XXV

End of the Burgos retreat—Cantonments in Portugal—Rest at last—
Shocking effects of excess in eating—The neighbourhood of Moimento de Beira—Wolves—The author employed to cater for his
regiment on St. Patrick's day—Is attacked by wolves on his return
—Measure for measure.

DAN CARSONS' prognostication, which closed the last chapter,
was not fulfilled, although a retreat on Portugal was
necessary.

Once clear of the Spanish frontier we arrived, by easy
marches, at the different towns and villages appointed for
our occupation, while the French army retraced their steps,
and, it is to be presumed, followed the course we had taken,
though not exactly the same route.

The village of Leomil was the one allotted to the 88th,
and was also the headquarters of Sir John Keane (the
General of brigade) and his staff. This town, distant about
five leagues from the city of Lamego, and two from Moimento
de Beira, was by no means a bad resting-place for men who
had for so many days, and in such inclement weather, inhabited no town, or slept, if sleep it could be called, under
any covering except their tattered uniforms; but the tran-
sition was too sudden, and it is not difficult for the reader
to see what the consequence was. An abundant supply of
money, a great plenty of wine, meat, and poultry were things

not to be lightly treated by a parcel of men in a state of nakedness and starvation. In a word, all were bought up greedily, and as greedily devoured. But the frames of the soldiers had undergone a great change; their stomachs were much weakened by the bad diet they had heretofore tasted, and the disordered state of their bowels was such, that in five cases out of six the soldiers were attacked with some complaint or other. The officers suffered little, because they had a greater command over themselves; but I knew an instance of a man of the company I commanded (his name was Travers) eating, for one week, independent of his rations, the head of an ox daily!

Reader, do not laugh at this. It is a true but melancholy picture, not a laughable one, of what a half-starved man will do when opportunity favours. The result, as might have been foreseen, was fatal. A violent inflammation of the bowels took place, and the poor fellow died in the most excruciating agonies. No remedy of our doctors could relieve him; they did all they could, but in vain.

The country in the neighbourhood of Leomil, and between that town and Moimento de Beira, is in the highest degree grand; it moreover abounded in game, and officers who were fond of their gun, or of coursing, had ample opportunities of enjoying both. There was, however, one drawback, which was an unpleasant one, and that was the vast number of wolves that infested the mountains. These fierce animals were so terrific when pressed by hunger, that in one instance they seized the head of a sheep which was in a house, having made their way under the door. The owner, hearing the cries of the animal, rushed to its assistance, and, catching hold of the hind legs, dragged it back, but the head and a part of the neck were carried away by the wolves. Another

instance of their ferocity soon after occurred. A young.
child, who had wandered into the street of a small village
earlier than usual, was carried off and devoured by these
animals. But this in no way damped the ardour of our
sportsmen. With a double-barrelled gun on his shoulder no
one feared danger, though he might guard against it; and
I never knew an instance of any one being attacked by a
wolf, although we saw many in our sporting excursions.

Our cantonments by this time, the first week in February,
had undergone so great a change for the better, that they
might be really termed comfortable. From the time we
were first settled in our present quarters we established an
evening club, which was superintended by Misthress O'Neil,
who was by this time re-established in health. We wished
to have a regular mess, but that was not possible, as the
difficulty and expense of purchasing materials would have
been too great; so we were necessitated to content ourselves
with our evening club, which was a source of great amusement and conviviality. It brought us together each evening
after our requisite duties to the soldiers had been gone
through; and we had no sort of gambling: whist, our
favourite game, was always played at a low rate, and each
night was wound up by a supper of such materials as could
be procured. Our commanding officer, Major Macgregor,
gave up his best room for our use, and, all things considered,
our club was most comfortable, and tended to keep up that
feeling of harmony and action for which the "Connaught
Rangers" were so remarkable during the Peninsular War.
In 1809, after the battle of Talavera, the 88th, while
quartered at Campo Mayor, established a mess. This circumstance, trifling as it may appear, was nevertheless attended
with a good deal of trouble and a heavy expense. I do not

remember that any other regiment in the army did the same. In 1812, after the battle of Salamanca, the 88th established a splendid mess, for which the officers paid a high rate. During both these periods the 88th was commanded by Colonel Alexander Wallace, whose name I have repeatedly mentioned in these pages for his distinguished conduct. Now the object of all this must be clear to any military man : it had but one object, and one only—the keeping up a gentlemanly and social feeling amongst the corps; and when, as has been seen, such feelings did exist, will any man give credit to the calumnies that have been attempted to be fastened upon the "Connaught Rangers" by the biographer of the late Sir Thomas Picton ?

Sir John Keane was to dine with the regiment on St. Patrick's day. Even at this early period I was their caterer, although in a far different way from that in which I am now employed : then I catered for their stomachs—their *faim ;* now I cater for their honour—their *fame!* At an early hour on the 15th of March, mounted on a good mule, with fifty dollars in my pocket, I left my regiment on the route to the city of Vizeu, with a *carte blanche* to do the best I could in the purchase of provisions. I was followed by my man Dan, who had for his assistant, or coadjutor, as he styled him, my batman, Jack Green, as handy a "boy" as ever "listed" in the ranks of the "Connaught Rangers." The mule they took charge of was little inferior to the one I rode, but their pace was of necessity slower, as he was encumbered not only with a pair of panniers, destined to carry the prog for our St. Patrick's dinner, but also with the weight of Dan and Jack, who arranged themselves in the best manner they could astride his back. Vizeu is five leagues from Leomil, but, as I knew the country tolerably well, I struck out of the high road, and, crossing the mountains, reached the town some hours before my servants.

Vizeu is a good town, one of the best in Portugal, and the shops are abundantly supplied with such commodities as would suit the taste of a general buyer. Brazil sugar, nearly as white as snow, green tea at a cheap price, cloths of every description, and a rich assortment of Braganza shawls, so much prized in England, were severally named to us as we passed the different shops; but Dan, who was, or at least made himself, spokesman on the occasion, shrugged up his shoulders and replied to each, " No, señor, me no care the chocolate, nor the suggera, nor the shawla; me care the peché."

We soon reached the market-place. There I found an abundance of what I most wished for—fish. I purchased a number of fine mullet, some hens and fowls, and a variety of other matters which I thought requisite to garnish our table the following day, and I despatched my two trusty servants on their route some hours before I departed myself.

Being mounted on a superb mule I did not mind much what road I took, but struck across the mountains above Leomil, bordering on Moimento de Beira. Before I reached the passes I so well knew it became dark, and I lost my way. On reaching a small village I was informed by the peasants that I was still two leagues from Leomil, had a bad and difficult country to traverse before I could reach the road, and that the mountains were infested with wolves. I was aware that the latter part of their report was but too true; and when they told me the name of their village, near which I had shot before, I was convinced that my knowledge of the country by night was not quite as perfect as in broad day. The peasants endeavoured to make me remain where

I was for the night; but notwithstanding their offers of hospitality, I preferred taking my chance with the wolves to the certainty of being half devoured by fleas, a commodity with which, I well knew, their houses were amply stocked. I therefore determined to proceed, as I was anxious to reach home; and I had no great fear of an attack, as I was well mounted, with a case of pistols in my holsters, and my sabre at my side. I left the reins loose on the neck of my mule, who, with wonderful sagacity, made her way through the different passes. We had nearly reached the high road without meeting any obstacle, save the different glens we were obliged to pass, when all of a sudden the mule became alarmed, and bounding to the right and left, made it difficult for me to keep my saddle. The distant cry of wolves soon, however, explained the cause of her uneasiness; and although I pressed on at as rapid a pace as the nature of the country would admit of, I found that the pack were palpably gaining on me.

I was within a few yards of the high road when three ringleaders of the pack came close to me. Two of them attacked my mule behind, while the other made a spring at her throat, and the remainder were coming rapidly into the field of battle, for so in fact it was. I discharged one of my pistols at the foremost, but whether I wounded him or no I cannot say; for, to speak candidly, I looked with more anxiety to secure a safe retreat than the honour of a splendid victory; and I can affirm, without the slightest qualm of conscience, that mine on this night was never surpassed—in rapidity, at least—in either ancient or modern times. Moreau was celebrated for his retreat through the Black Forest— Wellington for his to the lines of Torres Vedras—but what was the disparity of numbers in either case to what I had to contend against? Neither of those great men had more than three to one opposed to him, while I had—if I may judge from the howling of the reserve, and the daring of the advance—fifteen to two! for my mule must have *her* share in the exploit, because had it not been for her I firmly believe I should have never had an opportunity of relating what took place on the night I speak of. In a word, never was mortal man nearer being devoured.

The rest of the story is easily told. At length I reached the high road leading to Leomil. I gave my mule a touch of the rowels of my spurs, which might have been dispensed with, for she, poor thing, was to the full as anxious as myself to quicken our pace. In less than half an hour I reached the headquarters of the "Connaught Rangers," and no man, I will venture to say, ever rejoined his corps with greater pleasure than I did mine on that occasion.

The hour for dinner at length arrived, and the dinner was a good one; and I say it was such, although I was the person who provided it. The fish was excellent, the fowl of the best quality, and to any one who has ever had the good fortune to taste a Lamego ham, it would be but superfluous to descant on the merits of so delicious a morsel. For the beef and mutton I can't say much, but the wine was of the best quality. I had taken particular care on this essential point, and went to a convent where my friend Graham, with his Portuguese regiment, were quartered, and, through his interest, prevailed on the priests to send us some of their own best. In saying this I need not say more in praise of the wine, as it is well known those gentlemen never kept, for their own use, one drop of any wine that was not of the best quality.

The dinner went off well, the attendance was good, and

we were all as happy as any corps could wish to be; but our doctor, O'Reily, being a little "Bacchi plenus," mistook the veranda for the door, walked out of it and fell, uninjured, about fifteen feet! The spot in which he happened to fall, fortunately, was a soft one, and he himself, being a little moist, escaped as by a miracle, without any mishap. Next morning I examined the spot, and was struck with astonishment at the exactness of the impression his features had left. Had he sat to have his likeness taken, and undergone the troublesome process of having his face daubed over with paste, it could not have been more perfect, and thus in a second of time, without any trouble to himself, he performed what would have cost him a full half-hour at least, with a great deal of annoyance into the bargain, had he regularly allowed a sculptor to take his bust. He had no doubt taken his wine without measure, and it is clear that the wine, or the effects of it, had taken his "measure," and made him "measure" his length on the heap of mud upon which he fortunately fell, and it was in this instance "measure for measure."

Major Macgregor, who commanded the 88th up to this period, now left us on leave, and was succeeded in the command by one of the most gentlemanlike officers and best soldiers in the British army—Captain Robert Nickle. Sir John Keane, as I have before said, commanded the brigade, Sir Edward Pakenham the division; and from the period of our arriving at our quarters at Leomil, until our leaving it on our advance towards Vittoria, we had not one single syllable of annoyance with either our Brigadier or Major-General, nor do I believe we had as much as one court-martial in the battalion—and this embraced a period of more than six months.

Y

CHAPTER XXVI

Ordered home—Priests carousing—San Carlos gambling-house at Lisbon—Cocking the card—The author quits the Peninsula—Adventures on the road—The author's return to Ireland.

To those who have never seen service, or been present with the Peninsular army for a series of years, it would be rather a difficult task to make them comprehend the feelings of an officer upon active service, when ordered home. There are many, no doubt, who would say it was a lucky "turn up"; but there are many, I know, who would have a contrary opinion. Years of hard fighting, fatigues, and privations, that we now wonder at, had, nevertheless, a charm that, in one way or another, bound us together, though it severed some; and, all things considered, I am of opinion that our days in the Peninsula were amongst the happiest of our lives.

It was with feelings of regret that I was now on the eve of quitting the first battalion of the Connaught Rangers, but, before doing so, I resolved to spend a few days with my old friend and companion, Captain Graham. He was attached to the 21st Portuguese Regiment, quartered in a large convent half-way between Leomil and Lamosa; and here, for the first time, I had a full specimen of the manners and habits of the priesthood of Portugal. I had, it is true, met them occasionally before, and always found them pleasant, agreeable companions; but I had little idea of the depraved state they lived in until I became, in a manner, an inmate of the convent where my friend was quartered.

Dinner was about to be announced when some five or six priests entered, each carrying under his arm a small pig-skin of wine. They were all merry, gay lads, and looked as if they had—which I have no doubt of—tasted the contents of their *fardeau.* All were agreeable men; they talked upon all subjects; but the fair sex "had the call." My friend asked where the others were who had promised to come. He was told they were on duty; but what that "duty" was, I could not exactly define. Be this as it may, dinner was scarcely over when three monks entered the apartment. One, who seemed to be the provider, was loaded with an enormous pig-skin of wine, which he carried on his back; and, so soon as the door was flung open, he, with some difficulty, placed it in a corner, and then, with his two companions, joined our festive board.

Now, at the time I am speaking of, I was a very young lad. I had, nevertheless, seen something of the world; I had mixed in society, high and low; I had read books— some of them moral, some the contrary; but in all that I had ever seen, read, or heard of, I never could suppose that, amongst any set of men—much less priests—so great a scene of blackguardism could be amalgamated together as I witnessed on this night. Their songs and talk were as indecent as can be imagined. The fellows were so pleasant that, if you could forget they were priests, it would have been well enough; but it is disgraceful to see men in this calling adopt the manners and habits of the most profligate, by which means they not only disgrace themselves, but the religion they profess.

I took leave of my old regiment, and, with two hundred and sixty-five dollars in my pocket, bent my way towards Lisbon. My old friend D'Arcy accompanied me, and my man, Dan Carsons, took charge of our baggage-mule, which carried our kits. This, indeed, was a sort of sinecure to him; for, to say the truth, we were not overstocked with many extras. Little occurred worthy of notice until we reached Lisbon, and there we met with our companion, Simon Fairfield, so well known to the army.[1] Maurice Quill was also there, and as they were both, like ourselves, waiting for a passage home by the first fleet that was to leave the Tagus for England, we thought we could not do better than "club" together.

It was a rare circumstance to meet two such characters, and our time passed away agreeably in learning those anecdotes which have been told of both. Much has been related of Quill, but Fairfield was immeasurably his superior on some points. In the first place, he sang beautifully, while Maurice could not sing at all; and if Quill possessed that extraordinary humour, which it is so well known he did, poor Simon Fairfield was an overmatch for him as a punster.

Our stay in Lisbon was but short, as, in a few days after our arrival, the fleet was in readiness to sail for Portsmouth. But, short as our sojourn was, it was of sufficient length to nearly empty our purses. That sink of profligacy and nest of sharpers, the San Carlos gambling-house, was the constant resort of all the idlers in Lisbon; and, in a few days, I and

---

[1] Fairfield was better known in the army by his Christian name, and was almost invariably called "Sim," or, as Joe Kelly called him, "Simmy." He ended very badly, in abject misery caused by his own vices and thriftlessness, without a coat to his back or a roof to his head.

my friends were completely eased of all our loose cash. But we had one resource left, in the shape of a horse each, which was the same thing as ready money, and we determined to try our luck once more at the gambling table. Accordingly, the horses were sent to the fair, were sold, and brought a "fair" price. Mine fetched one hundred and twenty-five dollars. Those belonging to Hill, D'Arcy, and Adair, all of my corps, were also disposed of at a "fair" value. Poor "*Fair*"field had no horse or mule. He had an old jackass —his companion for years—which brought to the general fund only fifteen dollars. A sort of council of war was now held as to the line of operations we should follow, and it was unanimously agreed that D'Arcy, being a good judge of the game, should be the purse-bearer, and play according to his own judgment to any amount he might think proper, for the profit or loss of the entire party.

Matters were so far arranged, and we were ready and panting with anxiety to have another trial with the bankers of the San Carlos tables, when Hill, a young man of sound sense, hinted that, to prevent any mistake, and not to leave all on the "hazard of the die," we should deposit a certain number of dollars each for the purchase of our sea-stock. This hint was so replete with *rationality* that we all acquiesced, and fifteen dollars "*par tête*" was regularly pouched by Hill, who was understood to be our caterer. He laid in a capital stock of wine, brandy, fowls, and meat—and, so far, all went on right. The wine and brandy he purchased from the far-famed Signor Cavizoli; but, if he paid high for them, they were of excellent quality.

Meanwhile D'Arcy, who conducted his department in the capacity of Chancellor of the Exchequer, was regular in his attendance at the gaming-table. He marked with much circumspection the gains and losses of the numbers on his cards, for and against the banker; but his caution was of no avail. In the first night's play one hundred dollars had been scooped from him by the Portuguese banker, leaving a surplus of about seventy-five more at his disposal. As this was our last stake, and as the fleet was to sail the following day (I wish it had sailed ten days sooner), we all went to San Carlos to witness the luck of D'Arcy. Before him lay seventy-five dollars, and before him sat the banker, ready and willing to relieve him of their weight. For the first half-hour he played with some success, but afterwards the tide of luck was against him. Not one of the party interfered *pro* or *con*. Again he made a rally, and, like a ship at sea who has weathered the storm and begins to right herself, he went on, as it were, sailing before the wind. But, in a moment of exultation, and having, as he thought, calculated to a nicety the certainty of success, he staked the entire of our stock-in-trade on the turn of the card. He was right—the card turned up in his favour, and he was a winner of three hundred dollars and upwards. I looked on quietly, and expected to see him take the money or double the card (which means "double or quit"), thereby insuring his stake at the worst, or doubling it in the event of success. What, then, was our astonishment and dismay when we saw him "cock" the card, and heard him, in a loud tone, addressing the dealer of the pack in the single monosyllable, "Cock." Now, the meaning of the word "cock," and "cocking" the card, that is to say, turning up one of the corners of it, implies that you will have, if you gain, three times the stake on the table, but, if you lose, you lose all. So it was with D'Arcy; the wrong card turned up, and we, one and all, turned out, went home to our beds, sailed for Portsmouth next day, and I never wagered a shilling at

a gaming-table since. Perhaps it was the best "turn up" I
ever had.

Our passage home was pleasant and short. No incident
worth relating occurred; and, in twelve days after we left
Lisbon, we found ourselves off Spithead. The number of
Jews which crowded the vessel was astonishing. They all
sought for gold, but amongst us it was a scarce commodity.
One solitary guinea was all I possessed, and I believe I could
say as much as any of my companions. For this guinea I
received, from a Jew, thirty shillings; and it was then that
I really began to lament the loss of my "specie" in Lisbon.
It was, however, of no use to repine. We had, after a good
deal of peril, arrived once more on our native shore. We
saw ourselves, on landing, hailed by our own people, and,
though last, not least, had an order on the agent for seven
months' pay! We were all splendidly dressed, with braided
coats, handsome forage caps, rich velvet waistcoats, appended
to which were a profusion of large silver Spanish buttons—
some wore gold ones—and our pantaloons bore the weight of
as much embroidery as, poor Fairfield once said, would furnish
a good sideboard of plate! Thanks to the old German tailor
in Lisbon (I forget his name) for this. If he charged high,
he gave everything of the best quality; but, as we landed,
and saw the garrison of Portsmouth in their white breeches
and black gaiters, and their officers in red coats, long boots,
and white shoulder belts, we must have appeared to them, as
they did to us, like men who formed a part of an army of
different nations.

We took coach the morning after our landing for London.
After a few days spent there in sight-seeing and amusements,
I set out to visit my family in Ireland. I took my place on
the top of the Liverpool coach, and, with a light heart,

viewed the beautiful country we passed over. The contrast it presented to that which I had but a few weeks before left was great indeed, and I felt a pride when I reflected that I, humble as I was, was one of those who had fought and bled not only for my country's honour, but my country's safety.

My servant, Dan Carsons, sat behind, and kept all the outside passengers near him, either in astonishment at the tales he recounted as to what he had seen, or in roars of laughter at some of his adventures, which he told without any scrupulous qualms as to whether they were true or not. He had made himself so agreeable to those behind that, at the first stage, where we changed horses, some of the front passengers requested he would take his place with them; but there was no vacant seat, and no one seemed disposed to resign his place, so I thought the best plan was for me to go behind, which, I said, I preferred to the front; and my man Dan was installed beside the driver. The laughter in front was, if possible, louder than it had been before in the rear, while Dan was recounting his Peninsular reminiscences.

We reached Liverpool without any adventure, and next day sailed for Dublin. In those days which I write of we did not use steam, and a three-day passage from Liverpool to Dublin was quite a common thing, and it was the practice then to lay in a sea stock for a voyage of four or five days. This was a matter of easy accomplishment, and, having laid in a fair supply of edibles, etc., we set sail, and on the third day arrived in Dublin. After remaining in the capital one day, I parted from my old companion, D'Arcy, and took the first coach for the Kildare road, while D'Arcy brought himself to an anchor in the Ennis mail. Our leave of absence was for three months, and, before the expiration of that time, the second battalion of the regiment was expected in Ireland, so we did not calculate on a long separation, nor were we mistaken.

It would be tedious and uninteresting to give any minute detail of my reception amongst my family and friends. Those sort of adventures read well in novels, but I do not think my readers will be displeased with me for leaving them out. As a matter of course all my acquaintances got round me, and I had to recount all my four years' adventures in the Peninsula; and, while I was so employed in the drawing-room, my man Dan fulfilled his part in the kitchen, and, I have little doubt, did much more justice to the matter than I did.

When my leave expired, I took leave of my friends and joined the second battalion, which was stationed at Fermoy. The army of the Peninsula had by this time, the spring of 1814, established itself within the French frontier, and reinforcements were in readiness to be sent from Cork to join their companions in the south of France, but, as will be seen in the next chapter, there was no need of this augmentation of force.

CHAPTER XXVII

Breaking up of the British Peninsular army at the abdication of Napoleon—Separation of the soldiers' wives—The elopement—Sad story of Thorp, the Drum-Major—Conclusion.

AFTER six years of terrible war, the army of the Peninsula at length found a stop put to its victorious career, and the inhabitants of the city of Toulouse were the last who heard a hostile shot fired against their countrymen. From the commencement of this wonderful struggle, in August 1808, to April 1814, more battles had been fought (all of them won) than England could boast of for nearly a century; and the triumphant march of the army of Wellington was uninterrupted by one defeat, until the subjection of their brave opponents was complete, which forbade further hostile advance upon the French territory.

It would be a work of supererogation to bring events before the reader which have been so often and so well told. Suffice it to say that upon the news of the abdication of the Emperor Napoleon having reached the headquarters of the Dukes of Dalmatia and Wellington, the armies of the different nations which formed portions of those troops were so arranged as to be ready to return to their respective countries or destinations. Those of Spain returned to Spain, and those of Portugal returned to Portugal. The British

infantry embarked at Bordeaux, some for America, some for
England; and the cavalry, marching through France, took
shipping at Boulogne.

The separation of those troops from each other, after so
long an intercourse, and an uninterrupted series of victories,
was a trying moment. There were, no doubt, many at least
about to return to their native country and to their friends;
but they were also about to leave behind them, probably for
ever, those countries in which they had passed the most
eventful years of their lives, and to be separated from friends
whose claim to the title could not be doubted—because such
friendships as those I speak of were not formed by interested
motives, and were consequently the more sincere and lasting.
They left also behind them the bones of forty thousand of
their companions who had fallen, either by disease or by the
sword, in the tremendous but glorious contest they had been
all engaged in—a contest which decided more than the fate of
the Peninsula, for the very *existence* of England was the
stake played for, or rather fought for, in this terrible game;
the loss of one single point would not only have rendered the
game desperate, but lost it altogether. The players on both
sides were nearly equal in skill, and if Wellington could not
boast of the same evenness and perfection of some of the
materials he had in hand, as compared with his opponents,
he most undeniably held a few *trumps* that always decided
the game in his favour. Sixty thousand Anglo-Portuguese,
under their great leader, accomplished more on the southern
frontier of France than did HALF A MILLION of the allies on
the side of Germany.

These are heart-stirring facts, and the recollection of
them, even after so long a lapse of time, causes the pulse to
quicken, and the heart to beat high; for it can never be too

often repeated, or too well remembered, by those of the Peninsular army who are now living, that it was the imperishable deeds of that army that saved their country.

Their great leader now left them; but he did not do so without his marked expressions of what he thought of the past, and his promises for the future. His General Order contained the following words :—

"Although circumstances may alter the relations in which he has stood towards them for some years, so much to his satisfaction, he assures them he will never cease to feel the warmest interest in their welfare and honour, and that he will be at all times happy to be of any service to those to whose conduct, discipline, and gallantry their country is so much indebted."

How these promises have been kept is too well known, and it is difficult to say whether that he ever made them, or never kept them, is to be regretted most. However, the Duke of Wellington, no doubt, does not put the same construction on his words, and on his acts, that others do; and it will be the task of the historian and posterity to deal with a matter which can be better judged of by unbiassed persons than by the parties interested. That the Duke of Wellington is one of the most remarkable, and perhaps the greatest man of the present age, few will deny; but that he has neglected the interests and feelings of his Peninsular army, as a body, is beyond all question; and were he in his grave to-morrow, hundreds of voices, that are now silent, would echo what I write.

All the necessary preparations being made, the armies of the three nations parted, and proceeded on the different routes pointed out for them to follow. The breaking up of this splendid army of veterans, that for six years slept on the field of battle they had invariably won, was a trying moment. Many a bronzed face, that had braved every danger unmoved, was now moistened with a tear; but the proud consciousness that so long as their country required their services, and that nothing, save death, had separated them, until at last they stood triumphant on the threshold of the invaders' country, stifled every other feeling. In fine, the commands of the great man that had so often assembled them at his beck, now separated them—and for ever.

Several of the most effective regiments were ordered to embark for Canada, and as the war between England and America was at its height, the battalions destined for American service were restricted to a certain number of soldiers' wives. The English, Irish, and Scotch were sent to England, and proper attention paid to their wants and comforts. They had also on board the transports that were to convey them to England their own countrymen and their own countrywomen, amongst whom were many personally known to them, who had served in the same brigade or division. But the poor faithful Spanish and Portuguese women, hundreds of whom had married or attached themselves to our soldiers, and who had accompanied them through all their fatigues and dangers, were from stern necessity obliged to be abandoned to their fate. This was also a trying moment; many of these poor creatures, the Portuguese in particular, had lived with our men for years, and had borne them children. They were fond and attached beings, and had been useful in many ways, and under many circumstances, not only to their husbands, but to the corps they belonged to generally. Some had amassed money (Heaven knows how!), but others were without a sixpence to support them on their long journey to their own country, and most of them were nearly naked. The prospect before them was hideous, and their lamentations were proportionate, for many, though they had a *country* to return to, had neither friends to welcome them nor a home to shelter them; for in this war of extermination, life, as well as property, was lost. The soldiers were seven months in arrear of pay, and the officers were as badly off; nevertheless subscriptions were raised, and a fund, small no doubt in proportion to their wants, enabled relief to be portioned amongst all. This partial and insufficient aid did not, nor could not, however, lessen the real bitterness of the scene, for many of those devoted beings—now outcasts, about to traverse hundreds of miles ere they reached their homes, if homes they found any—had followed their husbands through the hottest of the battlefield; had staunched their wounds with their tattered garments, or moistened their parched lips, when without such care death would have been certain; they had, when such aid was not required, devoted days and nights in rendering those attentions which only they who have witnessed them can justly appreciate. Yet these faithful and heroic women were now, after those trials, to be seen standing on the beach, while they witnessed with bursting hearts the filling of those sails, and the crowding of those ships, that were to separate them for ever from those to whom they had looked for protection and support.

In this list there was one female, a lady—I call her so, for her rank and prospects entitled her to the appellation I have given her—who was as much to be pitied as the rest, though her circumstances were widely different. She was a beautiful woman, only daughter of the wealthy Juiz de Fora of Campo Mayor. During the autumn of 1809, when a portion of the Peninsular army, after the battle of Talavera,

was quartered in that town, this girl—for so she was then—
fell in love with the Drum-Major of the 88th Regiment.
His name was Thorp. As in most cases of the sort, both
parties had made up their minds to the consequences. The
girl was determined to elope with Thorp, and Thorp was
equally resolved to carry her off; but this required measures
as well as means. Touching the latter Thorp was amply
supplied, for he was pay-sergeant of a company, and, moreover, received constant remittances from his father, who was
a man of respectability in Lancashire. In a word, Thorp
was a gentleman, and lived and died a hero! As to the
lady, her tale is easily told. Her father, Señor José Alfonzo
Cherito, Juiz de Fora of Campo Mayor, was a man possessing
large estates, and having but one child, and that child a
daughter, he naturally looked forward to a suitable match
for her. Now, as poor Thorp could not boast of those
qualities or attributes which the worthy Juiz de Fora had
very naturally anticipated, when his daughter had made up
her mind to espouse Thorp, his rage and disappointment
may be easily imagined when he learned that she had left
his *quinta*, taking all her jewels with her. The regiment
was to march the following morning, and as all mode of
conveyance in the shape of cars or mules, for the wounded
or sick, was under the "surveillance" of the worthy magis-
trate, he apprehended no difficulty in tracing his runaway
daughter—but he was mistaken. The cars were examined,
the baggage-mules were overhauled, the commissariat mules,
carrying ammunition, biscuit, and rum, were looked at, but
amongst all these no trace of the fugitive could be found.
What, then, was to be done? There was but one other
chance of finding the girl, and this was a survey of the
officers' horses, as the officers rode at the head or in rear of

the column; but the Juiz de Fora, although a functionary
of high note and high authority in his own calling, and
amongst his own neighbours, did not much relish an inspection, though freely granted, which would place him amongst a
thousand shining British bayonets. However, he did accept
the invitation, and was allowed to make the inspection—but
he discovered no trace of his daughter.

"Are you satisfied?" said the Colonel.

"I am satisfied that my daughter is not with your
regiment, sir; yet I am anything but satisfied as to her
fate!" replied the old man.

The band played a quick march; Thorp, as Drum-Major,
flourished his cane; the daughter of the Juiz de Fora, in her
new and disguised character of cymbal-boy, with her face
blacked, and regimental jacket, banged the Turkish cymbals,
and Thorp, who as Drum-Major was destined to make a
noise in the world, was for obvious reasons silent on this
occasion. The regiment reached Monte Forte the same day,
and the *padre* of that town performed the marriage ceremony
in due form.

In detailing the history of the elopement and marriage of
Jacintha Cherito with Drum-Major Thorp, I have given but
a short outline of a very romantic and, as it was nigh turning
out, a tragical affair. But were I to sit down quietly, and
write of all the intrigues that were set in motion, or of all
the attempts that were made to assassinate this girl, and also
her husband, what I could truly write would be fitting for
the pages of a romance. Thorp's history shall be told in a
few words. It was this:—

He joined the 88th Regiment on its return from South
America in 1807. He was quite a lad, and being rather too
young to be placed in the ranks, was handed over to the

Drum-Major. He soon became so great a proficient that, on the regiment embarking for Portugal, at the end of 1808, he was raised to the rank of Drum-Major, in the room of his preceptor, who was invalided. In those days our Drum-Majors wore hats pretty much the same as those now worn by Field-Marshals; indeed, the only difference between them was that the hat then worn by the former was not only of a more imposing and capacious size, but more copiously garnished with white feathers round the brim than those of the latter now are. The coat, too, a weight in itself, from the quantity of silver lace with which it was bedizened, was an object sufficient to attract attention and respect from the multitude that witnessed the debarkation of the regiment at Lisbon. In short, Thorp was mistaken by the Portuguese for a General Officer, and some went so far as to guess at his being the Earl of Moira, who, it was rumoured at the time, was about to join the army. Absurd as those opinions were—and most absurd they assuredly were, because Thorp, neither in years nor appearance, resembled in the slightest degree the high personage he was mistaken for—Thorp felt gratified—and where is the Drum-Major that would not?— at being taken for a General Officer; and from that moment he made up his mind to pitch drums, drummers, and drumsticks, not only from his hands but his thoughts also, and fight his way to the honourable privilege of carrying the pole of a colour in place of the mace of a Drum-Major.

His wish was soon gratified, for when his regiment, at Busaco, was running headlong with the bayonet against three of Reynier's splendid battalions, Thorp, to the amazement of Colonel Wallace, was seen at the head of the 88th, not with his "mace of office" in his hand, but with his plumed hat, waving it high over his head, as he called out, "The

z

Connaught Rangers for ever!" During the action the Sergeant-Major had been killed while fighting beside Thorp, and Wallace, on the field of battle, named him as Sergeant-Major, in place of the one he had lost. From this period up to the battle of Toulouse, Thorp was a distinguished man. Four times had he been wounded, but he was always up with his regiment in time for the next battle, often with his wounds unhealed. At the battle of Orthes, his conduct was so remarkable that his name was forwarded for an ensigncy. Thorp knew this, and at Toulouse, the last battle fought by the Peninsular army, he was resolved to prove that his recommendation was deserved. In this action his bravery was not bravery alone—it was rashness.

Some companies of Picton's division had been repulsed in an attack at the bridge-head, near the canal—which attack it has been said, and in my opinion truly said, should never have been made—when Thorp ran forward, and assisted in rallying the soldiers. The fire from the firearms and batteries of the French was incessant, and many officers and soldiers had fallen. There was one spot in particular that had been the scene of much slaughter to those who occupied it, and five officers, besides numbers of soldiers, had been already struck down by cannon-shot, and others wounded by musketry. Amongst the latter was Captain Robert Nickle, one of the most distinguished officers in the army. While he was hobbling to the rear, he observed Thorp standing in the midst of those who had fallen, the rest having been withdrawn out of fire from a position that should never have been occupied. For in the front of the French battery, and running in a direct line from the canal to this position, was a low narrow avenue or hedge, which ended within a few yards of where our people had formed after their repulse, and this avenue served as a guide, or groove, for the enemy's range; they were now, however, more or less, under cover. In a moment of excitement, Thorp, with his cap in his hand, stood alone on this spot, saying, "Now let us see if they can hit *me!*" Nickle, who was passing at the moment, supported by two of his company—for his arm was badly shattered—called out to Thorp to leave the spot. "Oh, Captain Nickle," replied Thorp, "they can't hit *me*, I think." Those were the last words he ever uttered. A round shot struck his chest, and, cutting him in two, whirled his remains in the air. Thus fell the gallant Thorp, and though his rank was humble, his chivalrous deeds were those of a hero. The day after his death the English mail brought the *Gazette* in which poor Thorp's name was seen as promoted to an ensigncy in his old regiment; and though this announcement came too late for him to know it, it was a great consolation to his poor afflicted widow, and it was the means of reconciling her father to the choice she had made, and her return once more to her home was made a scene of great rejoicing; but nothing more of her was ever heard by the regiment.

The war in the Peninsula was now ended, after having continued for nearly six years with various changes; and gloriously, in truth, was it ended by the British General and his unconquerable army. "Thus the war terminated, and with it all remembrance of the veterans' services." And now, reader, I am about to take leave of you, for the present at least. In these "Adventures" I have told you many circumstances you never before heard of, and I hope I have not fatigued you, or trespassed too long on your patience. I have, without being, I trust, too tedious, told you of the wrongs my old corps has suffered. I have, without presuming to write a History of the Peninsular War, told you something of the services performed by the Peninsular army; and I have drawn your attention to the scandalous manner in which the never-to-be-forgotten services of that wonderful army were treated by the Government and by the Duke of Wellington. I leave the continuation of the *Adventures of the Connaught Rangers* dependent on the favour of which you may think the pages I have now presented to you deserving.

THE END

Printed by R. & R. CLARK, LIMITED, *Edinburgh*.